Exceptional Teaching

Ideas in action...

LEARNER-CENTERED • STRATEGIC • ENGAGING • RESOURCE-RICH • ASSESSMENT-DRIVEN •

EMCParadigm
PUBLISHING

Senior Developmental Editor	Sonja Felland Brown
Consulting Editor and Writer	Barbara G. Cox, PhD
Contributing Writers	William M. Mitchell, EdD, and Burton S. Kaliski, EdD
Cover and Text Designer	Leslie Anderson
Desktop Production Specialists	Lisa Beller and Patrina Nyhan
Copyeditor	Rosemary Wallner
Proofreader	Teresa Hudoba
Indexer	Nancy Fulton

Publishing Team: George Provol, Publisher; Janice Johnson, Director of Product Development; Lori Landwer, Marketing Manager; Shelley Clubb, Electronic Design and Production Manager

Care has been taken to verify the accuracy of information presented in this book. However, the editor and publisher cannot accept any responsibility for Web, e-mail, newsgroup, or chat room subject matter or content, or for consequences from application of the information in this book, and make no warranty, expressed or implied, with respect to its content.

Trademarks: Some of the product names and company names included in this book have been used for identification purposes only and may be trademarks or registered trademarks of their respective manufacturers and sellers. The editor and publisher disclaim any affiliation, association, or connection with, or sponsorship or endorsement by, such owners.

ISBN: 0-7638-1301-X

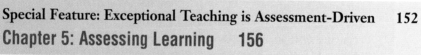

Special Feature: Exceptional Teaching is Engaging and Action-Oriented 112

Chapter 4: Delivering Engaging Instruction 116

Special Feature: Exceptional Teaching is Assessment-Driven 152

Chapter 5: Assessing Learning 156

Appendix: E-Learning (Distance Learning)—Frequently Asked Questions 186

Index 197

Preface

How often have you wished for a concise, highly readable handbook that presents the essential strategies for planning and delivering excellent instruction—plus the practical forms and files to translate these ideas into action? If you are like most instructors, you have been seeking just such a guide for a long time, particularly if you are an adjunct, or sessional, faculty member. We have been listening, and with the publication of *Exceptional Teaching*, we present our solution.

Today's college instructors face rigorous challenges, almost all of which result from continuous change—in the characteristics of the student population, in the jobs for which industry expects colleges to educate students, and in the educational delivery venues. Increasingly, today's postsecondary students are considered nontraditional learners, which the National Center for Education Statistics defines as students who attend part-time, work full-time, have dependents, are single parents, and postpone entering college until their twenties, thirties, or even later. One of the most striking and far-reaching changes in the postsecondary education field is the growth in online course offerings all over the country. And it is no coincidence that distance learning has expanded as the student population has become more nontraditional. With ever more students who are older, full-time workers, there is a greater need for anytime, anywhere course access. For college instructors, this means learning new techniques and technologies to communicate with students. Teaching completely or partially online demands different types of planning and modifications in the ways you assess learning. Added to these pressures are the continuous evolving of e-learning and the likelihood of being asked to teach a new subject with little advance time.

Exceptional Teaching prepares you to teach in today's changing and challenging educational environment. Its five chapters focus on the key questions of how to plan courses, how to plan individual sessions, how to teach in action- and results-oriented ways, and how to assess learning effectively and meaningfully. Every major topic includes a discussion of the implications for distance and hybrid learning, and a special appendix addresses the most frequently asked questions about e-learning. Insightful readings on learning theories and teaching approaches are offered at the book's Internet Resource Center (IRC) to enrich and extend discussions in the text. Planning forms, electronic templates, surveys, and expert guidelines at the IRC provide the tools to help you turn your goals into achievements. See the next page for a summary of the extensive resources available.

Ideas in Action

Once you have completed the reading and end-of-chapter activities of this text, you will be skilled in the following competencies:

Course Planning: envision and plan traditional, hybrid, and Web-based courses that foster learner responsibility, ensure authentic performance, value how students think, and honor best practices as identified by industry and subject matter experts

Session Planning: design clear roadmaps through instruction that recognize students' level of prior knowledge, reflect the importance of contextual and applied learning, and provide navigation checkpoints for self-evaluation and monitoring

Delivering Instruction: deliver instruction using multimodal techniques that recognize the importance of coaching, engagement, activity, reflection, and the opportunity for undoing and redoing

Assessment: construct an effective assessment plan involving multiple venues and best practices in the use of preassessments, course monitoring techniques, cognitive tests, and performance assessments; use the results to continually revise and improve instruction

We wish you success, and we thank you for choosing one of the most difficult, but important careers.

Internet Resource Center at <u>www.emcp.com</u>

Exceptional Teaching is

- ➤ Learner-Centered

- ➤ Strategic and Planned

- ➤ Resource-Rich

- ➤ Engaging and Action-Oriented

- ➤ Assessment-Driven

CALCULUS

Exceptional Teaching is

Learner-Centered

For decades we've been saying that exceptional teaching is learner-centered, yet many of our courses were limited to lectures, reading assignments, and tests, placing the learning responsibility entirely on the student. Such courses were lecture-centered, book-centered, text-centered, instructor-centered, and instructor-driven, but certainly not learner-centered. The instruction was effective for some, but many students did not succeed. Today, we realize that we need to center instruction on some important learner characteristics and that these characteristics vary among students. Our planning must be appropriate for the subject matter, the environment, and students with various backgrounds and approaches to learning.

What characteristics of a learner are we supposed to center our instruction on? At least these four: current level of knowledge or skill; communication preferences; effective learning experiences, sometimes called learning style;

and interests. Address these characteristics and add the learning goals for that student, and much of the groundwork for delivering instruction that is learner-centered will have been laid.

Learner's Current Level of Knowledge or Skill

Although some college courses require a certain level of competence or experience, sometimes in the form of prerequisites, many do not. Furthermore, even those that do have prerequisites often enroll students with diverse abilities and characteristics. Seldom will you teach a course in which all the students begin with the same level of knowledge or skill.

What do you do about it? Begin with some assessment of the knowledge or skills of the students. This might be informal and oral,

asking students to talk about what they know about a subject (as well as what they want to know, but we'll come to that later). It could be more formal and written, and might serve as a pretest for the course. For example, if you were setting out to teach a business math class, you might construct a written assessment that asks students to perform basic arithmetic functions and some estimations or "best guesses" based on a fact set, to answer questions about problem-solving steps, and to answer some questions about business concepts related to business math. Furthermore, you might add items about students' business or job experiences (paychecks are always important), other related background, and their particular learning interests or goals for the course. With this information, you will be much better prepared to implement (or adjust) your instructional plan for the class.

Learner's Communication Preferences

You have probably observed that some students will talk frequently in class, regardless of the topic. Some will become active participants in small groups but not in large class situations. Others will seldom talk in any educational setting, but demonstrate excellent writing abilities or will write numerous e-mails.

On the "intake" side, some students will absorb information from discussions better than from lectures; from small group peer interactions better than from instructor speak; or from visual representations, hands-on work, or reading better than from any oral communication.

Lots of educational research is leading to recommendations about personalizing our communications with students, that is, recognizing that lecture mode tends to be impersonal, especially with large class sizes. In practical terms, this "personalizing our communications" takes two forms, structural and style or content.

Structurally, this means we need to provide opportunities for students to participate in ways they are comfortable with and—something that is often overlooked—opportunities for students to develop a comfort level with new ways of learning. How does this happen? For both cases, we need to provide choices. Part of accepting our share of responsibility for

students' learning requires planning and implementing various communication modes—instructor to student, student to instructor, student to student, one-on-one, small group, large group. And we ensure that students can develop a comfort level with unfamiliar ways of communicating by providing the choices in "safe mode." That is, instructors provide positive feedback for communicating and for good work in the various situations.

Personalizing our communications also means ensuring that the style and content of our communications relates to students' learning, lives, interests, and issues. We do this by asking more questions and by incorporating what we know about students into examples and assignments.

Learner's Effective Learning Experiences, or Learning Style

Educators and researchers have defined learning styles in many different ways. For our purposes, we use the term to indicate the environments, activities, and thinking styles that have been effective for a student in the past—that student's effective learning experience. That experience will probably

be a combination of factors, including, but not limited to, lecture vs. small group discussion or independent study or discovery; reading vs. listening and speaking; writing, doing, or solving problems; intrinsic or extrinsic motivation; visual, auditory, or kinesthetic; and many others.

But how can instructors possibly deal with all of this? We can and we do. And part of the answer is, once again, providing *choices*. One of the most powerful strategies is to offer instruction using an array of alternative media and approaches: online tutorials, courses on CD-ROM or DVD, streaming video presentations, and hands-on demonstrations followed by student practice are just a few examples. Sometimes it is not practical to deliver instruction in alternative venues, but it is possible to assess students differently, allowing them to demonstrate what they have learned in alternative ways. Assessing learning in customized ways allows students to communicate their progress using their strengths and natural aptitudes, such as oral presentations or hands-on demonstrations.

Just as students have preferred ways of communicating and learning, instructors have preferred ways of communicating and teaching. To the degree that instructors are responsible for students' success, they may need to adapt their teaching styles, incorporating content and delivery modes that they haven't used in the past.

Learner's Interests

An important way of ensuring that instruction is learner-centered is to include learner interests in presentations, examples, and assignments. Some of those interests you will already know from talking with students, reading their papers or the student newspaper, listening, listening, and listening. When devising writing assignments or projects or activities, if your information or imagination fails you, give choices or let students propose their topic. In a graphic design class, for example, an instructor might get better results letting students decide their own project for a package design than by requiring a package design for plant food, cat litter, a movie DVD, or any other limited choice.

Using students' interests in lecture or discussion examples as well as in assignments and projects has two definite positive effects, one cognitive and the other motivational.

When students' interests are used for examples, they are more able to relate the information to what they already know, which improves their understanding and their remembering. They may also become increasingly motivated to learn because the information is relevant to their lives, to what they care about, do, or plan.

No single instructional model can be expected to work for all courses, instructors, and students. The challenge is for instructors to use, sometimes create, more varied instructional modes and alternative media in ways that will help them engage the intellect, imagination, and motivation of the majority of students.

Chapter 1

The Contemporary College Classroom: Teaching and Learning Challenges

Mouth dry and throat tightening, ears ringing, I felt a little weak. My notes spread out before me, I could hear a voice from somewhere in the distance, something familiar, something about the formation of a legal structure in the Colonies. As it droned on, I recognized it as my own. Not the warm, reassuring welcome to nervous students. Not the clever descriptions and dry humor holding promise of engaging dialogue in weeks to come. The sea of eyes, thirty-five pairs of them, met my gaze as I gathered my wits. I knew what they expected. I was supposed to be the font of wisdom, the expert on everything colonial, engaging and bright, entertaining and energetic. They wanted to be dazzled. I looked from face to face. Which ones would want an extension on the paper, or extra credit for attendance, or advice on finding a job? Which ones would ask for more online references or send an e-mail at 2 A.M. requesting immediate answers to impossible questions? Who would want tutoring in writing an essay or complain that the slide presentations were boring? Just who were all these students, and what did they expect, anyhow?

I drew in a deep breath. That faraway voice kept on. Gradually, I began to see individual faces—all ages, male and female, and many Asian and Indian students this time. And a guide dog appeared to snooze by one student's feet, but I suspected it would come alert instantly at a touch or word. Good heavens. Could that lanky kid be more than twelve? And the woman on the left with white hair—was that Jane Melton, known on campus as the oldest living perennial student, and a whiz at using the Internet? How would I be able to teach such a diverse class effectively?

The voice continued, now talking about the research and writing of a required report on colonial society. Then it happened. First one, then another and another. Hands in the air. Professor, how are we going to use the Internet in this class? Will you give us tutoring if we need help? My English is not perfect; what other resources are available to help me learn this material? Do you count grammar and spelling when you grade the report? Do we have quizzes? Do they count? The syllabus says we have online assignments. Can we use the computers in the library? Can we get a copy of the PowerPoint® presentations you use? Can I submit my report by e-mail?

The questions weren't as scary as I'd feared. I'd prepared for most of them. At last the voice was mine again.

Learning Outcomes

- Describe the significant challenges that faculty face in today's colleges
- Identify the important characteristics of today's traditional and nontraditional college students
- Describe adult students and name characteristics that differentiate them from younger students
- Describe the varying academic goals of different groups of students
- List common expectations that students have of instructors and indicate whether they are reasonable; indicate that instructors have the ability to shape the expectations of students and minimize unrealistic ones
- Describe the course structures or formats in which today's faculty must be prepared to teach

Pressing Challenges Facing College Instructors

The challenges I face today aren't any different from the ones I've been dealing with for the past decade. We never have enough money and we never have enough time.

The sentiment may not be uncommon, and it may well be having an impact on how colleges and individual instructors are able to meet the needs and priorities of today's students. Nonetheless, *changes* in allocations of financial resources and instructor time are creating new and pressing challenges.

For some instructors, the physical and equipment changes are the least of the matter. Planning and implementing diverse approaches to teaching a changing student population, allowing for collaborative as well as independent learning, and devising fair and representative assessments challenge even experienced "traditional classroom" instructors.

The discussions later in this chapter about changing student characteristics, expectations, and instructional environments, as well as new options and opportunities, demonstrate some of the key issues. Some of these challenges include:

- delivering instruction to higher numbers of students, that is, meeting a demand for increased "productivity"
- delivering appropriate instruction to an increasingly diverse student population
- mastering new technologies for instructional delivery alternatives
- teaching in off-campus, temporary, or ill-equipped classrooms or labs
- managing the increasing volume of teaching and administrative tasks, including meetings, course development, and committees
- meeting the certification and other requirements that set course frameworks

• meeting the challenges of increased pressure on assessment and accountability

A highly valuable resource that colleges rely on is their adjunct or associate faculty. Like regular faculty, these instructors have important teaching missions, but they may not be responsible for the committee work, office hours, and other administrative contributions. On the other hand, they often work without the same level of compensation, benefits, security, and support that is provided for the regular faculty.

"Learning is what most adults will do for a living in the 21ˢᵗ century."

—Lewis Perelman

Because associate faculty are less engaged with the administration, reaching continuity with other courses in the program may be more challenging. Scheduling and finding resources for classroom use, research, conferences, and other purposes can be more difficult. Sometimes associate faculty are included or invited to in-service programs, but not always. Associate faculty might also find less continuity in their student enrollments, that is, fewer students that they know from previous courses. Becoming familiar with the capabilities and learning styles of individual students is less likely.

Some administrations are superb in reaching out to adjunct or associate faculty; others are not. Where administrations lack the commitment to developing solid relationships with these instructors, they risk instructors perceiving themselves as being second-class citizens on campus. The instructors must challenge themselves to find ways to become engaged with the administration and other faculty to a level that is satisfactory to them.

Characteristics of Today's Postsecondary College Students

Today's college instructors face significant challenges, many of which are new faces on long-lived issues and others that are relatively new to college circumstances. Among the greatest of these is the increased diversity of student characteristics. The diversity among students, traditional and nontraditional, encompasses their goals, schedules, gender, race and ethnicity, language abilities, technology abilities, physical capacities, and preparation for college work.

Traditional Students

Who are today's "traditional" students? What characterizes them? And have they changed over the past five or ten years? Some subjective descriptions still apply: these are students who participate in a two-year postsecondary college curriculum directly after graduating from high school. They attend the college full time. Most work part time, not full time. For the most part, they are young (17 to 19 years), energetic, and interested in exploring the avenues of learning laid out before them. Among traditional students are those whose parents insisted that they go to college and some who attend because they do not know what else to do.

Full-time students fresh from secondary school tend to adjust quickly to schedules and classroom regimen. They are familiar with school culture and basic procedures and behavior policies. Some struggle with newfound social freedoms, a multitude of extracurricular distractions, and an array of tempting electives. These may lead to difficulties in developing disciplined, self-scheduled, effective study skills and habits.

Academic Goals

More than other students, traditional students participate in two-year college programs to prepare to transfer to a four-year institution. Transfer students sometimes begin without a clear educational plan. These students use the offerings of the two-year college to sample areas of interest before making a commitment to a discipline or educational path.

Other traditional students enroll in schools or programs of learning that result in a certificate or an Associate of Arts degree. The schools might be community colleges, or vocational, technical, or proprietary schools. The programs, particularly at community colleges, might well be vocational, technical, liberal arts, sciences, or any of various others. These students often have a specific career goal that is driving their endeavors, course choices, and educational planning.

Learner Preparation

Repeatedly, we see that learner preparation among traditional students at the outset of their college experience can be described as bimodal—that is, either as very good or unfortunately poor. Some poorly prepared students, for example, may be very capable and motivated, and quickly acquire the skills and knowledge needed to participate successfully in their college courses. Students who may have performed poorly in high school because they were not motivated or had no clear-cut goals perform well in the community college or vocational or other postsecondary school because their education goals are specific, realistic, and worthwhile, particularly when completing a program or series of courses that lead to a job.

While it might be convenient for instructors to view those students with good preparation as not requiring special attention, such is not necessarily the case. These students deserve growth in skills and knowledge that is paced for their abilities. They can lose motivation or become resentful if an instructor's time or focus is spent assisting the less prepared students or slower learners. Instructors must find ways to engage all their students effectively in the learning process, which may mean helping students overcome obstacles presented by poor preparation.

The first language of most traditional students is English. Also, students beginning their college career direct from high school have completed at least some of their precollege education in a local high school and have participated in that education in English. Some of these students may still require English language instruction, especially in vocabulary and writing, before they can benefit fully from college courses.

The number of female students continues to increase and is now greater than the number of males in many schools. The significance of this is, indeed, more related to learner preparation than social issues. Why? Often male students are better prepared than female students in mathematics concepts, reasoning, and mechanics.* (Sadly, this remains true today despite several decades of addressing the need for improved mathematics education for girls in our public elementary and secondary schools.)

One interesting characteristic that distinguishes today's traditional student from those of twenty years ago is their experience with high-energy information input or interaction. Today's 17- to 19-year-olds have grown up with lively television, from *Sesame Street* to *Reading Rainbow* to MTV; interactive games and puzzles; videos and CDs/DVDs; high-action video games; and computer programs that entertain while (we hope) they teach. Students now entering college have learned to learn in sound and video bites, are less patient with slower paced instruction, and want to know it all—*now*, and may have come to expect to gain that knowledge without effort.

Technology Skills

The world of learning demands a set of technology skills that was not required of students even ten years ago. To perform well in a community college, vocational, technical, or proprietary school, students need to use Internet research and communication tools. Traditional students whose high schools provided up-to-date equipment and instruction in their use, particularly for reports, e-mail writing, and other communications, enter the postsecondary arena able to use these tools fairly effectively. Others, however, may lack this preparation and may need to develop basic computing, research, and writing abilities.

Diversity among Traditional Students

Despite these similarities, we see remarkable diversity on our college campuses, diversity that continues to increase each term. And while the changes in student characteristics vary tremendously from area to area and even campus to campus, they are generally greatest in academic goals and learner preparation for college coursework. Racial and ethnic diversity increases noticeably nearly everywhere, and the nature of that diversity varies markedly by geographic area and even individual location. For example, students of Asian backgrounds are numerous in Orange County, California; Cuban-American students populate south Florida schools; and Mexican-American students constitute a high proportion of traditional enrollments in various areas of California, Texas, Illinois, Arizona, and elsewhere. Schools in and near cities enroll students of every racial and

---

* On the other hand, the differences once commonplace in reading and writing skills between male and female students, after controlling for other factors, seem to have greatly diminished. Have we done a better job of teaching these skills to high school boys? Have they become more motivated? Have our measures changed? For whatever reason, girls seem to have lost the slight advantage they once held.

ethnic group or national origin possible. At one time, these students were automatically characterized as nontraditional, but our immigrants now have a longer history of residence—and education—in the United States, and we cannot and should not make such assumptions.

Students with visual or hearing impairments or limited physical mobility now participate in college courses as successfully as those without. Policy changes over recent decades have resulted in greater accessibility for students with physical limitations. Improved building and classroom access, provision of learning assistants who sign for the deaf or read for the blind, and new technologies that convert text to voice are examples of some of the ways that the barriers previously standing between learners with disabilities and postsecondary education are being lowered.

Nontraditional Students

Nontraditional students bring with them certain characteristics that instructors need to recognize and address. For the most part, these students are further along in their lives than traditional students. Many have not participated in classes, written a paper, taken a test, prepared notes, applied new skills or concepts, or otherwise functioned as students in a very long time. They may need help with study skills, problem solving, organizing information, and other learning activities. Many have high anxiety about returning to school and need (sometimes, demand) assurances about their abilities or performance.

Nontraditional students are those who until recent years were not as commonly found in postsecondary schools. They are generally older than traditional students. Many—28 percent of community college students, for example—have already earned a bachelor's degree.[1] Nontraditional students often have goals that are very different from those of traditional students. In community colleges, for example, nearly half of the enrollments are not for purposes of earning credit toward a certificate or toward a transfer to another institution.[2] The most common groups of nontraditional students, whether full or part time, include:

- learners who worked for some time before deciding to continue their education
- learners who work full time and are following a slower plan to reach their educational goals
- recent arrivals to the United States, who are unfamiliar with school culture and may need English language learner (ELL) instruction
- students who have grown up and been educated in a community whose primary characteristic is the density of a particular ethnic or cultural group
- students who have not been able to enter the world of work or who have been squeezed out of employment from the downsizing of businesses, outsourcing, or other reasons

---

[1] William J. Flynn, "Why Not Assess and Document All Learning?" *Learning Abstracts* 7 (March 2004): 2, www.league.org/publication/abstracts/.
[2] Flynn, "Why Not Assess and Document All Learning?" 2.

Meeting a Challenge
Teaching Learners Who Are Disabled

Today's educators strive to teach all of their students effectively. Educators see the unique abilities that students bring to their learning and seek ways to help students apply and expand those abilities in the learning environment.

The Americans with Disabilities Act (ADA), enacted in 1990, encourages the development of policies and procedures in our colleges that promote respect for and active involvement of students with mobility, hearing, vision, and mental disabilities. This means that instructors must reconsider their teaching approaches, assignments, and classroom environments to eliminate any aspect that could be an obstacle for students with various disabilities.

Educate yourself about disabilities. If possible, attend a workshop or in-service training to familiarize yourself with the types of disabilities, their causes and characteristics. Learn about brain injuries, for example, and the huge range of resulting cognitive, physical, emotional, and social impairments. If your college does not offer such training, encourage them to do so—while you find other ways to get the information.

Study any available information about your school's policies, procedures, and services for students with disabilities. Find out what accommodations are required of you as well as what responsibilities students with disabilities must assume. In the years since the ADA was enacted, our schools have made great strides in providing elevators, ramps, and railings for students with mobility impairments. Providing accommodations for hearing and visually impaired students or learning disabled students has been more complicated and, often, more expensive. Find out what your school has to offer.

Distance education has provided access to postsecondary courses that was previously unattainable. Students who, for reasons of location or scheduling, are not able to participate in classroom courses, can do so via the Internet or through telecourses or audio courses. New technologies for computer use by students with a physical or sensory impairment have increased the importance of online education. Various associations provide guidelines for Web page and online course development that is consistent with these tools.

Find ways to provide the needed accommodations without compromising the quality of your course. Evaluate the performance of students with disabilities using the same criteria that you use for other students. Being too lenient with grading does students no favors: they develop a false picture of their accomplishments and underestimate what they need to learn. Nor should you grade students with disabilities more stringently because they were given additional time or some other necessary consideration. Check your grading procedures and decision points to ensure evaluation/grading equity.

And remember to respect students' privacy with regard to disability matters. File any information about their accommodations in a safe place and do not discuss disability-related issues with these students in the hearing of others.

- individuals who have decided to change career paths
- individuals whose personal life situations, goals, or finances have changed and who now can or need to or wish to embark on or return to their education or training. The growing numbers of single parents enrolling in college courses is a good example. Some older individuals are returning to the educational system after a long period of time spent in the workforce, service, or household management.[3] Others are returning to the educational system after dropping out of mainstream society due to substance abuse; physical, emotional, or mental illness; financial disaster; or other unhappy circumstance.

Many nontraditional learners actively participate in many of life's arenas, including family, social, work, cultural. They lead active, busy lives, and time taken from crowded schedules for learning is valuable and jealously guarded. Their various commitments may allow them to participate only in courses offered in alternative formats—distance education or hybrid courses—or nontraditional schedules. They insist that their learning time be productive, and can sometimes grow frustrated with the pace of conventional full-semester classroom instruction.

Traditional and Nontraditional Student Proportions

As you probably know very well, the proportion of students in a class or in a college who fit the description above has increased dramatically over the past five to ten years. Some schools whose enrollments included more than 75 percent traditional students now enroll as few as 10 percent.[4] The biggest single factor in this shift is not any of the characteristics we've described above, but rather the tremendous increase in part-time students, whether from economic necessity or growth in the returning student and adult student populations.

Academic Goals

A broad spectrum of academic goals motivates nontraditional students, particularly in community colleges. Many of them parallel those of traditional students—they intend to transfer to a four-year institution or they hope to complete the requirements for a particular certificate such as A+, Net+, or Microsoft Office Specialist or for an Associate of Arts degree.

Another familiar goal is found among students who enroll in one or a few courses: they wish to get training in a specific workplace skill or to prepare to pass a particular competency test that will open a career door.

Personal growth goals of improved basic reading, writing, and math skills, English language abilities, and various technological and computer skills are common.

Goals among students in vocational and proprietary schools tend to be somewhat less varied than in the community colleges, and are aligned closely with the school's focus or certificate offering.

---

[3] Flynn, "Why Not Assess and Document All Learning?" 2.
[4] Review of data from selected schools in the western United States, 2004.

Learner Preparation

Nontraditional students may be less prepared for learning in a structured environment, but they may also be very highly motivated. In some cases, these students adapt to the learning situations and processes quickly—and sometimes they "try harder." For the most part, these motivated learners take their learning seriously, apply themselves in and out of the classroom, complete assignments carefully and on time, and take initiative to get tutoring or academic counseling when needed.

Recent immigrants, not schooled in the United States or accustomed to U.S. educational conventions, may experience difficulties or stress adjusting to school culture and behavioral norms. Learners who were educated outside the United States and in a school culture very different from ours may be particularly outspoken in class, demanding, or critical—or they may seem withdrawn and not comment at all.

> "In 1999, the suggestion to a class of graduate students in educational administration that, by 2010, all campus courses would be a combination of face-to-face and online components was met with disbelief. By 2004, students were generally surprised if a course did not have online components and a web site associated with the class."
>
> —Judith Boetcher and Rita-Marie Conrad

We have learned to expect that students whose first language is not English might be slower readers or awkward speakers, or have difficulty with test vocabulary or lecture comprehension. However, we can forget that the solution does not lie entirely in additional ELL instruction, especially where the language obstacles create frustrations or misunderstandings. ELL instruction is seldom coordinated with the content of students' other courses, and students may need assistance with terminology, writing formats, and other language skills within the context of their non-ELL classes. They may also need assistance from academic or other counselors, or from tutors specializing in a given subject area.

Returnees to the world of learning may have an important area for catch-up: technology and computer literacy. For some, sending e-mail will be a challenge, searching for a book on the library catalog system will be painful, using the Internet for research will be a tremendous mystery, and the very thought of using a spreadsheet, database, or presentation program will trigger cold sweats.

Because returning students may have been away from schooling for significant periods, they may be unsure of their writing and other communication skills. But they are reengaging with learning because they have strong desires to do so, and they are strongly motivated to do well. Depending on the particular situation, returning adult learners tend to enter the learning place for one (or more) of the following reasons:

- mid-life career changes (retooling)
- professional development (continuing education in a profession or career)
- personal enrichment
- self-improvement

What Students Expect from Their Classes and Instructors

What do students say they expect from instructors and courses? What do instructors *think* they expect? And how do these views influence what instructors do?

While it is true that expectations students hold for their instructors and courses vary widely from student to student, course to course, as well as by school or location, a few expectations appear to be held almost universally; a few others also merit comment.

Some expectations are more reasonable than others. Instructors find that a few students have expectations of them that would be impossible for *any* instructor to live up to. And, then, some students just don't know what to expect. These points are very telling. Instructors can shape those expectations at the outset of a course, and the degree to which they do this successfully will influence students' satisfaction with their learning experience.

In the following sections we discuss a few expectations that students commonly hold of their instructors and courses, followed by some that are less common or less reasonable.

Instructors Are Knowledgeable of the Subject Matter

That instructors know what they're talking about is a basic expectation students (as well as other faculty and administrators) hold. Indeed, instructors expect this of themselves. Instructors are also expected to stay current with changes and additions of new information or perspectives to a knowledge base. Students are disappointed, even angry, when presented with outdated information.

Do students expect instructors to know all the answers? Yes, some do. But for the most part, instructors are able to disabuse them of this notion in short order.

Instructors Present Accurate Information in a Way That Is Clear, Well Organized, and Understandable

Knowing the skills and knowledge of a subject does not guarantee that someone knows how to present that information in a way that facilitates learning. A particularly learned history professor was once described as a "mainframe computer without a program." His head held a wealth of information, but he had great difficulty imparting it to students in ways they could understand, remember, and apply.

Similarly, students expect instructors to present the essential information of a course. They want to be certain that they have mastered the key elements of a body of knowledge—not just the areas that a particular instructor happens to enjoy or enjoys teaching. And students do expect to hear new and differing ideas and perspectives or approaches to skill development or concept mastery and application.

Questions, Discussions, Activities, and Assignments Clarify and Extend Learning

Teaching isn't telling, or at least it isn't *just* telling. Instructors who lecture for three hours, assign textbook readings, and then assess learning with one or two multiple-choice tests and Scantron® or other automated scoring forms are fast becoming aware that students are not happy with their learning experience.

Likewise, it isn't just what you *cover* that is important; it's what you *teach*. And instructors need to determine what they've actually been able to communicate to students. Only then can they provide learner-centered instruction. How? By asking questions, *listening* to what students have to say during class discussion, and by making sure that activities and assignments are based on what students know and what they need to know.

Students do expect in-class questions and discussions to contribute to their mastery of the subject matter or skill. They believe the instructor should shape the discussion and ensure that the flow of comments and information does clarify and extend their learning. At the same time, some students resent being "put on the spot" or embarrassed by questions they cannot answer, and they expect instructors to be sensitive to this.

Do students expect to be entertained? Yes, to a certain extent, they do. But they probably will not express it that way. They expect classroom learning to be interesting and active, and when it is not, they are bored, disappointed, and sometimes, if they feel their time has been wasted, angry.

Are activities and assignments interesting and meaningful and not "busy work"? Students expect activities that not only extend their learning but that require them to apply it. In many areas, they also expect their learning to have practical applications that contribute to their student, work, or personal lives.

Instructors Provide Frequent, Regular, and Fair Feedback and Acknowledgment

As many times as we hear this, instructors often fail to provide students with the amount and quality of feedback and acknowledgment they need, expect, and deserve. This is especially true for large classes. Formative evaluations throughout a course, including those based on quizzes, tests, papers, assignments, class discussions, and other sources of information on student progress and performance, all serve to enhance student performance by focusing attention on areas needing improvement—as well as by providing recognition of good work. Students who do not receive feedback they feel is necessary to keep them on the right path or redirect them into better learning can become frustrated and angry, and probably with good reason. On the other hand, students whose work or progress is acknowledged in clear, direct ways are further inspired to do well.

Students do expect evaluation and feedback to be fair and useful. (We will treat assessment and evaluation of students' learning more specifically in Chapter 5.) It is also the case that students will occasionally expect, and

> *"The secret of education is respecting the pupil."*
> —Ralph Waldo Emerson

sometimes demand, that their efforts be acknowledged, even when performance does not merit recognition.

Instructors Use Technology Appropriately

We know that some schools have been more able to keep pace with technological developments than others. Sometimes the reason is related to money; other times it is related to the interest of individual faculty and administrators to make good use of new delivery modes as they become available. Regardless of how up-to-date a school is in this regard, students expect their instructors to be savvy about using today's electronic resources in their teaching—both inside the classroom and out.

In the classroom, students expect instructors to use technologies for specific instructional reasons, and not simply for the sake of using them. Learners quickly recognize overuse or inappropriate use of presentation media, especially when it substitutes for quality instructor/student interactions. (A rule of thumb is to use presentation media no more than 40 percent of the in-class instructional time.)

External to the classroom, students expect instructors to make effective use of Internet resources and references, e-mail, course Web pages, and other online tools that enhance communication and understanding. Most of today's students have grown up with the Internet and assume they will find useful information and answers available to them online for just about everything. They may be surprised to discover that a school has not established a campus-wide wireless network for their instant access.

"The aim of teachers and the school curricula should be to awaken, not 'stock' or 'train' the mind. We need to help students be aware of what they don't know that is worth knowing."

—Grant Wiggins

Students, especially those in science courses, know that state-of-the-art research, lab, and field technologies are being used widely for college instruction everywhere. They expect their instructors to be using the latest tools in their fields.

Instructors Give Students Guidance and Advice

In some environments, students think of instructors as substitutes for reading or research. They expect instructors to act as learning consultants whose job is to coach them about how to learn effectively and to answer unending streams of questions. Establishing clear roles at the outset of a course can reduce this tendency greatly.

While academic counseling, program guidance, and career path advice are commonly in the domain of the student services programs, students still expect their instructors to be fonts of wisdom about their schooling decisions. This is especially true of students who are new to college and have arrived fresh from high school. Many view their professors as authority figures whose job is partly to help them navigate the college system. Some students bring personal problems to instructors expecting solutions. They may ask faculty to help them find jobs.

Various types of disabilities affect people's ability to use the Web and computers effectively. These include visual, hearing, speech-related, cognitive, physical, and neurological disabilities. Designers of Web sites and pages, and particularly designers of online learning courses, need to ensure that individuals with disabilities are not precluded from participation by design or function.

For example, students who are visually impaired may need audio descriptions of illustrations or videos. People who are hearing-impaired may need captions for any audio components. Some individuals may need alternate input devices for sites that use speech input. Designers should specify screens that do not flicker and images that do not flash or strobe because they can aggravate neurological disorders. For people facing cognitive challenges, the language/reading level(s) of Web page content and the navigation design are key usability factors.

Advocate Organizations

The World Wide Web Consortium (W3C), which promotes evolution and interoperability of the Web, works in four "domains": Architecture, Interaction, Technology and Society, and Web Accessibility Initiative. The fourth domain, the WAI, works to (a) ensure that Web technologies support accessibility; (b) develop guidelines for accessibility; (c) improve evaluation and repair tools for Web accessibility; (d) develop education and outreach materials; and (e) coordinate with research and development. (See www.w3.org/WAI/ for extensive, detailed information on this important work.)

The National Institute on Disability and Rehabilitation Research (NIDRR) provides leadership and support for a comprehensive program of research related to the rehabilitation of individuals with disabilities.

Evaluation, Repair, and Authoring Tools

Software developers are now providing evaluation, repair, and authoring tools that help course developers make their pages more accessible to people with disabilities. Developers now have many to choose from, ranging from free to expensive, easy-to-use to complex. Here are two examples.

- **Check and Repair: "A-Prompt" (Accessibility Prompt)**
  A-Prompt software will check Web pages for barriers to accessibility and will perform some automatic repairs. It assists Web authors with some manual repairs. The program is free and downloadable from www.websavvy-access.org/resources/aprompt.php.

- **MAGpie (Media Access Generator)**

  The National Center for Accessible Media (NCAM) produced a free application (MAGpie 1.0) that supports captioning/subtitles for major media programs, including Windows Media® (Microsoft), MPEG, QuickTime® (Apple), and RealMedia® (Real Networks). A text editing tool in MAGpie enables developers to transcribe a video while viewing it. MAGpie can also export the transcribed text files into three different caption formats (QuickTime Text, RealText® & SMIL, and SAMI) to be associated and played with the original video or audio. Visit NCAM for more details and to download the program: http://ncam.wgbh.org/webaccess/magpie/.

- **Speech-Enabled Web Applications**

  Early speech synthesizers "spoke" in a monotone, robotic pattern. In recent years, however, tremendous resources have been directed toward developing technologies for speech-enabled Web applications. These are among the most sophisticated programs developed and, often expensive, they may not be particularly user-friendly. The mechanics of producing speech from text, including the development of "grammars" and other components, is highly complex. See www.acoustics.hut.fi/~slemmett/speech.html for a list of speech synthesizer links.

- **Assistive Hardware**

  User hardware has made huge strides in the past decade, and many of the software tools available to developers are built to work with specific hardware. Assistive technology products must be compatible with the computer operating system and programs on the particular computer being used.

  Specific assistive devices include special keyboards, wands/sticks, sip-and-puff systems, joysticks, or track screens for use with on-screen keyboards. Technologies are available for Braille output, light signalers, screen magnifiers and readers, and speech recognition systems. To get a brief description of each of these, visit www.microsoft.com/enable/at/types.aspx.

INTERNET RESOURCE *Readings*

Faculty quickly learn, however, to refer students to appropriate counselors on campus, along with providing assurances that help can be found there.

Instructors Are Neutral on Controversial Questions

Students, especially in public education, do expect teachers to present all sides of an issue or argument objectively and fairly. They expect to be provided with the information and evaluative measures or tools that will enable them to reach valid conclusions of their own. Often, the expectation is a reasonable one, but it gets challenged regularly in ethics courses, political science and philosophy classes, and in some social and behavioral sciences, health sciences, and elsewhere.

Instructors of Online Courses Provide Well Organized Content and Are Available for Assistance

Along with comprehensive content, students expect clear directions, samples of required assignments, and "24-7" instructor availability. The continuing expansion of course offerings online and the competition for enrollments have been accompanied by an additional set of student expectations and instructor challenges. Course marketing has sometimes created the impression that the advantages of online learning include up-to-the-minute content, continuous instructor contact, and an easy, fun avenue to course or program completion.

Some experienced instructors report that they occasionally encounter students who expect to be rewarded with a passing grade for attending class and are surprised when their grades reflect lack of performance or mastery. Some students expect to be spoon-fed and are surprised if they need to apply themselves or develop increased discipline to perform well.

The short story is that students expect instructors who are knowledgeable and who know how to teach in today's environments. Furthermore, beyond caring about their learning, students expect instructors to care about them as individuals.

Challenges of Teaching in Various Course Structures

Every format in which we deliver instruction has its own challenges, and each has been marked by change. Influenced by research on effective teaching, learning styles, learning disabilities, concept and skill acquisition, and a multitude of variations on these, we have been challenged to make our approaches to teaching increasingly learner-appropriate—strategic, dynamic, communicative, relational, and resource-rich. While we will discuss these aspects of effective teaching in more detail in Chapter 2, the point here is that these changes have affected every environment in which we teach, and even added new ones.

Lecture, Lab and Field, Combinations

Constant change is the norm in postsecondary teaching environments, including course structures, classroom assignments, and class locations. When the new semester's room and course assignments are delivered, for example, you might discover that your art history class has been assigned to a temporary "bungalow" on the nearby high school campus. Cara Garza learns that she'll be teaching business finance in a large conference room that a local bank has made available to the college at no charge. Your office mate's political science class, which he organized to use small group collaborative learning in a movable desk or chair setting will meet in the humanities lecture theater. And the request you made for a "high-tech" lecture hall so that you can use your proposed but not-yet-developed sophisticated electronic presentations, including live streaming from the Web, has been approved at the last minute, giving you four weeks to prepare. Whatever the course format—lecture, lab, field, or combinations thereof—instructors must be flexible and prepared to adapt to change.

Lecture formats still constitute the core of college curricula, but these environments are far from being immune to change. Changes such as the above examples describe are not uncommon. Some happen because of crowded campuses or economic setbacks. Others, however, have improved with upgraded facilities and state-of-the art equipment for the latest of electronic resources.

Lecture format classes are not limited to instructor talk, or at least they shouldn't be. Instructors, even those enamored with the sound of their own voice, must use a mix of ways to impart information and to *cause learning*. Depending on what is appropriate for the subject matter, conducting a demonstration, guiding experiments, using quality visual examples, leading discussions, and asking questions are critical to causing learning. Effective instructors find ways to promote learning that engage students' thinking and doing, not just their hearing and listening.

"Every truth has four corners: as a teacher I give you one corner, and it is for you to find the other three."

—Confucius

Lab classes or courses with lab or field requirements continue to be an important part of the mainstream course, particularly in the sciences (and in technology courses—any course that requires learning hands-on skills). Yet these too have seen change or are feeling the need for change. For example, some nursing programs with students conducting field observations or participating in internships in different health facilities are now meeting virtually from their site, with live streaming, to report and discuss their experiences. Today's rich available resources are touching every discipline we teach, and we must meet the demands and challenges they pose. Being faced with the need to learn new sets of skills in order to provide the best possible instruction in today's environments and using today's tools is not unique to a handful of instructors. The ongoing development of materials and technologies requires continuous improvement for most of us.

Online and Hybrid

More than ever before, college instructors are faced with teaching in course formats that are unfamiliar to them (or many of them). New technologies and pressures to use them mean that instructors must find ways to master new teaching environments and do so quickly. In addition to traditional lecture courses and seminars, lab and/or field courses, and combinations of these, many instructors must master the art of teaching online classes or hybrids, also called "blended classes," or place themselves at risk of poor evaluations or fewer teaching assignments. On the other hand, some instructors view online courses within the college context as exciting challenges and dive into online course management, and sometimes course development, with unbridled enthusiasm.

Why the sudden popularity of online classes? Is it just the latest albatross hung on overworked instructors because it's the "in" thing to do? Not really. Our colleges are responding to the needs of larger communities of learners and to constraints on economic resources. It's market demand. Online instruction allows us to reach students who otherwise could not avail themselves of courses. Students with significant work and family scheduling commitments, students who do not tolerate classroom instruction well, who need additional time to read or digest information, who learn best with a self-paced situation, and others can now participate in and benefit from a much greater range of course options. And colleges can increase student enrollments with less stress on physical resources. This is resulting in greater stress, however, for instructors who must master the art of teaching effectively with online content, assessments, and communication tools.

"Sixty years ago I knew everything; now I know nothing. Education is a progressive discovery of our own ignorance."

—Will Durant

Online courses operate through course management systems (CMS), such as Blackboard®, WebCT®, and others. Educational publishers have developed many CMS-based online courses for use with their textbooks, and instructors nationwide are now using these as well as developing their own online courses using a CMS.

For the most part, CMS products are fairly user friendly, and students quickly master navigating within them and using the tools. Most CMS products have a set of important features or components, including the syllabus, instructor information, course documents, calendars, asynchronous communications (for example, announcements, surveys, discussion boards, e-mail), synchronous communications (for example, live chats, whiteboards), grouping of students into collaborative study or work groups, online assessments, and online gradebooks.

CMS products provide the means for addressing critical issues in online courses. They allow the chunking of information for ease of learning, review or repetition of key elements; multimodal learning options and ways for students to interact with content; online quizzes; timely, sometimes immediate, feedback; portfolio/performance assessments; and proctored tests.

Some instructors are discovering that their traditional classes are scheduled to become hybrid or blended classes, with up to half of the instructional time planned for online delivery. Hybrid classes maintain personal instructor/student contact plus provide self-study flexibility. In these situations, instructors are finding ways to decide which components or content of a course can be delivered most effectively online or in person.

We also find remnants of older telecourses being modified for online delivery. Video and live telecasts help convey the sense of personal communication, even when students are not physically convened. Much telecourse content, however, is outdated, and must be supplemented with online resources, assessments, and content.

Chapter Summary

- Today's college instructors face significant challenges, many of which represent new angles on classic issues and others that are relatively recent. Among the greatest of these are the increased diversity of student characteristics, instructional environments, and new delivery options. The number of teaching and administrative tasks has become overwhelming in many schools, and pressure on assessment and accountability continues to expand.

- The diversity among students, traditional and nontraditional, encompasses their goals, schedules, gender, race and ethnicity, language abilities, technology abilities, physical capacities, and preparation for college work.

- Expectations students hold of instructors have also shifted. Students still expect instructors to be knowledgeable of their subject matter. They expect discussions that contribute to their mastery, meaningful activities that avoid busy work, frequent feedback, and appropriate uses of up-to-date technology resources. Increasingly, students expect guidance and advice. They expect online courses that are fully developed, well organized, and entertaining; and they expect that the instructors are available for consultation by e-mail or in chat rooms "24-7."

- Instructors are also coping with constant change in course structures—lecture, lab, field, online, and combinations of all these. Each course type demands a customized set of teaching approaches and instructor characteristics.

Think About It: How Have Your Students Changed?

This checklist is intended to enhance your awareness of the characteristics of your students. If you are not currently teaching, base your answers on your observations or impressions of students at your local college. Mark each item as "mainly agree" or "mainly disagree" by placing an X in the appropriate column.

Mainly Agree	Mainly Disagree	Characteristic
		1. Fewer students seem to be motivated by desire for learning. They are more motivated by economic or career issues.
		2. More students are working or they are working more hours.
		3. More students have money problems.
		4. Older or returning students seem to be more anxious than they used to be.
		5. More students are recent high school graduates.
		6. More bright recent high school graduates seem to be going straight to a four-year institution or into the job market, because fewer of them are in my classes or attending two-year schools.
		7. Students seem to be less respectful and less courteous.
		8. I have (the college has) more students with learning disabilities.
		9. Students are more impatient. They want instant learning without applying themselves to the process.
		10. In general, students seem to have less knowledge at the outset of their college work. They are not as well prepared in various subjects, such as science, history, and math.
		11. More students need to improve their classroom verbal communication skills, their reading skills, and their writing skills.
		12. More students do not seem interested in reading.
		13. More students need instruction in English as a second language.
		14. More students need to develop thinking and problem-solving skills.
		15. Students are demanding more and more time and personal help from me (instructors).
		16. More students resent having to complete assignments. They seem to think that classroom attendance should be sufficient.
		17. More students are taking drugs or are recovering from addictions.
		18. "Good" students are becoming more resentful of the time I (instructors) take with students who need more help.
		19. An increasing proportion of enrollment consists of part-time students.
		20. More students want courses with consumer orientation or information such as inclusion of job search information or personal finance management.
		21. More students have low math skills.
		22. More students are single parents.
		23. Racial and ethnic diversity has increased significantly.
		24. More students have personal, family, or emotional problems that affect their learning.
		25. Students need technical skills for Web and hybrid learning.
		26. More students are interested in a personal or individual learning plan.
		27. Students need alternative and always-accessible learning media (CD-ROMs, DVDs, PDAs).

These characteristics are based on recent surveys and discussions among postsecondary professionals. The number of items you marked "mainly agree" indicates how similar your students and experiences are to the situations in other colleges. Remember, though, that the specific characteristics and experiences vary widely from place to place.

The importance of completing this short checklist is not really to see if your student characteristics are like those of students elsewhere. Rather, it is to help you think about your students and their learning.

After you have completed the checklist, think about what these characteristics imply for how you teach. Write one implication for each characteristic that you marked "mainly agree."

Discussion Questions

1. Are the characteristics of your students changing? Describe the students you think you will be teaching five years from now.
2. Should instructors be expected to develop online course content? Why or why not?
3. Describe the teaching structures in which you now work. Are you prepared to teach in other formats? Which structures work best for you? Which ones best meet the needs of most of your students? Which ones will best meet the needs of most of your students five years from now?
4. Which changes facing you and your college present the greatest challenge for you? Why?
5. What can you do to improve the relationship of adjunct faculty with regular faculty and the administration?

Field Work

Find out the following information as it applies on your campus.

1. What counseling services—academic and personal—are available to students?
2. Does the school offer tutoring in basic skills? Does the school offer course-specific assistance?
3. Can students obtain tutoring or consulting on computer use for CD-ROM, DVD, or online classes?
4. Does the school offer an array of classes at different levels for English language learners (ELL)? Are any of them tied to a particular discipline, such as the sciences?
5. Are signing services for students with loss of hearing available? Are testing and other arrangements available for students who are visually impaired?
6. Is a report on ADA compliance available to you and to the public?
7. What is the proportion of

   a. full-time vs. part-time students?
   b. classroom vs. online students?
   c. traditional vs. online courses?
   d. adjunct or associate faculty vs. full-time faculty?

8. Have you conducted a survey of students to obtain information on their goals? What are the chief ones identified?

Professional Portfolio: What are the Key Characteristics of Exceptional Teachers?

Opinions and research analyses offer an enormous range of ideas about what makes an outstanding teacher. Harry Wong, well known author of *The First Days of School: How to Be an Effective Teacher*, cites the qualities of positive expectations, good classroom management, and the ability to design lesson plans for student mastery. Dr. Mani Mina of the Department of Electrical and Computer Engineering, Iowa State University, has come up with ten key characteristics:

1. Knows the subject to the level that it can be communicated coherently
2. Is prepared for each class
3. Is interested in the subject and the students' learning of the subject
4. Shows expertise in the subject and shares it with enthusiasm
5. Is clear on expectations
6. Welcomes questions and comments
7. Is patient with the class and gives students time to learn and digest
8. Has an open mind throughout the term and is ready to change approaches to make the students learn more
9. Respects students and tries to understand their points of view
10. Can make the students look forward to going to class

Another of the many lists is one developed by Judith Lloyd Yero in "Teacher Quality," published by Teacher's Mind Resources at www.TeachersMind.com. According to Yero, researchers have discovered that outstanding teachers share the following characteristics:

- a belief that all students can learn, but not all in the same way
- a belief that teachers are learners and students are teachers
- a high level of respect for all students
- high expectations for all students, but not the same for all
- a humanistic rather than custodial approach to classroom control

How closely do your own beliefs about the qualities of an exceptional teacher align with the theories presented above? Using these suggestions and others from research or your experience, develop your own list of the key characteristics of exceptional teachers. For each characteristic, write a two- or three-sentence explanation and give at least one example of how you exhibit this quality in your teaching.

Exceptional Teaching is

Strategic and Planned

Exceptional teaching does not happen by accident. Instructors assess, plan, implement, and evaluate . . . repeatedly. They do this based on many of the factors that make teaching learner-centered and on several other variables.

Identify the Heart of the Course

Before students even think about entering or logging into the classroom, instructors make decisions about the course. These begin with identifying the heart of the course. That is, what, exactly, are the most important outcomes that students should achieve? And what plan of action can the instructor devise that will help ensure those outcomes? These intended outcomes must be realistic, and sometimes they must be flexible as well. Some instructors overestimate how much students can master in the duration of a course. Others underestimate. Bear in mind that you might need to make adjustments along the way. If you have only covered half the material and the course is three-fourths through, the best option may not be to rush through the other half of the material. Periodic reality checks and experience will be your best guides.

For example, Glen teaches basic English writing skills. Whether he wants students to recognize and use correct English grammar or wants students to be able to write a one-page description that is logical and coherent will drive his plan in different directions.

Greg is planning to teach an art history class. Which aspects of art history does he feel students should master? Names, dates, and styles? Influences of Dutch masters? Use of light, color, or form by Impressionists? And how well should students know these things?

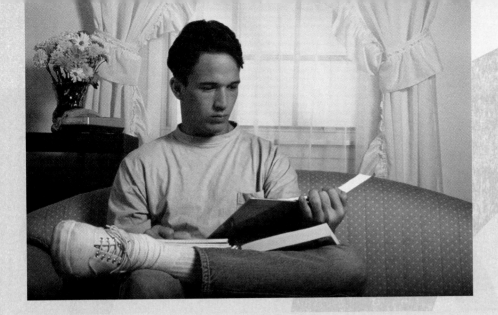

Well enough to identify them? Describe them? Compare them? What Greg decides about the key concepts of the course and how well students should know them will shape his action plan. He will decide what he really wants students to learn and then plan how he is going to make that learning happen.

How Will the Course Come Alive?

When Alice was planning her business math class, she asked a set of questions about the outcomes she intended for her students. For example, one outcome was that students would be able to graph profits over time, given a data set with revenues and expenses. With this in mind, she asked herself the following questions, and the answers helped define her action plan.

1. Does this require instructor lecture? If so, on what topics? What do I need to tell them? Show them? Structure for them?
2. Does teaching toward this outcome create opportunities for instructor/student or student/student dialog? At which points? How? How do I set them up?
3. How can I encourage/inspire students to interact with the content?

4. How can I shape the context so that the outcome is more relevant to student interests? How can I motivate students to think about this intended outcome, how to reach it, what uses it might have?
5. How can I provide opportunities for students to work as teams, small groups, or an interrelated community?
6. What resources can I provide or identify that will help students reach this outcome or enhance their understanding, skill, or performance?
7. How can I use technology creatively and meaningfully in this course?
8. How will I know that students have attained the intended outcome?

What you plan, your action plan for a course, is your intended approach to teaching the course. Is what you plan always what happens? Probably not. Maybe we even hope not. Events, questions, students, and other things happen to inspire you to make midcourse corrections. And sometimes an idea that seemed brilliant to you at the time of planning seems absurd under classroom lights.

This is why continuous questioning of your intentions and expectations for a course results in a better course for the students. Effective instructors ask themselves repeatedly, "Does what I am doing take us toward what I meant to accomplish?"

Chapter

2

Planning a Successful Course

I was stuck, and I could feel the panic creeping in. It was the first time the dean had given me responsibility for planning a course, and my brain was shorting out from overload. I'd read through a dozen textbooks looking at topics and assignments and chapter questions. I'd browsed at least forty reference books that I'd kept for just this situation. I'd looked at instructor editions, transparencies, charts, and illustrations until my eyes fogged. I'd found and invented and created lists of projects and assignments and questions and guest speakers and demonstrations and field trips. I'd previewed workbooks, journals, learning kits, CD-ROMs and videos and audiotapes and spent long hours searching the Web for solutions, sure to aggravate a hand already aching from the unfettered mousing. I'd diagrammed student hours and how they might be spent—diagrams that now I could not decipher. I made notes about student backgrounds and expectations, department and division requirements; pictured the available classrooms and facilities; and reviewed the curriculum where the course would fit. And oh the lists upon lists of objectives—intended outcomes—scratched out and scribbled over—outcomes related to knowledge and analysis and expression and behaviors plus ideas on how to evaluate them all.

I knocked over yesterday's coffee, thick with half and half, and silently watched it spread across the papers and trickle down the side of the desk. Is crying allowed in course development? I hadn't allotted time for that. Tired of it all, I gave in to the moment, put my head down, and waited. The coffee dripped onto the stack of books on the floor. I tried to remember what I thought I knew about course development, and my mind wandered to a question I'd once heard an instructional designer ask. "What's the point, Sue? What will the learners gain that is *important?* Answer that first. Then decide on the parts. What are the parts?" Okay, parts. Every course has parts. That's something I've dealt with time and again. Now I just had to figure out *which* parts make up the course content. Then come the resources, activities, and assessments—I'm on my way.

Learning Outcomes

- Write primary course outcomes, including related foundation, cross-disciplinary, and technical skills
- Choose a delivery method and instructional approach to suit the course content
- Structure course content into parts based on key topics and essential questions
- Design the major course activities to support achieving the course outcomes within authentic learning contexts
- Select text and media resources using established criteria
- Plan an assessment strategy that aligns with the course outcomes

Course Planning: Strategizing and Thinking through the Process

This chapter addresses the rationale for developing a course action plan (CAP) and the steps that culminate in an informal, working document to guide subsequent course planning, including creating the syllabus and writing individual session plans—topics addressed in Chapter 3. The CAP proposed and discussed in this chapter includes four sections:

Phase One: Developing the course outcomes, including related foundation, cross-disciplinary, and technology skills

Phase Two: Determining the course structure, that is, dividing the course content into parts and identifying outcomes for each part

Phase Three: Selecting the course methodology, including delivery mode, instructional approach, resources, and activities

Phase Four: Planning an assessment strategy, including the number and timing of cognitive tests and performance assessments such as projects, reports, and presentations

Developing a course action plan is really a thinking process in which you focus on what you want students to achieve by the end of the course and identify the strategies that will make this learning happen. Picture the thinking process as a type of flowchart consisting of four phases: (1) developing course outcomes; (2) dividing the course content into parts, each with a set of learning outcomes; (3) choosing instructional methods, resources, and major assignments; and (4) identifying a strategy for assessing students' achievement of the outcomes. These four phases mirror the steps in every teaching/learning situation, whether viewed from the broad course level or the single class session level: identifying measurable outcomes, structuring the learning content into parts, employing resources and activities to cause the learning to happen, and then measuring learners' progress—

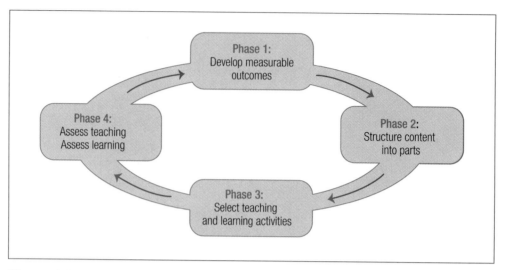

Figure 2.1. Phases of a Course Action Plan.

and your teaching success—against the course outcomes. Figure 2.1 illustrates the relationships among the phases and their components.

By answering the questions and developing the information called for in each section of this chapter, you will be able to create your own course action plan. And while this type of thoughtful planning is ideal, we also recognize that in certain circumstances, particularly if you are an adjunct faculty member, you may be handed the course outcomes along with a textbook that generally aligns with the outcomes and be expected to launch the course on a predetermined path. A previous instructor or the textbook publisher might have supplied the suggested outcomes and a syllabus. But even in these situations, you can use the course action plan thinking process to identify ways to enrich the course or perhaps identify additional outcomes and their related activities that will add value for students.

Preparing to Plan: What Do I Need to Know?

The first step isn't one that you find in most "how to design a course" descriptions. It doesn't start with a form or outline, and it doesn't have an order. The first step is immersing yourself in every aspect of the course, filling your brain with information about student characteristics; changes or trends in your discipline; your school's physical, technological, and other resources; textbooks and supplementary materials; ideas about activities to engage students' minds and motivations; options for contexts for teaching and learning; and creative, authentic ways to assess learning.

Some time along the way, probably when your head feels about to burst, your brain will begin making decisions about what you really want students to learn. And you'll begin to see the "big picture" as having five or six or nine or some other number of big chunks. And then, taking into account how much time you have, your resources, your students, and all the other pictures in your head, you will decide which big chunks, and which big outcomes, will be the basis of your course.

When you are thinking about the important outcomes that you want students to get out of the course, remember that we wish to produce learning, not just "deliver instruction." Consider, too, that some outcomes are more important than others. What changes do you want to see in students' knowledge or abilities or attitudes? Write "Most of all, I want students to learn . . ." or "I want students to learn how to . . . ." These statements should capture the significant learning that you want to happen. Tip: Yes, you could write, and probably will later write, "Students will learn how to . . . ," but making it personal by starting out with "I want . . ." can sometimes help you think. Even starting with "My students will . . ." can help make your thinking less abstract or distant.

Using Taxonomies

If you find yourself struggling with writing broad course-level outcomes, or if you are unsure about the value of what you have written, it may be helpful to consider outcomes within the framework of learning theories or learning taxonomies, which classify learning into types and levels. Taxonomies put to good use will help teachers with the following tasks:

- stating their goals for student learning
- categorizing the outcomes in terms of difficulty and challenge
- "thinking through" the level of thinking they want from learners; do they want the students to do higher-order thinking or just have a rudimentary understanding of basic facts?
- planning activities that align to that type of thinking by selecting different action verbs
- helping students to know where they are going and to be accountable for their learning (outcomes are designed to "expect" students to be accountable)
- assessing progress that aligns directly to the level and challenge of each outcome

Bloom's Taxonomy

Many theories of learning have influenced teaching throughout the history of education. Among the most influential in the latter half of the twentieth century was the work of Benjamin Bloom and his colleagues. Following the 1948 meetings of the American Psychological Association, Bloom and other educational psychologists classified levels of intellectual behaviors they considered important in learning. Their work developed into a taxonomy with three overlapping domains: the cognitive (mental), psychomotor (skills), and affective (attitudes, feelings, and values).[1]

Bloom divides each domain into hierarchical (ordered) levels, as shown in Figure 2.2. Further, each level can be associated with certain action verbs in order to focus on the learning at that level.

---

[1] Benjamin Bloom's 1956 book with David Krathwohl, *Taxonomy of Educational Objectives,* was the first of several books on this topic.

CLASSIFICATION OF PERFORMANCE OBJECTIVES	
Cognitive Domain (Mental)	
Level	**Definition**
1. Knowledge	Recalling of previously learned material. VERBS: define, describe, identify, label, list, select
2. Comprehension	Making use of knowledge without relating it to other material. VERBS: describe, discuss, explain, give example, illustrate, summarize
3. Application	Using learned material in new and concrete situations. VERBS: classify, complete, demonstrate, generalize, relate, solve
4. Analysis	Breaking down material into its component parts. VERBS: analyze, compare, contrast, discriminate, separate, transform
5. Synthesis	Putting together elements/parts to form a whole. VERBS: arrange, combine, develop, integrate, organize, synthesize
6. Evaluation	Judging the value of material for a given purpose. VERBS: appraise, assess, evaluate, decide, rate, recommend
Affective Domain (Attitudes, Values, Feelings)	
Level	**Definition**
1. Receiving	Willingness to pay attention to a stimulus. VERBS: ask, choose, follow, locate, reply, use
2. Responding	Actively participating. VERBS: answers, discuss, greet, help, present, tell
3. Valuing	Attaching value or worth to a behavior or object. VERBS: describe, explain, join, select, share, study
4. Organization	Building a value system from individual values. VERBS: arrange, combine, explain, integrate, order, relate
5. Characterization	Acts in a way to demonstrate values. VERBS: discriminate, display, modify, perform, question, use
Psychomotor Domain (Skills)	
Level	**Definition**
1. Perception	Becoming aware of objects through senses. VERBS: be aware, recognize, sense
2. Set	Getting ready for a specific action. VERBS: achieve, position, prepare
3. Guided Response	Imitating or trying out the actions of others. VERBS: follow, imitate, perform
4. Mechanism	Demonstrating a habitual response. VERBS: carry out, demonstrate, perform
5. Complex Overt Response	Performing a motor skill on one's own. VERBS: operate, perform, set up
6. Adaptation	Altering a motor skill to meet a new situation. VERBS: alter, develop, revise
7. Origination	Creating new motor responses to situations. VERBS: create, demonstrate, react

Figure 2.2. Bloom's Taxonomy of Learning Domains. (Adapted from Benjamin S. Bloom and David R. Krathwohl. *Taxonomy of Educational Objectives: The Classification of Educational Goals.* New York: Longman's, Green, 1956.)

Typical verbs for each level are indicated in the list, although this is not an exhaustive list of possible verbs. Note that more verbs are found on the cognitive and affective levels than on the psychomotor level. Consult Bloom and other sources for additional lists of verbs.

Fink's Taxonomy of Significant Learning

During the past decade or so, educators have come to recognize the importance of other areas in learners' education, and they have worked to broaden the learning outcomes taxonomy. The taxonomy of significant learning[2] developed by L. Dee Fink identifies six categories of important learning outcomes: foundational knowledge, application, integration, human dimension, caring, and learning how to learn.

> *"when you commit to something, the universe conspires to assist you...."*
>
> —Barbara Streisand

Fink's six categories and brief examples of each are described below. As you read the information on Fink's taxonomy, note that Bloom's and Fink's taxonomies are not mutually exclusive. Fink's work is in some ways broader than Bloom's, while Bloom gives us many helpful descriptions and verbs to define intended outcomes in detail.

Foundational Knowledge

Foundational knowledge is necessary for other learning. It includes general basic knowledge of, for example, math, history, basic science, geography, art, citizenship, or major ideas. Course outcomes would be related to understanding and remembering information and ideas.

> Examples: Students will apply the principles of small business in a free market. Students will learn the functions of key components of a computer system (hardware, software, data).

Foundational knowledge is similar to Bloom's cognitive domain levels 1 and 2, viz., recall of previously learned material and making use of knowledge without relating it to other material.

Application

By application, Fink means that students use foundational knowledge to think or act in new ways. In this sense, it is putting foundational knowledge to use. The thinking might be practical, analytical, creative, or some other form. The acting refers to development of certain skills. Course outcomes would be related to thinking and doing.

---

[2]L. Dee Fink. *Creating Significant Learning Experiences: An Integrated Approach to Designing College Courses*, San Francisco: Jossey-Bass, 2003.

Meeting a Challenge
Planning for English Language Learners

One of the fastest growing groups of students in higher education is composed of students whose first language is not English and whose English is not yet equivalent to that of native English speakers in lexicon and syntax. The wide differences in fluency among limited English speakers makes your planning for meeting their needs somewhat more complex—and very important.

Chances are that you already know you will have some students whose language skills are not up to the level we expect or want. What? You're not the English language learners instructor? Not your job? Think again. Your job is to help *all* the students in your course meet the intended outcomes. So plan how you're going to do this for your English language learners. Begin by assessing early on the language abilities of your students. Try these measures:

1. One method is a "one-minute preview." Tear some sheets of paper into four parts and give each student a piece. Ask them no more than two questions and give them one minute (okay, two) to write their answer. The question *could* be about their language skills, but it might be better to ask them something else. That way you get a short writing sample plus information about something else, such as why they are taking the course, something they would like to learn, the types of activities they enjoy, or what they are most worried about in the course. You don't need to be an English teacher to see which students will need help. Use your common sense.
2. If your class is small, conduct a discussion early in the course. Make sure you hear each student answer a question or ask one.
3. If you are conducting a pretest for the course, include some questions that ask students if they need to improve their English or their writing skills.
4. Tell students to e-mail you if they think they will need language help or extra exam time for reading assignments or tests.

Evaluating Resources and Activities

When you are planning your course, the following questions should be among those you ask:

- Do your textbook and other materials (including online course work) provide clearly stated definitions of terms in a glossary?
- Do you need to provide glossary items in addition to those provided?
- What is the best way to provide glossary terms? Lists or cards that you prepare? On the Web? Photocopies of annotated pages? In a workshop that shows students how to do this?
- Do you have or need a list of terms for each session or part that might be troublemakers for English language learners?
- Do you have or need a list of "tips for learning the language of botany" (or whatever your subject area)?
- Do you need to devise additional activities to require students to *use* the language you want them to learn?

- Do your materials use plenty of examples, charts, graphs, diagrams, and illustrations to convey concepts?
- Do you need to have students arrange for tutors to assist with writing reports and essays? Do you need to dedicate a session or part of one to instruction on how to write the report, essay, or other work you expect?

Rethinking Course Outcomes

Seldom are assessments language-free. Even art, woodworking, auto mechanics, and other such courses usually have a written component included. How will you know that students have reached the outcomes you set? Examine the assessments that you have created or selected *again*, from the specific perspective of evaluating the language used by the assessments and the language being required of students for responding. Also ask if the assessment provides varying ways of presenting information and questions. Does it use graphics, diagrams, and illustrations? Does it ask students to match things or sketch relationships? In other words, maximize the probability that students have ample opportunity to demonstrate their mastery of concepts and skills rather than big words and grammar.

Examples: Students will analyze the major components of a dramatic work. Students will describe and compare the main functions of various types of applications, including spreadsheets, databases, and word processors.

Application is similar to Bloom's cognitive domain levels 3 and 4, viz., using learned material in new and concrete situations and breaking down material into its component parts.

Integration

Students' ability to recognize or make connections between things is considered the focus of the integration category. This is important learning that gives students a new power of thinking. Course outcomes are related to synthesizing, organizing, and developing ideas, systems, projects, etc., and include creativity and arriving at new "works," physical or intellectual.

Examples: Students will write a critical review. Students will design a database; they will design and generate reports from the database using sample data.

Integration is similar to Bloom's cognitive domain level 5, synthesis.

Human Dimension

"All learning has an emotional base."
—Plato

The human dimension category is related to students' learning about themselves and others— the personal or social implications of their learning. They recognize and understand the human significance of what they are learning. This learning could come about from participation in activities with others or from course content. Outcomes might include developing a better understanding of others or interacting more effectively with others.

Examples: Students will conduct effective interviews. Students will participate in cooperative brainstorming to design databases to address specific needs.

The human dimension is most closely allied to Bloom's affective domain levels 1, 2, and 3, receiving, responding, and valuing.

Caring

Caring refers to developing new feelings, interests, or values—including motivation for learning. Fink notes, "When students care about something, they then have the energy they need for learning more about it and making it a part of their lives. Without the energy for learning, nothing significant happens." Outcomes will be related to interests, attitudes, values, and motivations, whether expressed or demonstrated in other ways.

Examples: Students will place a higher value on their mathematical skills for their everyday living. Students will value the efficiency of a database as compared to older approaches to records management.

Caring is most similar to Bloom's affective domain level 3, valuing.

Learning How to Learn

This category refers to students' becoming better learners. In the past, helping students learn how to learn may have been among the least appreciated categories of learning. This learning does not mean that students master twelve different theories about how people learn. It does mean that they discover the environments in which they are most successful learners, the techniques that help them remember information, and the questioning tools that help them connect related information or skills. They might learn to monitor their comprehension, use a particular method of discovery, or direct their own learning process. Outcomes might include any of these.

Examples: Students will use strategies for identifying the significant facts presented in a scientific article. Students will use strategies for testing their own comprehension of database design by evaluating and comparing database evaluations.

Learning how to learn is related to Bloom's cognitive domain level 6, evaluation, although Fink's category focuses more on internal strategies for learning whereas Bloom's cognitive domain refers to a level of thinking.

For Fink, these six groups are the *significant* categories of learning, and courses that bring about learning in two or three of these areas are accomplishing important learning.

Applying Bloom's and Fink's Taxonomies

Note that we have been discussing outcomes in general ways. Intended outcomes for your courses will be more specific and relevant to those courses. As a course plan is defined in greater detail, it will delineate how students will demonstrate their achievement of the outcomes and what the course will do to bring about that achievement. For example, an English course on the plays of Tennessee Williams might list the following among general intended outcomes (using Fink's categories and Bloom's verbs):

Application: Students will analyze the text of a Tennessee Williams play.
Integration: Students will compare the written version of a Tennessee Williams play to a performance of the same play.
Human Dimension: Students will describe ways that Tennessee Williams' life influenced his writing.
Caring: Students will demonstrate greater interest in American drama.

Another example is a first-term college accounting course for which you might use Bloom's taxonomy to establish the following course-level outcomes:

- analyze accounting transactions (cognitive, analysis)
- develop a set of financial statements for an organization (cognitive, synthesis)
- evaluate the financial health of an organization (cognitive, evaluation)
- discriminate between ethical and unethical financial behavior of an organization (affective, characterization)
- carry out data entry of transactions into accounting software (psychomotor, mechanism)

PHASE ONE: Developing Course Outcomes

With some background knowledge of learning taxonomies, you are ready to attack the process of developing outcomes and objectives. How do you decide? What questions do you ask?

1. **Course outcomes:** When this course is over, in what ways will the learner be *permanently* changed? Should instruction result in

- building knowledge?
- developing higher-order thinking?
- changing attitudes or emotions?
- developing interpersonal skills?
- developing psychomotor skills?
- developing independent learning skills?
- developing technical literacy?

Then evaluate your course goals from another perspective by thinking about the essence of the course. In a graphic design course, for example, if the essence is art, design, originality, beauty, symbolism, and creation, do your outcomes reflect that emphasis?

If your course essence is technical problem solving, troubleshooting, crisis management, learning new systems all the time, and interpreting technical documents, do your course outcomes reflect this emphasis?

2. **Authentic context:** Think of your course in terms of providing an authentic context for learning. Ask these questions about the course content to help you arrive at the related foundational, cross-disciplinary, and technical skills that should be stressed:

- What types of problems are faced? How?
- What decisions are made?
- What must be communicated?
- What do learners have to read or write?
- What technical skills are required to perform the work?
- Under what conditions is the work performed on the job?
- Will the work be done alone or in a group?
- How will the performer learn the work is satisfactory?
- How will the performer receive feedback?

3. **Taxonomies of learning:** Using the taxonomies and related contextual skills presented earlier, write the end-of-course outcomes first. In phase two of your course planning, when you divide the content into parts, you will write the part outcomes.

Looking ahead to planning activities and tests, examine the verb list (Bloom's, Figure 2.2) and think about what type of thinking you are looking for. This guides the activities you will design for learning, review, and eventually assessment. Notice that some of the differences among the verbs are clear and direct; others are more subtle. Consider, for example, the verbs "debate" and "negotiate." Asking students to debate an issue or the pros and cons of an argument may imply that someone else will judge their arguments and their effectiveness. Negotiation, on the other hand, implies that students will need to come to some agreement about a question or issue. Another example might be the verbs "identify" and "label." At a glance, these seem very similar. To identify something, you might ask students to indicate which item from a list of descriptions is the XYZ, as in "Which of the following is an example of XYZ?" On the other hand, you might ask students to give a name to each item described in the list, that is, label them.

4. **Audit of the work:** As a final step, revisit the work from the perspective of "realism" and authenticity. Do the statements communicate *importance* and convey *relevance*? Do they look like busy work or do they look like work worth doing?

The Phase One Course Outcomes section of the CAP includes primary course outcomes and related contextual skills in foundation, cross-disciplinary, and technology areas. See Figure 2.3 for an example of how these might be written for a Pharmacology and Pharmacy Practice course for pharmacy technicians.

COURSE: PHARMACOLOGY AND PHARMACY PRACTICE
PHASE ONE: Course Outcomes
PRIMARY COURSE OUTCOMES
At course conclusion, the student will be able to
✓ Demonstrate sufficient knowledge of drugs to function as a pharmacy technician in a community or hospital setting.
✓ Calculate, measure, and dispense drugs accurately.
✓ Perform administrative duties and adhere to pharmacy ethical/legal guidelines.
✓ Demonstrate best practices in customer relations and patient care.
RELATED CONTEXTUAL SKILLS
Foundation Skills
✓ Use medical vocabulary accurately and appropriately.
✓ Read technical material (labels, packaging, specifications, reports) and extract pertinent information.
✓ Make decisions in accordance with pharmacy and business ethics.
✓ Demonstrate an ability to resolve conflicts.
✓ Appreciate the value of the scientific method.
✓ Appreciate other cultures and how cultural values affect and interact with pharmacology and pharmacy practice.

continued on next page

Communication and Cross-disciplinary Skills
✓ Write concise and effective e-mails.
✓ Read e-mails and faxes and interpret written documentation correctly.
✓ Speak clearly and directly.
✓ Build positive, ongoing relationships with employer, staff, and customers.
✓ Work in a team/group environment.
Technology Skills
✓ Use medical resources on the Web to find and verify medical and technical information.
✓ Conduct effective Web searches on medical queries and questions.
✓ Understand and download information from the Internet.
✓ Use pharmacy software-based dispensing systems.

Figure 2.3. Sample Primary Course Outcomes and Related Contextual Skills.

PHASE TWO: Determining Course Structure

In Phase One of the CAP process, you established performance outcomes for your course. These statements of performance are essentially the educational targets for the student. In Phase Two, planning for the course parts and units begins. This phase involves four steps: (1) determining the subject areas that need to be taught and chunking the course into parts (typically four to six parts); (2) specifying the part- or unit-level performance outcomes; (3) validating your courses by formulating the essential questions of the course; and (4) thinking through sequence, the order of learning.

Structuring the Course into Parts

Defining subject boundaries is an important but difficult task. You need to identify which subjects students need to learn in order to demonstrate the course outcomes by the end of the quarter or semester. Begin by analyzing the outcomes and determining which subject areas or curriculum areas are implied. Looking at the Primary Course Level Outcomes for the Pharmacology and Pharmacy Practice course shown in Figure 2.3, it is clear that the areas of pharmacologic agents, human relations and communications, and calculation and measurement are subjects that would encompass the desired learning. Here is where curriculum planning really gets interesting. We all know that you do not have the time to teach everything. In fact, you cannot even teach everything of importance, but you can begin to narrow down the subjects by asking these questions:

- What topics in each subject area are essential for demonstrating the course outcomes? List those topics.
- Do some of the topics complement or require each other for authenticity and thus should be taught together in the same part? If so, group them accordingly.
- Are the skills taught to mastery level in another course either preceding or following this course? Often the related skills (writing, math, speaking) have been taught but need to be modeled and applied in the functional context.

In this case, students also take a full-credit course in pharmacy math, so the math work done in the Pharmacology and Pharmacy Practice course will be at the applied level and a high level of skill will be assumed. The same is true for communications; students take a full-credit course, so applied skills will be emphasized.

- Is this the only course that will address this subject and skill set? Human relations, pharmacologic agents, and pharmacy methods are subjects that are not taught in any other course. Full, direct instruction in those parts will be required in this course.
- What do students already know about each subject? What can they learn on their own independent of your direct instruction?
- Where in each subject will the instruction "begin" and "end"?

Specifying Part Outcomes

Outcomes developed at the part or unit level build to the performance of the course outcomes, so the most important question to ask yourself is, "Will these unit outcomes prepare students to successfully perform the end-of-course outcomes?" Figure 2.4 shows how outcome-based curriculum planning is organized hierarchically. Throughout instruction, the learner will be working toward meeting various objectives and outcomes. The broad course outcomes are marked by higher and more challenging skill sets and typically require the integration of many skills, while unit or part outcomes are more narrowly defined and focused. Note that the terms *outcomes* and *objectives* are frequently interchanged. For the purposes of this text, we will use *outcomes* at the course and part level and *objectives* at the lesson or session level. As you develop your outcomes, ask yourself: "What must my students be able to demonstrate or reveal to indicate that they have a thoughtful grasp of the essentials?"

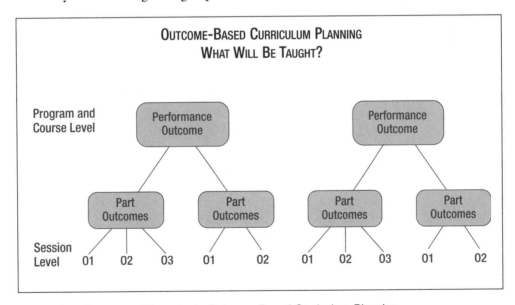

Figure 2.4. Outcomes Hierarchy in Outcome-Based Curriculum Planning.

Formulating the Essential Questions

One way to ensure that your course is focused on the most important skills is to formulate the essential questions that form the heart of the course. Essential questions are historically the most important questions, issues, problems, and debates in the field. The goal is to get students to practice thinking like experts in the field and to use course knowledge and skills to address the fundamental problems of each discipline. Frequently, instructors are so bogged down with the enormity of course planning that the larger picture is lost. Formulating essential questions helps instructors and students see the big picture, the recurring themes, and the questions that when answered lead to enduring understanding. For example, in math courses, these kind of questions prevail: What does it mean to reason mathematically? How does *what* we measure affect *how* we measure? Can everything be quantified? For additional examples, review the essential questions developed for the Pharmacology and Pharmacy Practice course (see Figure 2.5) and the Plays of Tennessee Williams course (see Figure 2.6).

> *"Many instructional arrangements seem 'contrived,' but there is nothing wrong with that. It is the teacher's function to contrive conditions under which students learn. It has always been the task of formal education to set up behavior which would prove useful or enjoyable later in a student's life."*
>
> —B. F. Skinner

COURSE: PHARMACOLOGY AND PHARMACY PRACTICE
PHASE TWO: Course Structure
COURSE PART 1: PHARMACOLOGIC AGENTS
Key Topics and Areas of Study:
A. Receptors, mechanisms of drug actions, pharmacokinetics, drug effects, and interactions
B. Administration of pharmacologic agents
C. Classes of drugs: anti-infectives, narcotics, respiratory, cardiac, GI, non-narcotic analgesics, chemotherapy, vitamins and supplements
D. Medical/pharmacological terms
Essential Questions: How does each drug act on the target body system? What other physiological processes are impacted? When are drugs more damaging than helpful? Which combinations of drugs and OTC drugs can cause illness or death? How can one drug be healthy for one person and not for another?
Part Outcomes:
✓ Demonstrate a working knowledge of the principles of drug action in the body and individual cells, drug dosages, routes of administration, and interactions.
✓ Interpret drug labels and dosage information and dispense as prescribed.
✓ Use drug references to accurately identify generic and brand equivalents.
COURSE PART 2: PHARMACY METHODS
Key Topics and Areas of Study:
A. Pharmacy law and ethics
B. Sources and uses of drugs
C. Types of drug administration
D. Extemporaneous compounding
E. Dispensing and inventory

continued on next page

Essential Questions: Should drugs be regulated and how? Do customers and pharmacies share the same values and concerns? When do the needs of the customer conflict with the goals of the pharmacist? How much should drugs cost? Who decides and what determines the cost? What latitude does the technician have to interpret the doctor's order? What latitude does the pharmacist have?

Part Outcomes:

✓ Perform pharmacy technician duties, meeting or exceeding the performance requirements and ethics standards required by the industry.

✓ Perform record-keeping functions associated with dispensing pharmaceuticals, processing insurance claims, and maintaining drug inventory.

✓ Recognize potential prescription errors related to conflicting, inadequate, or excessive administration of drugs.

COURSE PART 3: HUMAN RELATIONS AND COMMUNICATIONS

Key Topics and Areas of Study:

A. Cultural and language differences

B. Issues in community settings

C. Issues in hospital settings

D. Communications and human relations

Essential Questions: Can a person hear but not listen? How do you know when someone understands? How does technology enhance expression? In what ways might technology hinder it? How can I improve my communication with customers who speak a different primary language? What are the differences in procedures and job responsibilities in community settings vs. hospital settings?

Part Outcomes:

✓ Translate and communicate prescribed dosage and administration instructions to customers or patients, ensuring patient understanding.

✓ Be a customer/patient advocate; resolve potential conflicts and misunderstandings.

COURSE PART 4: CALCULATION AND MEASUREMENT

Key Topics and Areas of Study:

A. Business math as used in pharmacies

B. Solutions, IV rate, dosages, electrolytes

C. Basic math used (fractions, ratios, decimals, percents)

D. Metric and apothecary systems

Essential Questions: When is the correct answer not the right solution? To what extent are science and common sense related? Can I explain math to customers and patients who speak a different language or who are not math literate?

Part Outcomes:

✓ Follow the correct procedures related to compounding and admixture operations.

✓ Perform calculations required for the usual dosages and solution preparations.

✓ Adhere to quality assurance processes and improve systems on a continuous basis.

Figure 2.5. Essential Questions for a Pharmacology and Pharmacy Practice Course.

THE PLAYS OF TENNESSEE WILLIAMS		
PART AND OUTCOME	ESSENTIAL QUESTIONS	KEY TOPICS/ AREAS OF STUDY
1. Play Analysis. Outcome: Students will analyze dramatic text. (Application)	What are the basic or common structures or forms in dramas? How do dramas develop their primary themes? What are character "types" and how are they developed or communicated? What is meant by dramatic flow? What are different ways to use space for different purposes? What are different ways that authors use to represent, organize, or communicate time and its passing?	*The Glass Menagerie* and *The Rose Tattoo*
2. Text vs. Performance Comparison. Outcome: Students will compare the written and performed versions of a play. (Integration)	What are the similarities and differences in the read, heard, and viewed experiences of plays?	*Cat on a Hot Tin Roof* and *The Glass Menagerie*
3. Human Influences. Outcome: Students will describe ways that writers' lives influence their writing. (Human Dimension)	How do an author's experiences influence his or her writings? What experiences might be most influential? Consider experiences of family, loneliness, social interactions, culture, sexuality, and others you identify. How are they reflected in *Clothes for a Summer Hotel* and *Cat on a Hot Tin Roof?*	*Clothes for a Summer Hotel* and *Cat on a Hot Tin Roof*
4. Being Inspired. Outcome: Students will demonstrate greater interest in American drama. (Caring)	What aspects of drama might relate to today's society? Which aspects do you observe in your own life? Which aspects do you observe in the lives of your family members, your heroes, successful people, people you admire or dislike, people who share your political or social views?	*American Blues*

Figure 2.6. Essential Questions for a Course on the Plays of Tennessee Williams.

Sequencing the Learning

Once you have identified the course parts, topics, and essential questions, you have defined the scope of your course and are ready to think about sequencing. It is important to note that scope (the extent of content) and sequence (the order of learning the content) are not the same thing but are often treated as if they were. The main questions that should drive sequencing decisions are:

- How can the course be sequenced to keep students engaged from day one, and interested and stimulated by the course materials?
- How can early authentic work and early successes be "arranged"? To motivate students, can you build instruction around applied contexts, preventing the too frequently asked question: "Why do I have to learn this?"
- Can instruction focus on problems worth solving and issues worth discussing? If so, student engagement is more likely.
- What sequence of parts will facilitate and produce effective learning?

The questions listed above focus on building and sustaining interest in the course, a key goal regardless of how you choose to sequence or organize your course. Experienced curriculum developers agree that there are a number of correct ways to sequence the course parts. Courses can be arranged in any of the following ways:

- chronologically
- simple to complex
- from description to analysis (deductive)
- from illustration to broader principles (inductive)
- from unified picture to specific parts
- by recurrent themes or patterns
- by case study methods
- by inquiry and discovery
- by application and problem solving

Though courses can be arranged in alternatively correct ways, some disciplines and their inherent habits of mind are best taught using a particular approach. For example, the inquiry approach is the strongest way to teach science and the scientific method. A topic/deductive approach would be far less effective. On the other hand, a topic/deductive approach would work well for the pharmacologic agents part of the course discussed in the CAP example.

Pharmacy methods would become more lively and engaging if the application and problem-solving approach were used and given this, methods should likely be presented first in the course followed by pharmacologic agents, calculations, and human relations and communications (the latter could be reinforced throughout the full course).

The Tennessee Williams plays example seems well suited to emphasizing recurrent themes or patterns. The order of parts seems reasonable as presented, assuming learners are given repeated opportunities to explore and understand the learning goals using different literature selections.

PHASE THREE: Selecting Course Methodology

Phase Three of the course action plan addresses the following elements of course planning:

1. Delivery method
2. Instructional approach
3. Course resources
4. Course activities
5. Out-of-class work and expectations
6. Adaptive plans

We'll address each of these in turn.

Instructors do not necessarily need Blackboard™ or WebCT™ to offer online instruction to students. Various software programs offer an array of authoring or development tools for instructors to use in creating online material and tools for students. Among the most useful and friendly, both important criteria, are the programs available from Half-Baked Software, Inc. Better yet, the programs are free to instructors who teach courses for public institutions and who agree to post their materials on the Internet with open access.

Programs by Half-Baked

The three major programs offered by Half-Baked are Hot Potatoes™, Hot Potatoes Masher™, and Quandary™. The Research and Development team at the University of Victoria Humanities Computing and Media Centre created the Hot Potatoes program, which includes six applications. Instructors can use the applications to create interactive multiple-choice, short-answer, scrambled-sentence, crossword, matching/ordering and fill-in-the-blank exercises for students to complete via the Internet, as shown below.

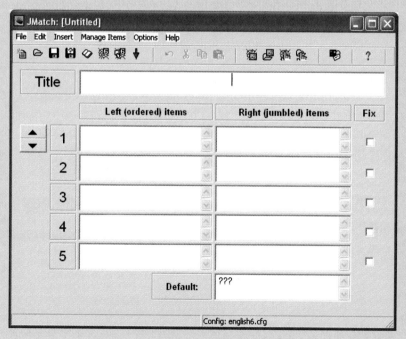

MATCHING ITEMS EXERCISE CREATION SCREEN FROM HOT POTATOES™ SOFTWARE.

The software supports foreign language instruction, including languages that use other characters such as Chinese, Japanese, or Arabic. Instructors of math-related courses can create items with formulas and mathematical symbols. Exercises can be time-limited, and questions can be weighted. Scoring even allows for partial credit on more complex questions. The interface is clean and colorful. With a little imagination, instructors can develop engaging, useful, professional-quality activities and assessments.

Hot Potatoes Masher

The Hot Potatoes Masher program compiles groups of Hot Potatoes exercises into units. Instructors can use the Masher to combine exercises into a single unit and build the Internet files from all of the exercises with the same look and feel. Navigation buttons link the exercises together in a particular order for administration. Also, Masher creates an index file for the unit. See the Integrating Technologies sidebar in Chapter 3 for a description of Quandary, another Half-Baked application.

Delivery Method and Instructional Approach

Questions to consider include: Are you are planning this course as a traditional classroom course, a distance education course, or a hybrid? Will your course be primarily instructor-led, instructor-facilitated, or a combination? Specify main approaches, including Web/distance learning components. Indicate how often meetings are held and the length of each session. Note the reviews, quizzes, small group work, and other features that you expect to include on a regular basis. If your course is a traditional on-campus course, then the typical approaches are:

- lecture
- lab/hands-on
- lecture and small group discussion

If the course is an online course, the typical approaches are:

- independent study
- whiteboard presentations
- live discussion in chat rooms (synchronous)
- threaded discussions (asynchronous)
- project or problem solving by individuals or teams

If the course is a hybrid, the typical approaches are

- lecture/discussion plus an online component
- self-study and discussion group plus an online component

In many (or most) cases, your college or some administrative office will decide whether a course is going to be offered as classroom instruction, lab, distance learning, or some combination of approaches. The decisions are often driven by financial considerations, enrollments, availability of faculty or adjunct faculty, balance of offerings in a department, and other factors. Whether the content or intended outcomes of a course might be better addressed by one approach or another is not always one of the key considerations in the decision.

However, because pressure to serve more students and to offer a greater array of courses is operating in many college environments, and because budgets, especially in community colleges, are also under pressure, some schools seek to offer more online courses or more combination online and classroom courses. Also, whether a publisher, developer, or school has created engaging, rich, accurate, and easy-to-use interactive online material, including various learning options and authentic assessments, will drive many decisions about instruction offered online.

Course Resources

In some cases, a faculty committee or the lead instructor already have determined course resources. If so, list your primary text and other printed materials, multimedia, guest lecturers, field trips, and so forth. If you have the opportunity to choose resources, take some time to reflect on ways to identify and evaluate the materials that will best serve your needs.

Reviewing and evaluating course resources is a more complex task now than it was even a decade ago. The array of textbooks and other products for both instructors and students has expanded to proportions well beyond the time instructors have to review them. Remember to consult with others in your field at conferences, meetings, or other occasions to help narrow the field. Sales representatives may be delighted to boast of their products' qualities and advantages to get the adoption, but you will need to limit the time you allow them. And watch for book and materials reviews in the journals in your discipline. These can save you a great deal of time by helping you avoid weak products or by pointing out features or benefits that you might have otherwise overlooked.

Selecting a Textbook

Selecting an appropriate textbook is a key step in preparing for your course. Though the Internet and media-based products have expanded teaching resources immeasurably, the textbook still remains the base for on-campus and much online instruction. While the form of text continues to evolve from hard copy to various electronic media, the printed textbook retains its dominance in today's real and virtual classrooms.

In some ways, evaluating a textbook is something of an art. Experienced educators know what to look for; they have learned firsthand which features or characteristics are a must and which are good but not necessary. Instructors without such experience, however, will benefit from using a list of criteria, preferably one prepared for their discipline, perhaps by an academic association. Figures 2.7A and 2.7B show one such list. NurseScribe®, a resource for nursing professionals, students, authors, and educators, developed this particular list. We have chosen to include it here because, while it is an excellent example of a discipline-based set of criteria, many of them apply to a wide range of courses. Also, the developers of this list considered criteria from a wide range of sources when creating their own.

TEXTBOOK EVALUATION BY NURSESCRIBE®

- *Consistency with philosophy of the program and curricular model of nursing*
- *Organization:*
  - ✓ The table of contents, appendices, glossary, and index are useful for students and faculty members.
  - ✓ Objectives are laid out for each section.
  - ✓ The material covered is complete.
- *Content:*
  - ✓ The conceptual model of the book is clearly carried out in the content.
  - ✓ The content is balanced; i.e., one topic is not discussed to the detriment of others in terms of length.
  - ✓ The sequence of content is appropriate; i.e., anatomy and physiology of a system is presented prior to information about pathology.
  - ✓ Examples are realistic.

---

continued on next page

Figure 2.7A. Suggested Textbook Evaluation Guidelines. (Reprinted with permission of NurseScribe, www.enursescribe.com.)

A key section missing from this evaluation is an appraisal of the assessments included in the book. Consider these questions as well:

- *Assessments:*

  ✓ Does the book include sufficient assessments?

  ✓ Does it provide intrachapter assessments?

  ✓ Does it include chapter assessments and more cumulative ones?

  ✓ Are assessments clearly appropriate for the material being tested?

  ✓ Are assessments of appropriate length?

  ✓ Do they use a variety of assessment approaches or techniques? Do they include objective items and subjective ones?

  ✓ Do assessments require various levels of ability, from recall to higher-order thinking?

  ✓ Are assessments interesting?

  ✓ Will assessments contribute to students' learning?

  ✓ Will assessments provide the information that you desire for evaluating students' accomplishments?

Figure 2.7B. Suggested Assessment Evaluation Guidelines.

Evaluating Media Resources

For many modern courses, media resources are fast becoming as important as textbooks. Instruction delivered by CD-ROM/DVD, the Web, or audio or video presentation may actually engage students' cognitive activity more readily or more effectively than reading. Evaluating content, whether for students or instructors, in media resources is not different from evaluating content in print resources. You will use criteria related to organization, accuracy, clarity, level, timeliness, options, objectivity or perspective, and so forth. (See the list for textbook evaluation criteria in Figure 2.7A.) Evaluating other aspects of media resources, however, will vary from one media type to the next. Web resources, for example, should be examined for basic approach: Is the resource content-rich or simply a page of links? Is it easy to navigate? Is it engaging and interactive? Do animations, video, sound, and other features enhance understanding or learning? Are pages current and links active?

> *"Education is not the filling of a pail, but the lighting of a fire."*
> —William Butler Yeats

Consider the basic approach of software resources and how you will use them. Are they designed for review, drill, or practice? Are they tutorials or simulations? Are they suitable for concept and/or skills development?

If you are considering a course E-Pack, ask these questions: Is a quality syllabus posted? Are content materials posted? Is it clear how you will use them in your class? Is material complete and accurate? Are the links helpful to the course and do they function correctly? Are tests and quizzes provided? Are study aids provided? Is the material presented in an engaging and visually appealing way? Do students "do" things, rather than just read screens full of print? Does content include charts, graphs, illustrations, animations? Does content include vocabulary or other pop-ups?

> *"Our professors know amazing information. They even know your names."*
> —Hamline University Billboard
> St. Paul, Minnesota

And for all electronic media, is the resource user friendly? Does it provide feedback? Is it linear, requiring progress through a fixed path of learning or presentation? Or does it allow learners to access sessions out of order? And is its cost a factor?

Figure 2.8 presents a checklist for evaluating a multimedia or computer-assisted instruction course.

MULTIMEDIA/COMPUTER–ASSISTED INSTRUCTION EVALUATION CHECKLIST

Curriculum Area: _____

Inspection Copy//Demo Disk Availability
- ❏ It is free.
- ❏ It is not free; costs _____
- ❏ The cost of the demo is deducted from the purchase price. ❏ Yes ❏ No

Trial Period
- ❏ The full version is available on a trial basis.
- ❏ The trial period length of time: _____

Reviews
- ❏ References/testimonials are available. These reviews are available at: _____

Cost of Product
Stand-alone set (One copy of CAI)
Lab Pack (How many copies are
included – 2, 5, 10?) _____
Network Version: _____
Site License: _____

What are the system requirements?
- ❏ Windows version _____
- ❏ Web browser _____

What are the hardware requirements?
Floppy drive required? ❏ Yes ❏ No
Hard disk required? ❏ Yes ❏ No
Hard disk space needed? _____
CD-ROM or DVD required? ❏ Yes ❏ No
Minimum speed of CD/DVD drive _____
Network storage space required?
❏ Yes ❏ No
Describe: _____
RAM memory requirements: _____MB
Video memory requirements: _____ MB
Printer ❏ Yes ❏ No ❏ Optional
Monitor
Color monitor ❏ Yes ❏ No
- ❏ 16 colors (standard VGA)
- ❏ 256 colors
- ❏ Millions of colors
Special size monitor? ❏ Yes ❏ No
Size and resolution
Sound Output ❏ Yes ❏ No ❏ Optional
Mouse ❏ Yes ❏ No ❏ Optional
Other _____

What is the instructional format?
- ❏ Tutorial   ❏ Problem Solving
- ❏ Drill & Practice   ❏ Assessment
- ❏ Game   ❏ Simulation
- ❏ Other describe): _____
_____

Documentation Availability
Print-based ❏ Yes ❏ No
Online ❏ Yes ❏ No

Objectives
Instructional objectives are clearly stated.
❏ Yes ❏ No
The content matches the instructional
objective(s). ❏ Yes ❏ No
The program achieves its defined purposes.
❏ Yes ❏ No

Design
The product includes high-interest, challenging
material. ❏ Yes ❏ No
The product offers material for advanced and
remedial students. ❏ Yes ❏ No
The media product is engaging and visually
appealing. ❏ Yes ❏ No
The interactivity of the media product meets the
learning requirements. ❏ Yes ❏ No
The activities will produce effective and lasting
learning. ❏ Yes ❏ No
Students control pace and sequence.
❏ Yes ❏ No

Content
The content is comprehensive. ❏ Yes ❏ No
The content is accurate and free from errors.
❏ Yes ❏ No
The content is up-to-date. ❏ Yes ❏ No
The content is free of racial/sex/age/ethnic
stereotypes. ❏ Yes ❏ No
The reading level is appropriate to the intended
audience. ❏ Yes ❏ No

Continued on next page

Media

The graphics are appropriate for the intended audience and are state-of-the-art.
❑ Yes ❑ No

Video is used appropriately. ❑ Yes ❑ No

Audio is used appropriately. ❑ Yes ❑ No

Responsiveness to User Needs

There is appropriate feedback for correct answers. ❑ Yes ❑ No

There is appropriate feedback for incorrect answers. ❑ Yes ❑ No

There is help/reinforcement after an incorrect answer. ❑ Yes ❑ No

Failure is not rewarded. ❑ Yes ❑ No

Assessment

The product includes quizzes and tests and students are able to monitor their own progress.
❑ Yes ❑ No

The product includes a pretest and conditional branching depending on performance.
❑ Yes ❑ No

Navigation

The product is easy to operate (user friendly) and follows best practices. ❑ Yes ❑ No

The menu can be returned to easily.
❑ Yes ❑ No

The screen advance is user-controlled.
❑ Yes ❑ No

If appropriate, instruction can be bypassed.
❑ Yes ❑ No

Records

The student management system is easy to use.
❑ Yes ❑ No

Records can be printed. ❑ Yes ❑ No

The management system prescribes instruction to an individual. ❑ Yes ❑ No

Instructors utilizing the management system can prescribe instruction to an individual.
❑ Yes ❑ No

Figure 2.8. Sample Multimedia/Computer-Assisted Instruction Evaluation Checklist.

Selecting Support Materials

While the textbook and/or multimedia program may be the basic resource for a course, a large number of other resources are available to you and your students. For example, if you were a user of an accounting textbook, the tools could include some or all of the following:

For Students

- Study guide
- Working papers/workbooks
- Web sites/Internet-based projects
- CD-ROM/DVD-ROM
- Software program
- Spreadsheet templates
- Simulations: manual and software

For Instructors

- Annotated instructor's edition
- Solutions manual
- Solutions transparencies
- Teaching transparencies
- PowerPoint® presentations
- Videos
- Test banks
- Printed achievement tests
- Discussion questions

Factors in Choosing Instructor Resources

Choose instructor accessories for their convenience and help to you as an instructor. The annotated instructor's edition of a textbook, for example, includes many teaching tips and added materials for you in the margins of the text pages. Teaching transparencies and PowerPoint presentations will be of value in your lectures and presentations, enabling you to show forms and provide notes to your students. Test banks and printed tests will help you in developing effective assessments.

Factors in Choosing Student Resources

Three broad categories should be considered prior to choosing a particular item:

- **Cost.** Student accessories may have a cost factor. You do not want to increase the cost of course materials for your students in an arbitrary way.
- **Value.** Does the resource add value to the course or to all or some of the students' learning of the material in the course? For example, you might direct some students to use a CD-ROM that comes with the textbook for further review of material. Or you may suggest that some students work on an advanced simulation kit to expand their knowledge.
- **Time.** This factor has three aspects to be taken into account. The first is the course time. Do you want to use X number of course hours for a simulation, for example? The second is time for the students to learn how to use the supplement properly. The third is time for you to learn to use it properly and to do it yourself. If, for example, you expect your students to complete a simulation packet, you must first do it yourself.

Planning Major Assignments and Activities

As you develop your course, you will want to pay particular attention to the assignments that you plan for your students. These tasks need to be meaningful and have purpose, and they must relate to the broad outcomes for the course. Assignments are given to students either to present topics you have not covered in class or to reinforce, extend, or enhance the learning of course concepts and skills.

Assignments fall into two categories: daily homework and comprehensive. Daily homework assignments are typically used to strengthen learning as developed in specific lessons. For example, in a mathematics class you might assign as homework a set of problems from the end of a chapter. (See Chapter 4 for a discussion of incorporating effective and worthwhile assignments into daily lesson plans.)

Comprehensive assignments are more integrative and cover learning from many lessons and many sources. Develop these major assignments during course planning, when you are taking a broad view of the course and your expectations for the critical learning students accomplish (the intended course outcomes). Here are some examples of comprehensive assignments:

- Analyze the plan for an annual report and determine which software applications to use to prepare it and how the report parts might be enhanced with specific software features. (Office Systems course)

- Design a layout for a retail display window of your choice. (Marketing course.)
- Prepare a portfolio of four different types of business reports. (Business Writing course)

Encouraging Higher-Order Thinking

What is common to the sample assignments presented above is that they tend to rank at the higher end of a learning taxonomy and often require problem solving, creative thinking, and decision making. They go far beyond any one lesson and are culminating in nature. And although all students must complete the major assignments of a course, you can also inject an element of individuality. The assignment to design a layout for a retail display window *of your choice* offers the student freedom within expectations. This type of assignment addresses a major course outcome but also allows for individual choice. Another approach is to use a core of assignments for all students and a menu of additional assignments from which the student must choose.

Shown in Figure 2.9 are examples of assignments for the course example presented earlier in Figure 2.6 (page 46) as they would relate to two of those intended outcomes.

EXAMPLES OF OUTCOMES WITH RELATED ASSIGNMENTS	
OUTCOME EXAMPLES	ASSIGNMENT EXAMPLES
Outcome: Play Analysis. Application: Students will analyze the text of a Tennessee Williams play.	Read. Read aloud. Participate in discussion. Answer a set of questions that requires answers of a paragraph or more. Write a critical analysis of structure/form, theme, and characters. Create a graphic representation of the play's structure. Prepare an annotation of the text, commenting on structure/form, theme, and characters.
Integration: Students will compare the written version of a Tennessee Williams play to a performance of the same play.	Participate in class reading or performance. Observe dramatization in class. View film version of the play. Create chart of similarities and differences for text versus performance for flow, space, and time.

Figure 2.9. Examples of Outcomes with Related Assignments.

Establishing Checkpoints for Major Assignments

Checkpoints for major assignments will help make your expectations of students clear and direct. Checkpoints will also keep your students on track. Try to have at least one checkpoint about two weeks after the start of a semester-long course so that students cannot get too far behind or too far off target without your knowing it and being able to assist or redirect them.

Make major papers, projects, and reports due in parts, not all at once. If you are requiring a research paper in your Business Communications course, for example, ask your students to submit the problem statement this week, the background literature next week, the research method the next week, etc. Give students clear directions along with standards or criteria for each assignment so that they will learn to recognize when they are preparing quality work. Giving them an example of an assignment completed well can often improve their understandings, self-expectations, and, ultimately, their work. Discuss the assignments and the characteristics of quality work in class before the students begin work on them.

Out-of-Class Work and Adaptive Plans

Out-of-class work includes homework assignments, library research, online reading, online research, assessments, field work, field trips, study group sessions, and so forth. While this work can add huge interest for students, select carefully so you include only those activities with learning implications directly relevant to the course. When you are planning out-of-class work, consider the amount of time students will have available to complete the activities. Align the out-of-class work with your outcomes and in-class work. Three to five major assignments or activities correlating with course outcomes might be a reasonable goal.

Your course should meet the learning needs of all its students. Depending on your location and your school's enrollment characteristics, your class likely will have English language learners (ELL), remedial learners, students with disabilities, and advanced or under-challenged learners at one time or another. When you plan your course, decide how to adapt the learning for these students. Here are some examples.

- **For English language learners:** See the sidebar in this chapter, pages 36–37. Provide online and/or multimedia tutorials. Provide extra vocabulary study. Use many diagrams, illustrations, and charts. When possible, assign hands-on tasks that allow students to demonstrate their learning.
- **For remedial learners:** Many of the adaptations you make for English language learners will also be effective for remedial learners. Find and assign software or online programs for language and math reviews. Some in-class reviews will benefit all students, including remedial learners.
- **For underchallenged (bored) students and students in need of acceleration:** Provide many options that require more advanced application of learning and in-depth research. Involve these students as much as possible in the planning of their learning activities. See also the sidebar, page 162, on teaching advanced students.
- **Students with disabilities:** See the sidebar in Chapter 1 on teaching students with disabilities, pages 18–19.

PHASE FOUR: Planning Assessments

The final phase of course planning is developing a testing strategy. Plan your assessment strategy to align with the intended learning outcomes that you decided for the course. When you do this, consider the following:

- Do you wish to conduct assessments only for major intended outcomes or for each part?
- Will you use multiple venues?

- Do you wish to conduct assessments for more detailed, more narrowly defined intended outcomes or objectives?
- What level of difficulty is each intended outcome and how does that guide the assessment strategy?
- Will all assessments be in a traditional test format? Or will you use performance tests and projects as part of the assessment plan?
- How much student time can you allot for assessments?
- What should be included in the content of those tests or performances?
- What are your college's assessment requirements for courses like yours? How much flexibility do you have?
- Will you assess students' knowledge or abilities at the beginning of the course?
- At what other points during the course will you conduct assessments?

Figure 2.10 shows a few examples of relating assessments to outcomes. This figure also includes the assignments and activities developed earlier (refer to Figure 2.9) as they relate to the part outcomes.

PART	OUTCOME EXAMPLES	ASSIGNMENT EXAMPLES	ASSESSMENT EXAMPLES
I. *The Rose Tattoo*	Outcome: Play Analysis. Application: Students will analyze the text of a Tennessee Williams play.	Read. Read aloud. Participate in discussion. Answer a set of questions that requires answers of a paragraph or more. Write a critical analysis of structure/form, theme, and characters. Create a graphic representation of the play's structure. Prepare an annotation of the text, commenting on structure/form, theme, and characters.	Pre-assessment test to determine what students already know about the structure of drama. Checkpoint Assessment 1: multiple-choice test on structure/form. Checkpoint Assessment 2: multiple-choice test on theme and characterizations. Outcome Assessment: Use the written critical analysis essay as an outcome performance (non-test) assessment.
	Integration: Students will compare the written version of a Tennessee Williams play to a performance of the same play.	Participate in class reading or performance. Observe dramatization in class. View film version of the play. Create chart of similarities and differences for text versus performance for flow, space, and time.	Outcome Assessment: Use assigned chart of similarities and differences for text versus performance for flow, space, and time as outcome performance (non-test) assessment.

Figure 2.10. Examples of Assignments and Assessments Related to Outcomes.

THE COMPLETED COURSE ACTION PLAN

So, you have carefully thought through the course outcomes, the content and its key parts, the teaching and learning activities that will guide students to achieving part and course outcomes, the resources you need, and the types of assessments that will indicate if students have accomplished the course goals. Now you have your master plan, whether it's a bare-bones one-page summary or a detailed course action plan in the format presented in this chapter (see Figure 2.11 below). You have completed a key element of exceptional teaching: planning and strategizing at the course level.

COURSE ACTION PLAN
COURSE NAME: PHARMACOLOGY AND PHARMACY PRACTICE
PHASE ONE: Course Outcomes
PRIMARY COURSE OUTCOMES
At course conclusion, the student will be able to
✓ Demonstrate sufficient knowledge of drugs to function as a pharmacy technician in a community or hospital setting.
✓ Calculate, measure, and dispense drugs accurately.
✓ Perform administrative duties and adhere to pharmacy ethical/legal guidelines.
✓ Demonstrate best practices in customer relations and patient care.
RELATED CONTEXTUAL SKILLS
Foundation Skills
✓ Use medical vocabulary accurately and appropriately.
✓ Read technical material (labels, packaging, specifications, reports) and extract pertinent information.
✓ Make decisions in accordance with pharmacy and business ethics.
✓ Demonstrate an ability to resolve conflicts.
✓ Appreciate the value of the scientific method.
✓ Appreciate other cultures and how cultural values affect and interact with pharmacology and pharmacy practice.
Communication and Cross-disciplinary Skills
✓ Write concise and effective e-mails.
✓ Read e-mails and faxes and interpret written documentation correctly.
✓ Speak clearly and directly.
✓ Build positive, ongoing relationships with employer, staff, and customers.
✓ Work in a team/group environment.
Technology Skills
✓ Use medical resources on the Web to find and verify medical and technical information.
✓ Conduct effective Web searches on medical queries and questions.
✓ Understand and download information from the Internet.
✓ Use pharmacy software-based dispensing systems.

continued on next page

PHASE TWO: Course Structure
COURSE PART 1: PHARMACOLOGIC AGENTS
Key Topics and Areas of Study:
A. Receptors, mechanisms of drug actions, pharmacokinetics, drug effects, and interactions
B. Administration of pharmacologic agents
C. Classes of drugs: anti-infectives, narcotics, respiratory, cardiac, GI, non-narcotic analgesics, chemotherapy, vitamins and supplements
D. Medical/pharmacological terms
Essential Questions: How does each drug act on the target body system? What other physiological processes are impacted? When are drugs more damaging than helpful? Which combinations of drugs and OTC drugs can cause illness or death? How can one drug be healthy for one person and not for another?
Part Outcomes: ✓ Demonstrate a working knowledge of the principles of drug action in the body and individual cells, drug dosages, routes of administration, and interactions. ✓ Interpret drug labels and dosage information and dispense as prescribed. ✓ Use drug references to accurately identify generic and brand equivalents.
COURSE PART 2: PHARMACY METHODS
Key Topics and Areas of Study:
A. Pharmacy law and ethics
B. Sources and uses of drugs
C. Types of drug administration
D. Extemporaneous compounding
E. Dispensing and inventory
Essential Questions: Should drugs be regulated and how? Do customers and pharmacies share the same values and concerns? When do the needs of the customer conflict with the goals of the pharmacist? How much should drugs cost? Who decides and what determines the cost? What latitude does the technician have to interpret the doctor's order? What latitude does the pharmacist have?
Part Outcomes: ✓ Perform pharmacy technician duties, meeting or exceeding the performance requirements and ethics standards required by the industry. ✓ Perform record-keeping functions associated with dispensing pharmaceuticals, processing insurance claims, and maintaining drug inventory. ✓ Recognize potential prescription errors related to conflicting, inadequate, or excessive administration of drugs.
COURSE PART 3: HUMAN RELATIONS AND COMMUNICATIONS
Key Topics and Areas of Study:
A. Cultural and language differences
B. Issues in community settings
C. Issues in hospital settings
D. Communications and human relations
Essential Questions: Can a person hear but not listen? How do you know when someone understands? How does technology enhance expression? In what ways might technology hinder it? How can I improve my communication with customers who speak a different primary language? What are the differences in procedures and job responsibilities in community settings vs. hospital settings?

continued on next page

Part Outcomes:
✓ Translate and communicate prescribed dosage and administration instructions to customers or patients, ensuring patient understanding.
✓ Be a customer/patient advocate; resolve potential conflicts and misunderstandings.
COURSE PART 4: CALCULATION AND MEASUREMENT
Key Topics and Areas of Study:
A. Business math as used in pharmacies
B. Solutions, IV rate, dosages, electrolytes
C. Basic math used (fractions, ratios, decimals, percents)
D. Metric and apothecary systems
Essential Questions: When is the correct answer not the right solution? To what extent are science and common sense related? Can I explain math to customers and patients who speak a different language or who are not math literate?
Part Outcomes:
✓ Follow the correct procedures related to compounding and admixture operations.
✓ Perform calculations required for the usual dosages and solution preparations.
✓ Adhere to quality assurance processes and improve systems on a continuous basis.
PHASE THREE: Course Methodology
Delivery Method: Hybrid
Instructional Approach: Combination of lecture/discussion and Web component
✓ Classes held three times per week, two hours per session. Two sessions will be on-site and one will be off-site (Web-delivered).
✓ The on-site sessions will be primarily classroom instructor-led but supported with guest speakers from industry; question-and-answer sessions will conclude each lecture.
✓ The off-site session will revolve around a structured question-and-answer session; participation and quality of contribution to the discussion will be monitored and evaluated.
✓ An underlying theme of the course is to build medical knowledge and medical vocabulary. Vocabulary reviews will be scheduled each week.
Course Resources: Primary text and other printed materials, multimedia, guest lecturers, field trips *Pharmacology* by Don Ballington and Mary Margaret Laughlin *Pharmacy Practice* by Don Ballington *Encore CD-ROM* – multimedia CD for concept rehearsal, skill practice, and online tests Guest speakers from hospital and community pharmacies
Course Activities: Kickoff activity and major part activities (aligned with outcomes)
✓ Kickoff Activity: Use a Discovery Channel show on forensic science, a Web site by *Court TV* and crime-scene software developed by the University of California to excite students about biopharmacology agents and the topic of DNA.
✓ Create a pro/con debate: U.S. citizens cannot purchase drugs from other countries yet the government is outsourcing drug research and development to India. Discuss key perspectives on this issue.
✓ Major Course Activities: Research assignments will be conducted online; research questions will be discussed in the chat rooms and projects will be posted using the WebCT LMS software. Students will participate in a peer review of the documents posted. Performance role plays will be used as an assessment addressing the communication and problem-solving issues.
Out-of-Class Work and Expectations: The course will require an average of about five hours out-of-class work per week.

continued on next page

Adaptive Plans:
✓ For English language learners: Provide multimedia tutorials on fast drugs facts. Provide CD-ROM of audio presentations of medical terms.
✓ For remedial learners: Provide same resources as listed for ESL. In addition, offer remedial math software for math reviews. Review measurement systems in class (all students will benefit).
✓ For underchallenged (bored students) and students in need of acceleration: Use advanced students to teach segments of the lesson, to lead structured discussions, and to perform role plays. Assign challenging Web-based research questions and have students present findings in class.
PHASE FOUR: Assessment Strategy
✓ Administer a course pretest to assess background knowledge of pharmacology.
✓ Administer a course pretest to assess requisite math skills for the course.
✓ Knowledge quizzes and tests for each chapter will be taken online with scores maintained in WebCT.
✓ The midterm and final tests will be taken on-site and proctored by a teaching assistant.
✓ Administer a progress check (cognitive test) at the end of each part of the course with structured feedback loops where all missed items will be corrected and discussed. Create turnaround plan if students are not getting the material.
✓ Assess end-of-course understandings using performance simulations and cognitive tests.

Figure 2.11. Completed Course Action Plan.

Special Considerations in Planning Online and Hybrid Courses

While the core planning considerations are the same for on-campus and online courses, the instructional delivery differences create distinct needs you must address in the course planning stage. For starters, online courses do not offer the daily face-to-face contact between and among the students and instructor that is provided in most on-campus courses. This represents a critical challenge. How will you communicate with your students? How will they submit assignments and tests? How will you deliver feedback to students? How will you get to know your students? How do you keep your students from falling behind? These are only a sampling of the questions that an instructor has to answer before beginning to teach an online class.

"Setting an example is not the main means of influencing another. It is the only means."
—Albert Einstein

The same basic questions that apply to traditional courses regarding schedule, student characteristics, outcomes, resources, and so forth, also apply to online courses. In addition to these, you will need to answer the following questions for online courses:

1. What course management system will be used: Blackboard, WebCT, or some other platform?
2. Will you offer a Web course where everything is done online? Or, will you teach a course where students work independently offline and use the course management system to review course outcomes, the syllabus, assignment due dates; communicate with the instructor; take online quizzes; transmit completed work; and participate in chat sessions?

3. Will you have an on-campus orientation meeting with your students at the beginning of the course? In some situations, because of the distance factor, students will not be able to come to campus. However, if feasible, by all means do so. Many students will likely have the same questions that can be answered at one time, and the face-to-face contact at an orientation will benefit both you and the students.

4. Will the students come to the campus or school to take exams? If not, will students be directed to offsite locations where exams can be administered to verify that the person taking the exam is indeed the person getting credit for the course? It is critical that this step be set up before the online class begins.

5. What PC configuration and/or software requirements must a student have to participate in your online course?

If you are teaching an online course for the first time, consider "walking in the students' shoes" by enrolling in an online course of the same type you will be teaching. Also, if possible, select a course that uses the same course management system platform. This will give you an opportunity to appreciate the challenges students face.

> "The highest result of education is tolerance."
>
> —Helen Keller

Once you have been assigned to teach a Web course (all student work is done online) or a hybrid course in which student work or another component is done offline, check to see what the publisher provides. Remember, in the latter case, the student uses the course management system (Blackboard, WebCT, others) to check on assignments and due dates, transmit completed work, and communicate with the instructor. Whether you are teaching a Web course or a hybrid course, publishers generally offer online demonstrations of the course itself or the content they provide. Examples of typical material included in a publisher's online course are:

- course objectives
- course syllabus
- course assignments
- course content
- lecture notes
- self-tests (a type of study guide that allows students to check their progress)
- quizzes (done online whether students are in a Web course or a hybrid course)
- external links (additional support for students)
- glossary

Keep in mind that whatever the publisher provides, the course management system allows you to go in and add, delete, change, and/or replace what is there. For example, in addition to the content the publisher has included in the course management system, the publisher may also offer general product ancillaries such as pretests, test banks, video clips, graphic presentations, and student data files, much of which you might want to import into your WebCT or Blackboard course. Check the publisher's catalog for available supplementary materials. Also, most publishers have some type of e-learning resource center with materials available to instructors and students.

Course planning isn't easy, but it is certainly not unmanageable. If you approach it as a challenge and an opportunity, you will find yourself engaged in exciting, creative activity, at least part of the time. Take it in small steps, check and double-check each piece you complete, and then put it to work. Where it doesn't work, be prepared to adjust.

We recommend that new course planners get plenty of feedback from experienced colleagues and even students. Be prepared to listen seriously to what they have to say and then weigh it for yourself before making changes.

CHAPTER SUMMARY

- The goal of course planning is to create a course action plan (CAP) that includes course outcomes and related foundation, cross-disciplinary, and technology skills; the course structure (parts and part outcomes); course methodology; and an overall assessment strategy.

- Learning taxonomies, such as Bloom's and Fink's, can help instructors identify and categorize outcomes, determine the thinking they want from learners, plan activities that align to that thinking, assess progress that aligns directly to the primary course outcomes, and help students be accountable for their learning.

- Phase One of the course action plan focuses on developing course outcomes that reflect the essence of the course and provide an authentic context for learning. A key question to ask is "In what ways will the learner be permanently changed?" Written in the language of taxonomies of learning, outcomes should communicate importance and relevance—work worth doing.

- The goal in Phase Two of course planning is to structure the course content into parts and then develop the learning outcomes for each part, based on key topics and essential questions. The final step in structuring the course is thinking through the sequencing or ordering of learning with the goals of making learning both meaningful and motivating.

- In Phase Three, planning centers on choosing the course delivery method, the instructional approach, course resources, and major activities, all of which must take into account the necessary adaptations for ESL learners, advanced learners, remedial learners, and the underchallenged. Sets of questions for evaluating resources can help instructors choose the most effective printed and/or multimedia materials.

- The final planning stage, Phase Four, is devoted to developing an assessment strategy that aligns with the learning outcomes for the course. Considerations include levels at which to test (part as well as end-of-course level?), use of multiple venues, level of difficulty of each outcome, traditional or performance-based testing, and the amount of time to allot.

- For online and hybrid courses, the core planning considerations are the same as for on-campus courses. However, the instructional delivery differences prompt some additional considerations, including determining how to communicate with students, which class management system to use, how much course work is done online, how to conduct assessments, and what software configurations are necessary for student participation. Typically, publishers offer online content and tests to accompany their textbooks, and instructors can modify these materials to suit their needs.

Think About It: Evaluate Your Course Planning Skills

Mark each item on a scale of 1 to 5. For Like/Enjoy, 1 represents "enjoy very much" and 5 represents "dislike intensely." For the Ability column, 1 represents "very able" and 5 represents "need extensive training or help."

Skill	Like/Enjoy	Ability
1. Analyze student learning styles, abilities, needs, and other characteristics.		
2. Identify characteristics that need alternate approaches: disabilities, literacy, technology, ELL, etc.		
3. Identify, develop, and/or evaluate approaches that meet the needs related to those characteristics.		
4. Identify potential course outcomes and decide which are important and useful.		
5. Determine order (organize) of course components; decide sequence of instruction, course structure.		
6. Identify varying teaching/learning approaches (and related activities) for course components or chunks.		
7. Identify and incorporate varying resources that will support diverse learning options, including online resources, cases, problems, community resources, experts, etc., *and* that are most likely to engage and motivate students.		
8. Create real-world, relevant activities and materials.		
9. Evaluate and select textbooks and other materials for use or adaptation.		
10. Design needed materials and tools as appropriate for in-class or online learning.		
11. Devise solutions for blending various teaching approaches, e.g., lecture, small group, independent; online; in the field; laboratory.		
12. Create clear course descriptions, outlines, and instructions for students.		
13. Create new ways to communicate with students.		
14. Evaluate or devise *teaching* assessments at all levels: activity, session, part, and course.		
15. Evaluate or devise *learning* assessments at all levels: activity, session, part, and course.		
16. Visualize a "course map" or CAP.		
17. Evaluate course designs or plans from the perspectives of different groups of students or educational professionals.		
18. Set course effectiveness criteria or goals and review/revise a course plan accordingly.		

Discussion Questions

1. Are there courses in which the learner outcome of developing an understanding of basic facts is an acceptable goal vs. guiding students to achieve higher-order thinking? If yes, which courses? If no, why not?
2. The chapter discussion on learning taxonomies suggests that teachers can use them to help students be accountable for their learning. To what extent should students be accountable for their own progress? Are there levels of accountability? If so, do you adjust them for individual students or do you hold a minimum expectation for all students? How can you facilitate that accountability?
3. In establishing educational goals, what are some effective approaches to capturing the "habits of the mind"?
4. From your experience, which aspect of course planning is most difficult for teachers? Why? What are some strategies for overcoming those difficulties?

Field Work

1. Are the intended outcomes for a course you are currently teaching more aligned with Bloom's or Fink's taxonomy? In what ways? If you do not have outcomes that align with the levels Human Dimension and Caring, reevaluate your course outcomes and write outcomes for these taxonomy levels.
2. Consider Fink's taxonomy of significant learning for a course you currently teach. Choose three or four of Fink's categories and list one or two outcomes for each category.
3. This chapter talked about the importance of discovering the essence of your course. Select two courses and define the essence of each course.
4. Using the same two courses, write the essential questions for each one.
5. Select the course that needs further development and audit the list of outcomes. Revisit the work from the perspective of realism and authenticity. Do the statements convey importance and communicate relevance to the learner? Do they look like work worth doing? Do they align at the right level on the taxonomy? Do they capture the thinking habits required by a skilled practitioner in the field?

Professional Portfolio: Identify Contextual Skills

Using the following questions, determine the cross-disciplinary, foundation, and technical skills essential to the learner's success in the course you selected for question 5 under "Field Work."

- What types of problems are faced? How?
- What decisions are made?
- What must be communicated?
- What do learners have to read or write?
- What technical skills are required to perform the work?
- Under what conditions is the work performed on the job?
- Will the work be done alone or in a group?
- How will the performer learn the work is satisfactory?
- How will the performer receive feedback?

Foundation Skills and Prerequisites:

Cross-disciplinary Skills:

Related Technical Skills:

Exceptional Teaching is
Resource-Rich

Too many instructional methods—too little time. How do I decide which methods to use? Why do experts argue that we have changed the role of the textbook? What is a blog and how is the Internet changing how we teach?

Select a Diverse Set of Resources

With the multitude of resources available to instructors today via the Internet and elsewhere, instructors can be overwhelmed by the choices. But resource-rich does not mean using or making available every resource you can identify. It means carefully reviewing and selecting a set of resources that will provide diverse means for students to extend their learning. In addition to some mandatory resources, offer students a set of choices that will empower and intrigue them, but not so many that they will be overwhelmed. Guide them by indicating "where to start" or tell them

a little about each resource to help them choose.

Textbooks

"Textbooks aren't what they used to be." True enough, and thank goodness. Today's textbooks should be leading the way toward more personalized and diverse instructional strategies. Selecting a textbook is no longer a process of checking the accuracy and looking to see if it has sufficient review questions and a test bank. Instructors check for variety of presentation, optional activities and readings, and useful material to help students master the terminology of the subject matter. They examine texts to see how students might interact with the content, and they look to see if the text is idea-rich.

In addition to providing written and visual instructional material, today's textbooks need to act as guides to exploring additional learning sources, including companion Web sites, multimedia CDs, assessment CDs, library materials, and more. Textbooks are no longer the beginning and end of a student's educational experience.

Companion Web Sites, Multimedia CDs, and Assessment CDs

Many of today's publishers extend or expand their textbooks for your students by making available companion Web sites, multimedia CDs, and assessment CDs. Companion Web sites are especially useful because of their accessibility and because the publishers can keep the material up to date, even up to the minute. Some publishers provide access free of charge with purchase of the textbook; others sell a "key" that grants access to the site and its materials and functions. Some of the features you might find on a companion Web site include the following:

- reference material for each chapter or topic
- learning materials for additional reading to clarify the textbook or expand on its topics
- material for advanced learners
- material for limited-English-proficient learners
- illustrations, images, slide shows, and animations to enhance or clarify students' understanding
- glossaries
- games and other activities to reinforce learning
- chat room availability
- discussion boards
- streaming audio/video
- self-assessment tools for students to check their progress
- links to additional material on the Internet—possibly reference material, "real-life" examples of what students are

learning, more depictions of concepts or processes, sites with news or alerts related to the course

The sites also often include quizzes and tests that are scored and submitted to the instructor.

Some courses will come to life with the use of multimedia and testing CDs. Many of the same things offered on a companion Web site can be made available by CD (or DVD), and students do not need to use the Internet to access them. The CDs can take students step-by-step through the main points of the course, clarify or enhance learning, and engage students in solving problems, writing assignments, designing procedures, and so forth. Audio clips can be made to run concurrently with text or images so that students have both aural and visual avenues to the material. Units on the CDs can include reviews and self-assessments. Many of these are high-end, polished products. Others still appear clunky. Test the CDs for yourself before adding them to a purchase requirement for the course.

Assessment CDs are most commonly large test banks with hundreds of items for instructors to use to generate tests, either for classroom administration on paper or to post online. Test banks ensure that instructors have plenty of items to select from, rotate from term to term, or use randomly for repeated administrations. They provide answers, and sometimes explanations of answers, as well as suggested reading for students who respond incorrectly.

Book References and Library Browsing

In some schools, the easy access that the Internet provides to a wealth of information has made use of libraries and hard copy books less attractive

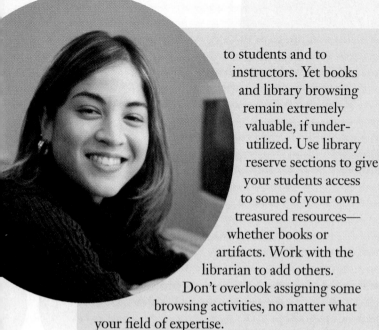

to students and to instructors. Yet books and library browsing remain extremely valuable, if under-utilized. Use library reserve sections to give your students access to some of your own treasured resources—whether books or artifacts. Work with the librarian to add others.

Don't overlook assigning some browsing activities, no matter what your field of expertise.

Films/Videos/DVDs

Films, videos, and DVDs will give students different perspectives than an instructor can provide by lecture alone. These often help students visualize what you cannot adequately describe with words. They may engage students' brains in ways that oral-only presentations cannot. Much of the fuss and bother of using audiovisual equipment is now gone, especially for classrooms set up with computers that handle DVDs and computer projection equipment. Work with your audiovisual department to identify new resources.

Guest Speakers

Professionals and experts in a field who are also good presenters bring new viewpoints and have a different status appeal for students. Use them judiciously, and be sure that they are willing to spend some time interacting with students and answering their questions. Use a little imagination when thinking of guests. They do not need to be well known or professional speakers. Find guests who can address topics in detail that you cannot, who can add new dimensions or details to a topic in your textbook or on your syllabus, and who will quickly earn students' attention and respect.

Community Connections

Think outside the classroom! Many post-secondary schools are continually searching for community partners, and the best level for doing this is in the context of courses. Assign students projects that require interviews or observations in the community. Do you teach botany? Send them to parks or preservation areas, growers or nurseries. Do you teach art? Send students to galleries, museums, or even kindergarten classes to observe art in the making. Numerous small businesses are eager to reinforce the concepts of entrepreneurship—try local printers or binders, copy shops, surfboard makers, bookstores, repair shops, anything that will interest your students. Arrange tours of city hall, the courthouse, banks, title companies, financial institutions, law offices, or other businesses where an executive will answer student questions. Sometimes just the change of venue will inspire students to delve more deeply into a question. You know the ones in your field better than anyone. What are they?

Internet Content

The vast amounts of information available to students online are almost unimaginable. But this is a mixed blessing. Much of the information is worthless, misleading, or just plain wrong. Instructors need to take care about online assignments on two fronts: usefulness and, unfortunately, shortcuts to grades (a euphemism for cheating).

To ensure usefulness, review what you find online to see if it will extend students' learning in interesting ways. This is your primary yardstick. Make sure the site is free, accessible, does not require exotic plug-ins, and is easy for novices to use. Then assign specific sites for students to use as part of a larger assignment or project. Sometimes asking students to find and review online resources and report on them can also be useful, as it helps them develop some critical thinking skills.

As for shortcuts to grades, all we wish to say is that you need to be alert. If student papers sound achingly familiar, they might be. It will not hurt to remind students at any level that the writing must be their own original writing and that they should cite their sources.

Other Students!

Don't overlook the possibility of viewing your students as content resources. Find out what they might know about a given topic and give them choices about presenting what they know (or what they learn). Some subjects lend themselves better than others to group projects, but most instructors can identify projects that will work for groups of about four students. Project or work groups, or even small study groups, will provide students with peer communications and a sense of community that just might be what they need to be motivated and succeed with a task or course. Remember that providing choices may be the key to effective group assignments.

Include Process Resources

The Internet is providing a venue for communication unlike any we've had before. Using blogs (online journals or diaries, often shared or public), bulletin boards, live chat, and/or whiteboards and other tools can change the character of student interactions and reduce the distance between and among them and you.

Various e-instruction programs will support collaborative inquiry among your students. Assign students to groups that can share resources and information while working on a project. You can also assign mentors to these groups, or to individual students for that matter, giving them access to a wide range of experts who can be of assistance with specific learning issues, experiences, or questions.

Online tutors, "intelligent" ones, can help personalize students' learning by allowing them to target specific questions or objectives.

Use Resource Choices to Extend the Classroom

Courses that are entirely textbook and lecture dependent can present serious challenges for students whose first language is not English, students who are slow readers, students who need a solid review of some foundation skills and concepts before they can participate at an optimal level, students who learn quickly and leave others behind, and students who are not excited about learning. Here are a few examples of how to use resources to extend the classroom.

Guest speakers can be inspirational to students who are struggling. Typically, a guest speaker is knowledgeable, a warm and engaging speaker, and will provide in-person evidence of how interesting the subject can become.

Ventures into the community to learn about the subject or topic in the real world can be highly motivational. All students benefit. This is also a strategy that students who are not expert readers can learn from without frustrations. Encourage them to ask questions, and then have them report what they learned.

One of the significant benefits of using Internet resources and multimedia CDs and DVDs is that these provide students with opportunities to work at their own pace, whether accelerated or more slowly. These resources meet some of the needs of students who need more visual representations or audio reviews. They provide "safe" environments for students to interact with material; that is, without being in the view of their peers. Students who need more time to formulate their communications can use bulletin boards, e-mail, and other forms of threaded discussions to participate as effectively as others.

Chapter 3

Planning Effective Course Sessions

"**N**ow I get it!"

It doesn't get much better for a teacher. I'd been working with George for several weeks of the semester in a basic bookkeeping class. Debits were a mystery to him. I'd demonstrated time and again. I found different descriptions in various textbooks (I kept some in my office for just that purpose) and had George read those. I found exercises on the Internet. I paired him with another student, thinking maybe my five-foot-one-half-inch 101-pound prematurely gray-haired persona might be intimidating him. I checked his math skills. They were fine. I guided, cajoled … stopping just short of bribery. It wasn't that he didn't try, but every time it came to completing the spreadsheet, George would freeze. "Subtract this one? This is an expense. That's a debit?"

So I said to myself, "Well, Self, some you just can't reach. And the others are doing fine."

Monday it happened. I started to present a case about Springer's Gardens, a nursery and landscaping business. "What types of expenses will Springer's have? What things will they pay for?" The hand shot up. George started naming and kept naming. "What are those, George?"

"Debits?" A grin.

Why didn't George tell me he worked for a nursery? Why hadn't I asked?

Learning Outcomes

- Identify intended outcomes for course sessions and determine the ideal sequence of sessions and topics
- Create a student-centered syllabus that includes the essential course information
- Describe best instructional practices and other important considerations for planning lessons
- Identify the key elements of a session plan, including the purpose of each element and some effective tools and techniques for executing it
- Evaluate lesson plan formats and templates
- Describe parallels between planning online and classroom sessions

Why Plan at the Session Level?

Instructors with many years of experience might tell you that their lesson plans are in their heads or that they "wing it." Maybe some do, and maybe some of these even do so fairly effectively. But chances are that they didn't start out that way.

Most instructors will be much more effective in the classroom if they know what they are going to do in any given session. Instructors who plan are more confident and secure about the session's progression, student activities, evaluations, and other components. They avoid last-minute scrambling for equipment and materials. They know what questions they want to ask, and what performances they expect of students. Planned sessions run more smoothly, and topics are more likely to get the amount of time and coverage they deserve. Planned assessments, whether casual or formal, contribute to the instructor's knowledge of student progress on a regular basis and become part of planning subsequent sessions. And, furthermore, students can recognize when an instructor is not prepared, which affects their own confidence and learning.

Before the Syllabus: Planning and Sequencing Sessions

What goes into planning course sessions? You did much of this work when you were planning the overall course, including establishing course outcomes, dividing the course into parts with specific outcomes for each part, and establishing the topics, skills, and concepts you will address to help students achieve the part outcomes. Now you will take your course action plan to the next level, which is to fit the course parts into the course time frame, whether it's ten weeks, a quarter, or a semester. This planning is the basis for the student syllabus and for planning individual sessions. Answering the following questions will help you get started.

- Considering the total number of weeks available and the relative importance of the course parts, how many weeks should be set aside for each part?
- For each part, which topics or skills require full sessions and how many sessions will you allocate to the part?
- Do students need to review some basic information or skills before you begin the main content of the course?
- Do you need to include activities or options to help ESL students master some of the terminology before they can participate effectively in other course components?
- Does the school require approximately fifty hours ("Carnegie clock hours") of in-class or online instruction for a three-credit course (not counting reading, research, study, etc.)? Do you need to abide by other guidelines for two- or one- credit courses?
- Realistically, how much out-of-class work can you assume? Does the school have guidelines for the in-class:homework hours ratio? For example, for an on-campus class, some colleges expect students to spend two hours reading and doing other course-related work for every one hour of in-class time.
- Is the schedule flexible or fixed?
- Is there an expectation for independent study and teamwork?
- Are some of the classes designated for on-campus instruction and some for off-campus/distance options?

This should give you a reasonable sense of instructional time. For example, you might schedule the fifty hours of your on-campus three-credit class as twenty-four 2-hour sessions plus a 2-hour final exam. Or you might schedule a three-credit hybrid class to have eighteen 2-hour sessions on campus, plus six 2-hour sessions online, plus a 2-hour online final exam.

Then, considering that you may need the first session for possible course pre-assessment and orientation and the last session for final assessment and feedback, do you have enough instruction time for the topics you have identified? Does each topic need to be taught in an on-campus session or could some be addressed through off-campus instruction or through a homework or independent study assignment? Are online components included in the time designated for instruction or part of the time designated for homework?

Consider this example. June Burton is going to teach real estate math. She knows right away that her four "big parts" will be Price and Value, Measurement, Real Estate Finance, and Real Estate Practice. She has listed the part outcomes and the topics for each part, and has estimated the total course hours required of students, including on-campus instructional sessions, online assignment hours, reading time, and project time. Further, she has estimated the number of session hours for each topic within a part and whether that time is class time or online assignment time. Her planning is displayed in Figure 3.1.

SESSIONS FOR REAL ESTATE MATH COURSE			
COURSE HOURS: 50 IN-CLASS HOURS AND 100 OUT-OF-CLASS HOURS			
✓ 24 classroom sessions, 2 hours each plus in-class 2-hour final ✓ 20 online assignments, 2 hours each ✓ 50 textbook reading hours ✓ 10 project hours			
Part I: Price and Value OUTCOMES: (1) Students will use fraction, decimal, and percentage calculations with a T diagram. (2) Students will solve problems related to list, sale, and net prices. (3) Students will solve compensation problems. (4) Students will solve appreciation and depreciation problems. (5) Students will solve problems related to ad valorem and property taxes.			
Part I Topic Groupings	**In-class Hours**	**Online Hours**	**Reading and Project Hours**
A. Review fractions, decimals, percentages	1 session	2 sessions	6
B. T diagram	1 session	0 session	2
C. List, sale, and net prices	1 session	2 sessions	4
D. Profit	1 session	1 session	2
E. Compensation	1 session	1 session	4
F. Appreciation and depreciation	2 sessions	1 session	4
G. Taxes	1 session	1 session	2
Part II: Measurement OUTCOMES: (6) Students will solve problems related to legal descriptions. (7) Students will solve problems related to area. (8) Students will solve problems related to volume.			
PART II TOPIC GROUPINGS	**In-class Hours**	**Online Hours**	**Reading and Project Hours**
A. Metes and bounds	1 session	0.5 session	1
B. Rectangular survey system	1 session	1 session	1
C. Measuring distance and area	1 session	1 session	3
D. Measuring volume	1 session	1 session	1
Part III: Real Estate Finance OUTCOMES: (9) Students will solve problems related to simple and compound interest. (10) Students will solve problems related to loans.			

continued on next page

Part III Topic Groupings	In-class Hours	Online Hours	Reading and Project Hours
(11) Students will solve problems related to real estate investments.			
A. Simple and compound interest	1 session	1 session	2
B. Loans	3 sessions	1.5 sessions	6
C. Investing	1 session	1 session	3
PART IV: REAL ESTATE PRACTICE **Outcomes:** (12) Students will solve appraisal problems. (13) Students will solve problems related to prorations. (14) Students will solve problems related to closing statements. (15) Students will solve problems related to leases.			
Part IV Topic Groupings	In-class Hours	Online Hours	Reading and Project Hours
A. Appraisal	2 sessions	2 sessions	6
B. Prorations	2 sessions	1 session	3
C. Closing statements	2 sessions	1 session	4
D. Leases	1 session	1 session	4

Figure 3.1. Session Planning Example for Real Estate Math Course.

How much planning should you do in advance? How many sessions should you prepare for? Experienced instructors prepare two or three sessions ahead. Session planning that is not too far ahead keeps the learning tied to where the students are thinking and working and learning. And session planning for at least two or three sessions will give instructors flexibility to use something from the next session if the current session has finished quickly or has an obstacle such as malfunctioning equipment or a no-show guest. Furthermore, and importantly, instructors can provide students with a more useful preview of what is to come if the details have been decided.

Preparing a Syllabus

The course syllabus is probably the first interaction that students have with you in your course. It will build on the information you developed in the CAP and will help students prepare for each part of the class. Robert Diamond[1] provides a useful list of what an effective learning-centered syllabus should do:

- Define students' responsibilities.

---

[1] R.M. Diamond. *Designing and Assessing Courses and Curricula: A Practical Guide.* San Francisco: Jossey Bass Higher and Adult Education Series, 1997. Also, Diamond, R.M., "Forward" in J. Grunert, *The Course Syllabus*, Bolton, Mass.: Anker Publishing Company, 1997.

- Define the instructor's role and responsibility to students.
- Provide a clear statement of intended goals and student outcomes.
- Establish standards and procedures for evaluation.
- Acquaint students with course logistics.
- Establish a pattern of communication between instructor and students.
- Include difficult-to-obtain materials such as readings, complex charts, and graphs.

Elements of a Student-Centered Syllabus

A comprehensive syllabus generally contains the following elements.

1. Course identifying data
2. Instructor data
3. Prerequisites
4. Course outcomes
5. Required course resources
6. Major assignments
7. Grade determination
8. Class structure
9. Course schedule
10. College/school requirements

Each of these elements is discussed and can be observed in the model syllabus in Figure 3.2. Spend some time looking at the model and the descriptions of the elements. Think about how these might apply to the syllabus for your course. Notice how the use of "you" makes the syllabus *student-centered* rather than *instructor-centered*, although it is intended to be used by both parties. Notice also that you do not necessarily need to follow the order of the chapters in the text.

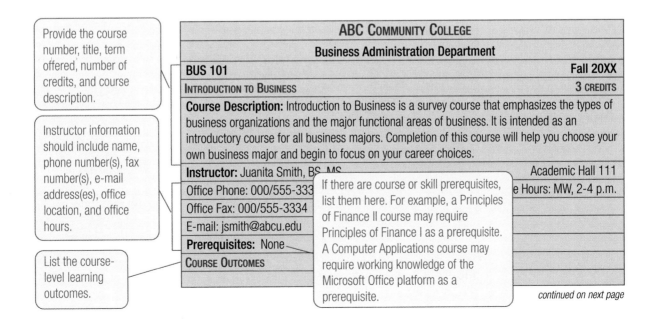

Provide the course number, title, term offered, number of credits, and course description.

Instructor information should include name, phone number(s), fax number(s), e-mail address(es), office location, and office hours.

List the course-level learning outcomes.

ABC COMMUNITY COLLEGE

Business Administration Department

BUS 101   **Fall 20XX**

INTRODUCTION TO BUSINESS   **3 CREDITS**

Course Description: Introduction to Business is a survey course that emphasizes the types of business organizations and the major functional areas of business. It is intended as an introductory course for all business majors. Completion of this course will help you choose your own business major and begin to focus on your career choices.

Instructor: Juanita Smith, BS, MS   Academic Hall 111

Office Phone: 000/555-333   e Hours: MW, 2-4 p.m.

Office Fax: 000/555-3334

E-mail: jsmith@abcu.edu

Prerequisites: None

COURSE OUTCOMES

If there are course or skill prerequisites, list them here. For example, a Principles of Finance II course may require Principles of Finance I as a prerequisite. A Computer Applications course may require working knowledge of the Microsoft Office platform as a prerequisite.

continued on next page

Include the name of the text and other course materials, such as workbooks or simulations, software, or Web sites.	At the end of this course, you will be able to:
	1. Discuss the major theories of management and leadership.
	2. Describe the major types of business organizations.
	3. Analyze a business to determine its functional parts.
	4. Assess the condition of a business.
	5. Explain your view about the place of ethics in a business.

REQUIRED COURSE RESOURCES

Text: MacGreevy, Collin. *Introduction to Business,* Eighth Edition. New York: XXX Publishers, 20XX.

Cases: *Cases to Accompany Introduction to Business*

Web Site: http://CourseName.edu

MAJOR ASSIGNMENTS

(Note: List the major assignments for the course. These may include papers, projects, and presentations.)

1. A 10- to15-page paper analyzing the condition of a business of your choice.

2. A 15-minute oral presentation on Item 1.

GRADE DETERMINATION

(Note: List the elements that comprise the course grade along with the percentage value of each one.)

1. Two exams @ 15% each	30%
2. A final exam	20
3. Paper	15
4. Oral presentation	10
5. Case preparation	10
6. Other assignments	15

Class Structure: This class will include a range of learning environments such as lecture and small-group discussion and a wide variety of activities, including Web-based projects.

(Note: Identify the primary learning environments or instructional approaches around which the course is designed.)

COURSE SCHEDULE (SUBJECT TO REVISION)

(Note: List day-by-day or week-by-week the topics to be learned, including related readings.)

Week	Topic(s)	Text Readings
1	Introduction; Forms of Organization	Chs. 1 and 2
2	Forms of Organization (continued)	Chs. 2 and 3
3	Management and Leadership	Ch. 6
4	Management and Leadership (continued)	Ch. 7
5	Case Work; Test 1	
6	Accounting	Ch. 12
7	Finance	Ch. 13
8	International Business	Ch. 15
9	Marketing	Ch. 9
10	Case Work; Test 2	
11	Entrepreneurship	Ch. 8
12	Integrative Activities	
13	Careers	Ch. 16
14	Presentations	
15	Review; Final Exam	

COLLEGE AND COURSE POLICY INFORMATION

(Note: Every institution tends to require specific policy reminders in course syllabi. Examples include an academic honesty policy, attendance and withdrawal policies, and ADA policies.)

✓ This community college conforms to the provisions of the Americans With Disabilities Act. You are invited to report any special needs to your instructor.

✓ Your attendance is expected at all class sessions. Excessive unexcused absences may result in withdrawal from the class.

✓ We subscribe to the community college policy on academic honesty found in the school catalog.

Figure 3.2. Sample Student-Centered Syllabus.

Instead, you can choose an order that makes sense to you, so long as you are not overriding standards of the college or school.

Two issues concerning the course syllabus must be kept in mind. The first is that if you are a part-time instructor, you may have no choice but to use the syllabus of the full-time faculty for that course. This does not prevent you from giving input about the syllabus, but you are not the person ultimately responsible for the course; the full-time faculty member is that person.

The second issue is the nature of the syllabus. It is, in effect, a contract between you and the student. However, since it is also a plan for the course, you may not be able to fulfill that plan exactly as indicated for a variety of reasons. For example, you may discover that Chapter 8 needs more time, reducing the time spent on the planned integrative activities. Or you may discover that the planned guest speaker for Chapter 16 is only available during the fourteenth week. This will cause a rescheduling of dates. Or you may discover that you need less time for Chapter 7 than planned and will have extra time for something else. For each of these and other similar reasons, the wording "subject to revision" appears in the course schedule section.

Preparing to Teach Effective Sessions

Before addressing the details of teaching at the session level, we need to consider some factors that are foundational to effective sessions. The first of these is a set of six instructional practices that are essential for good teaching and learning. These practices are related to students' overall learning, not just the course-specific content. Then we shall turn attention to identifying topic or session intended outcomes and thinking about overall session structure issues.

Best Instructional Practices

Instructors new to teaching and individuals outside the world of education are sometimes not aware that the best instruction develops students' abilities in various areas, even within a specific or narrow subject. Here are some of the instructional practices that might be overlooked, but that are critical to effective teaching.

- Build background knowledge.
- Teach essential vocabulary.
- Include reading, communication, and writing.
- Address technical literacy skills.
- Provide opportunities for students to learn independently.
- Make learning emotional.

An exciting addition to the Half-Baked Software repertoire is Quandary. (See the Chapter 2 Integrating Technology sidebar on page 48 for an introduction to Half-Baked.) What Quandary calls "action mazes" are similar to some popular adventure or mystery games. The program, which is useful for both instruction and assessment, presents learners with information or a description of a situation and a set of choices. The program engages learners' problem-solving and analytical skills, assesses content

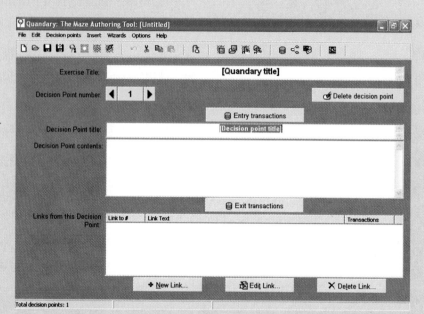

OPENING SCREEN OF QUANDARY'S MAZE AUTHORING TOOL.

comprehension, and guides learning content, whether new or review. Students' performance is assessed and recorded.

Quandary can challenge instructors' creativity. The program can be used for problem solving, diagnosis, surveys, procedures training, and more. Shown above is the opening screen of the maze authoring tool. Get an idea of the breadth of uses by visiting http://www.halfbakedsoftware.com/quandary_tutorials_examples.php. Here are two examples.

1. Middle Ages Tour by Russel Tarr. The situation presented to learners says "You are a fantastic inventor who has created a magnificent TIME MACHINE. You set the dates for the time of the dinosaurs, but due to a mechanical fault the machine has crash landed in the MIDDLE AGES. Your task is to find the missing pieces of the time machine, which have been scattered around this area. When you have found all of the missing pieces, you must then get back to the machine to return home. You should have a worksheet to help you with this."

The "worksheets" include a mapping activity for users to create a map of the town or village; a sights, sounds, and smells outline; a jobs in the Middle Ages worksheet; and a higher-level activity with structured questions.

2. Michael Krauss's ELL students at Lewis & Clark College used Quandary to make their own mazes on a variety of topics. (See www.lclark.edu/~krauss/quandarytasks/home.html.) Examples of student projects include "You Only Get One Chance" (a parody on James Bond) and "How Will He Spend Time on the Weekend?" (with unexpected events plus scenes around Portland, Oregon).

Quandary provides tutorials, examples, a clip art library, and a selection of tools to assist instructors in creating their own action mazes.

Build Background Knowledge

Building background knowledge is important for two major reasons. First, chances are that among your students will be some who do not have as much foundational knowledge for the course as others. Building this knowledge will help those students participate and learn more effectively. Second, background knowledge will add breadth to all students' learning. This is the knowledge that will add to the relational database, so to speak, in their heads. Having more information to which new learning can be tied will help people learn better throughout their educational experience and beyond.

Teach Essential Vocabulary

If you want to raise test scores, teach vocabulary.

Instructors can be so familiar with the vocabulary of their discipline that they forget that many terms and phrases are not familiar to their students. Furthermore, generally speaking, instructors are more well read than their students, which means their overall vocabulary is greater both for comprehension and use. The best instructional practices include ways to help students master the terminology for the subject matter and extend their general working lexicon.

Think of the terminology of your discipline as a foreign language, and then use foreign language teaching techniques to help your students acquire this language: word lists, terminology quizzes, cloze (fill -in-the-blank) techniques, crossword puzzles, bees, etc.

To build students' general vocabulary, do not shy from "big words." Use them in appropriate contexts and *explain them in plain language*. For example, an instructor might say, "For this assignment, you need to write an *explication* of [XYZ]. That is, you need to write a detailed explanation." Getting students to use a dictionary usually requires a specific assignment and can be received more positively if you make it an online assignment using an online dictionary, such as Merriam-Webster at www.m-w.com. The Web has many dictionaries for specific disciplines. Find some of them for your courses by looking at www.dictionaries.com or conduct an online search for "botanical dictionary," "art dictionary," and so forth. Remember that dictionary activities can be fun! (Try the rhyming dictionaries at http://dictionaries.com/?show=Rhyming+Dictionary.)

Include Reading, Communication, and Writing

No, maybe you aren't teaching an English class. But very few concepts and skills can be put to use without good communication skills. The best instructional practices include diverse assignments that require students to develop and use these skills, whether visual, oral, or written and whether with you, with other students, or with themselves (reading, writing). The key is to *plan* specific activities and assignments that foster this development in-class, online, and independently. When you are preparing your session plans, include at least one communication builder for each session or assignment. Examples include question-and-answer sessions, team projects that require students to coordinate their learning or participation with one another, conducting interviews and reporting them, and so forth. If you assign a piece of writing, be sure to convey to the students that it is important to them and to you. Read and comment on what they have written!

Address Technical Literacy Skills

Good grief. I teach sculpting (potting, woodworking ...). Why must I bother with "technical literacy"? Technical literacy refers to two areas: (1) the technical side of a discipline, and (2) using technologies.

Most subject areas have their own technical tools, that is, special mechanics. Technical literacy in sculpting, for example, might include knowledge of clays, glazes, molds, kilns, and firing. Literacy in technologies includes those used in a specific discipline, such as CAD/CAM programs, spreadsheets and databases, and three-dimensional imaging. They also include technology literacy that is important for every student, and these emphasize basic computing and communications. All students need to develop and practice their technology concepts and skills: basic computing, word processing, Internet searching, discussion boards, e-mail, and so forth. Not only does good instructional practice help students use these tools in course-specific ways—which will build their technology competencies in general—but these skills are already absolutely necessary for full participation in today's economic, social, and educational life.

Some ways to use technology in your classes are the following:

- showing a marketing class how to do an electronic survey on the Internet
- using a software program to time your students' keyboarding speeds
- including QuickBooks® or Peachtree® or some other software in your accounting course to record accounting transactions and to retrieve data for the later steps in the accounting cycle
- assigning an Internet research problem
- meeting in a chat room

Provide Opportunities for Students to Learn Independently

Part of the job of positive instruction is to foster students' abilities to learn independently—that is, to enable them to continue learning long after the formal education process has been completed. Provide choices that require independent learning. By this we mean activities that do not just review what has been presented in class. This is new learning, and students do it on their own and submit some evidence of that learning.

> "Education's purpose is to replace an empty mind with an open one."
>
> —Malcom S. Forbes

A good (and fairly common) example is a research project on a specific topic or question related to a course. For example, a course in modern architecture might assign students to learn about and report on a particular architect or building or style that is not covered in the textbook or in class.

Make Learning Emotional

Emotional learning? No, not learning *about* emotions. Using emotions to make learning happen and help ensure that it sticks. Here are a few examples.

1. Provide learning activities that are truly enjoyable, that students might find engaging, interesting, and fun.
2. Show your own high level of interest and enjoyment of a topic or activity.
3. Use emotion when talking with students. "Can you **belieeeeeve** they could do that?" "Just *imagine* what this means!" "Doesn't it really make you furious that … !"
4. Provide feedback in a way that shows you *care*. "What a huge improvement, Tony." "What's this little gem here? Build on that piece!"
5. Engage students' interest. Captivate them. Motivate them. Encourage them. Exhort them.

Elements of a Session Plan

Many models for creating session plans have been developed and are available for your use via the Internet. We have reviewed several of these, and have incorporated the essential elements into our own model. Here it is.

- Warm-up
- Purpose and kickoff
- Instructional approach and methodology
- Development and practice
- Session assessment
- Wrap-up and assignments

Figures 3.3 and 3.4 provide examples of how completed session plans for specific courses might look.

LANDSCAPE DESIGN	
Session Plan	
Session Name: Country Gardens	
1. Warm-ups	Slides: Country Gardens
2. Purpose and kickoff	Plant materials. Ask about/discuss country vs. retro or modernistic containers/hardscape. Parallels to plant materials.
3. Instructional approach and methodology	Continuation of slide show. Hands-on selection of plant materials in the greenhouse for class project.
4. Development and practice	Greenhouse teams.
5. Session assessment	Plant lists.
6. Wrap-up and assignment	Summary and feedback. Assignment reminder: rationale for plant selections.

Figure 3.3. Session Plan for a Landscape Design Course.

COLONIAL HISTORY	
Session Plan	
Session name: Colonial Jobs	
Warm-ups	Quick review by Q & A: goals of the Virginia Company
Purpose and kickoff	Jobs. Story of John Chambers work. Need for salt. Segue to other jobs.
Instructional approach and methodology	Lecture and discussion: jobs in Virginia.
Development and practice	Discussion (small group): job descriptions.
Session assessment	Two-minute writing: favorite colonial job.
Wrap-up and assignment	Summary and feedback. Assignment reminder: Letter from colonist to family in Europe comparing job in Virginia with same job at "home."

Figure 3.4. Session Plan for a Colonial History Course.

Warm-Ups

Getting students' attention and engaging their thinking from the very start of a class session can influence the success of the remainder of the session. What we call "warm- ups" could be a quick question-and-answer exchange with the instructor calling on individual students, questions requiring students to answer in chorus to improve memory, a short audio interview replay, review of homework in small groups, a session pretest or checklist, or some other activity to focus students on the instructor or on the course material.

Some instructors will conduct a quick review of a previous session to reinforce or clarify students' understanding. You might plan this as part of regular warm-ups or in addition to warm-ups for sessions that were particularly complex or introduced large amounts of new material. For example, assume that in your previous class your students learned how to record cash sales of merchandise. You have reviewed this entry (debit to the cash account, credit to the sales account). Now you ask, "What if the buyer could not pay cash immediately? How else can the sale occur?" A student replies, "On credit." You say, "If it is on credit, one of these two accounts for a cash sale will stay the same and one will change. Which is the one that stays the same?" Hands go up, the correct answer will be given, and the lesson will go on.

Generally, you will spend between five and ten minutes on warm-ups.

Purpose and Kickoff

Using two or three minutes, tell students what you expect to be accomplished during this session. Tell them what information or skills you expect them to learn as well as what participation you expect of them. This is a key opportunity to excite, interest, and motivate students.

What you say and how you say it will influence students' attitudes and energy levels for the remainder of the session. Think about what will be more engaging. For example, which of the following would get more attention? "Today we are going to talk about (aside: this usually means 'I'm going to lecture on') prorating interest, taxes, and insurance. We prorate interest and taxes in arrears and insurance in advance." Or, "When do you pay for insurance? Before or after your house burns down?" (Students respond.) "And if you paid your insurance for a whole year and then sold your house in six months, would you want part of your money back?" (Students respond.) "Now we have to figure out what's fair for you to get back." Or "Today we're going to pretend we're back in kindergarten! We're going to suspend our disbelief for two hours while we generate ideas about how to create an [XYZ]."

How you say something also affects motivation. If you sound and act bored or tired, you students will feel bored and tired. Use emphasis, humor, and gestures and other body language to communicate that this, whatever it is, will be enjoyable, will engage their thinking, and will be something they can relate to!

Instructional Approach and Methodology

What choices do you have to *cause learning* during class sessions? Which activities will work best for the time, students, and subject matter? Instructional approaches can be broadly classified as instructor-led, instructor-facilitated, or a combination of the two. We've grouped these in Table 3.1. In instructor-led approaches, the instructor leads, or chooses the direction and strategy, and students follow. In instructor-facilitated approaches, the instructor provides the opportunities and the tools for learning, and students create their own individual paths toward achieving the learning outcomes.

Instructor-Led	Online Counterparts	Instructor-Facilitated	Online Counterparts
Lecture	Multimedia Readings Flash® animations Video segments	Lab	Home-based computer or laptop
Discussion	Chat rooms	Group projects	Team assignments
Question and Answer	Bulletin boards	Independent study	Web quests Drop-box assignments
Demonstration	Video demonstrations Software simulations	Peer mentoring	Collaboration by e-mail and telephone

Table 3.1. Major Instructional Approaches.

In most cases, you will want to use some instructor-led and some instructor-facilitated instruction, including some online components. You need to do this to discover which approaches work best for your topics, students, and time. Vary the activities during a session and from session to session to avoid boredom (yours as well as the students) and also to maximize the probability that all students will find opportunities to learn in ways that work best for them. Be prepared with "backup" activities, just in case something you planned doesn't work as well as you had hoped or expected. This is the main content of your session, and will probably use about 85 to 90 percent of the available time.

Most of our students are not one-trial learners. You will increase the likelihood of successful learning with each iteration. Repeat stuff? Usually, but not literally. Provide students with *varying* ways to review and then extend learning, solidifying recently presented concepts or skills and adding to them. Think of this as a circular process, or perhaps as a spiral, in which learning and teaching circle back before moving forward.

Instructor-Led Teaching Approaches

Four primary types of instructor-led approaches are lecture, discussion, question-and-answer, and demonstration. We'll describe these briefly below and then discuss the specific techniques for each approach in Chapter 4.

A traditional, classic methodology, lecturing is widely used on college campuses and is familiar to most students. *Some* lecture is appropriate for just about any course, but, unfortunately, it is sometimes used to excess because this is the teaching approach that many instructors have the greatest experience with. Some instructors may never tire of hearing themselves talk, but lecture will not provide the most effective teaching for all students all of the time. Remember that "telling isn't all there is to teaching," and look for additional approaches to help students learn.

If yours is an online course, activities that parallel the classroom lecture include students' reading the "lecture" material, video and Flash presentations, and instructor-led whiteboard sessions.

Discussion is an approach in which the instructor or a facilitator (maybe a student) leads the group talk and students participate. Good discussion leaders guide discussions, elicit comments and questions from students, and make points along the way so that the discussion stays on topic. In discussions, students build on each other's comments and questions. Related to discussion is the method of brainstorming, which is designed to generate ideas from the students. The instructor presents a topic area or questions, and then helps spark ideas among the students, recording the thoughts without comment or judgment. A subsequent phase of brainstorming can be evaluating the ideas.

Brainstorming can be led by the instructor, especially if students have not participated in brainstorming sessions previously. After they have mastered the steps and "culture" of brainstorming sessions, however, students can do this in smaller, instructor-facilitated groups.

Discussion and brainstorming are used less than other approaches for "hands-on" courses that teach students skills. An auto mechanics instructor, for example, will probably conduct fewer classroom discussions about repairing a carburetor than demonstrations of how to do it. This does not mean that the discussions do not have their place in such courses. Often they will be very useful in helping students think about possible diagnoses (for example, "The computer hard drive is making a sound like it's an icemaker. What could that be?") or engendering ideas about ways to solve a problem (for example, "The clay is too loose. What could make it loose? What should we do about it?").

In online courses, discussions and brainstorming can be conducted synchronously ("live") in chat rooms or asynchronously via bulletin boards or threaded e-mailing. As with classroom discussions, the online discussion will need guidance and steady prodding.

Question-and-answer is a time-proven teaching method in which the instructor poses questions to the students who in turn reply. Question-and-answer differs from discussion in that the instructor is more directive and responses are expected to be specific to a given question, rather than building on other comments. Online question-and-answer sessions differ from online discussions in similar fashion. The instructor or online leader will present questions that are much narrower than those that drive general discussions—and the instructor will be looking for specific responses. The main tool will still be chat room sessions, although bulletin boards can be adapted for the purpose.

Question-and-answer sessions can be useful in most courses for previewing content, reviewing content, and for quick assessments of the class's mastery.

Demonstration is presentation by the instructor of how to do something; for example, the operation of a machine, the completion of an eight-column work sheet, or an artistic technique. The students watch, perhaps copy, and learn.

Demonstration for online courses requires use of drawings and illustrations, animations, and possibly streaming video. Slide presentations, such as those created in PowerPoint, are easily added to most online learning programs and can be very effective.

Instructor-Facilitated Teaching Approaches

Lab work is a major instructional mode, important to certain disciplines and critical to others. Some may think of labs as falling primarily in the science curricula, and perhaps in "computer labs." This widely used approach, however, takes diverse forms and is often combined with lecture for courses focusing on various hands-on skills such as computer applications, medical assisting, and other allied health courses; vocational courses such as carpentry, upholstery, auto mechanics, or computer repair; and science courses such as biology, chemistry, physics, and geology.

Lab work typically includes both guided practice in which the instructor demonstrates a skill and independent practice in which students rehearse newly learned skills solo. Depending on the objective, students can work in pairs, but more commonly they work individually. They work at assigned tasks while the instructor moves from station to station checking on progress, understanding, or skill development and answering student questions.

Field work might well be considered a form of lab in which the laboratory is larger. Collecting botanical samples, conducting field water tests, examining geological formations firsthand, comparing full-size architectural elements, collecting time/motion data in a factory, or interviewing a CEO or a social worker are but a few examples of an unimaginably large set of possibilities for field study in the "greater lab."

Group work, or collaborative learning, is a highly effective method if used properly. Group work can be a disaster if the groups' attention wanders from the task. For group work, the instructor organizes students into small groups, assigns a task, and lets the group function, providing guidance as needed and assessing informally. Courses that include homework assignments often provide situations for students to pair up or work in groups of three or four to check their work and share their strategies for arriving at certain answers or completing certain tasks. (This can also be categorized as peer mentoring.)

Independent study is an approach to learning in which students work on their own at a specific task during class. Often independent study is used outside of class to allow for more instructor/student or student/student interaction in class. Use in-class independent work when students must access school equipment, when you need to assess individual student learning, or when you determine that students need to have you available while they attempt to master a concept or skill.

Work sheets are independent "seat work" activities that can allow students to practice what has recently been taught. They provide built-in checks of learning for you and your students.

Peer mentoring is a teaching/learning method in which each student is paired with another, one being the helper/tutor of the other. The instructor is then free to provide help as needed. The student who is being helped improves his or her learning. The mentor learns more of the subject area through the process of teaching the other student.

Bringing in Outside Resources

Your classroom can be expanded considerably by bringing in outside resources—or by going to them. Resources can be real, such as guest speakers and field trips, or virtual, using technology. Bringing in the CEO of a local business to talk about leadership or a human resources director to talk about the content of a résumé provides an element of realism beyond what you can offer as an instructor. To obtain maximum value from a guest speaker, prepare for the event by doing the following.

- Have your students read any background material needed for the topic. Ask them to be ready with questions and suggest key points to look for in the presentation.
- Give the speaker background about your students: their interests, their goals, and their content learning to date.
- Allow your speaker adequate but not excessive time to present, leaving time for questions and discussion.
- Follow up the presentation with your students. Discuss what was learned to see if the purpose of using the guest speaker has been met.
- If your speaker is online in a chat room, be sure to monitor or assign a student to monitor the process so that the questions are clear and the speaker has time to reply. If you have the technology, live stream the speaker and follow with chat room questions and answers.

Trips and observations outside the classroom can also add considerable educational value so long as the time and effort in planning and executing the trip do not outweigh the benefits. Seeing a manufacturing process in operation, for example, can bring a concept to life for students in a management course. Visiting the reservations center for an airline can quickly reinforce classroom instruction for a group of travel and tourism students. To decide if the experience will have a net positive value, consider student travel time, especially if the field trip is scheduled at a time that differs from class time. Also, determine whether the field trip is accessible to all students, and is there a cost that could impact some students?

As an alternative, instructors can create virtual field trips so students need not leave the classroom. For example, take a field trip and photograph key elements with a digital camera. Then build the photos into a file (PowerPoint, ofoto.com, or other) with captions to share with your class. If you have the resources, use a digital video camcorder and upload the video to your online course.

You may be able to find pertinent virtual tours online that illustrate the steps of a process or display how something works. Screen them carefully to find exactly what you need. Find out if a representative of the organization or business might be willing to participate in a live chat with your students after they have viewed the virtual tour.

Development and Practice

The major section of every session centers on the teaching-learning process. What concepts and/or skills are being developed and what type of practice will bring about the intended learning? We've been looking at planning from the instructor's side of the table. What are the students doing during each type of instruction? Table 3.2 shows a sampling.

Instructional Mode	Student Activity
Lecture	Listening and taking notes; asking questions
Online lecture reading	Reading, taking notes
Discussion	Commenting and questioning
Brainstorming	Generating ideas, then evaluating ideas
Demonstration	Observing; following the model
Lab work	Experimenting, collecting, observing, interviewing, examining, comparing, operating, problem solving
Group work, collaborative learning	Participating, sharing, helping, joint learning, problem solving
Independent study	Researching, writing, analyzing, problem solving
Peer mentoring	Learning by teaching

Table 3.2. Student Interaction during Instructional Modes.

Note the differing levels of engagement, from "listening and taking notes" during lecture to "experimenting, collecting, observing, ...operating, problem solving" during lab work. Research on productive learning clearly indicates that learners retain more information when they participate actively, when the lesson has meaning for them, and when they are provided ample opportunities for guided practice (scaffolding) and independent practice. In a phrase, the goal of all learning is to provide purposeful practice. But does this mean that real learning can only take place during lab work or group work in which students are involved with hands-on activities? No, but it does mean we need to incorporate active learning—true learner participation—into each session, no matter the subject.

Begin with understanding how students approach new material. When faced with new material, the first thing students do is a "mind scan" to assess what they already know about the subject. In this process, students try to relate the new subject matter to what they already know. The degree to which the instructor or the materials help bridge the content to what the student already knows determines the amount of time the student can devote to learning what is new. Many instructors use stories, examples, analogies, and metaphors to help students make an early connection. Others spend a concentrated session on finding what the learner already knows and work hard to address any and all learner misconceptions.

> "Let me tell you the secret that has led me to my goal. My strength lies solely in my tenacity."
>
> —Louis Pasteur

Madeline Hunter and other educational theorists have suggested that in addition to the issue of what students already know, two other factors increase motivation on a task: early success in performing the task, and feedback/knowledge or results.

The only way to *know* if students know is to have them practice. Nothing is truly learned until it becomes embedded in long-term memory, so practice to the point of over-learning is essential. Practice is made of two distinctly different phases: guided practice and independent practice. Guided or scaffolded practice helps to determine if the skill or concept is being learned or transferred. Students are asked to verbalize, demonstrate, or perform with assistance from the instructor. Throughout guided instruction, instructors ask students questions that check for understanding. Identifying and overcoming student misconceptions (students think they know but they do not know) is key to productive learning, because unlearning something that is known is more difficult than learning new information. Once the instructor believes students understand, he or she allows them to practice independently.

Independent practice helps to ensure mastery and increases the likelihood of retention. More often than not education operates by the motto, "teach and then test" and, in the process, we wait too long before we allow students to "try it out" themselves. In real life we have learned that the opposite is often true. That is, experience tests and then teaches. The challenge for instructors is to decide when it is best to teach then test versus test (experience) and then teach.

In general, practice sessions should be more intense at the beginning of learning a new skill, and by more intense we mean frequent review sessions. When you feel students are closer to consolidating their skills, practice can be distributed over increasing intervals of time. Practice should commence at the earliest point in the instruction that allows authentic work to be performed.

The teaching mode and the type of content affect the type of practice sought. Skills or applications such as a course in Microsoft® Excel, medical assisting, or massage therapy are best practiced in three states: direct step-by-step demonstrations, then guided practice with coaching throughout, and finally independent practice. Concepts and academic skills such as information technology, technical writing, biology, or history are best practiced in modules of increasing cognitive challenge: first in familiar contexts, then transferred gradually to new and more complex settings, and finally demonstrated in the target goal or authentic setting.

Developing new competencies and habits of the mind is the goal of all learning. Providing purposeful practice with feedback is the system that tells you if your students are building the skills they need. Why is practice with feedback so important? Students cannot improve their skills without candid feedback about their work. They not only need to know how they are doing, they need to know how they are doing relative to the end goal and they need to know what their deficiencies are. This puts pressure on the instructor to communicate with students on a frequent basis and to make sure that their comments address the specific and individual needs of the student. It is only through well planned recursive feedback loops that the instructor knows if students are beginning to think like the masters or performing like the experts in the subject area.

So how do you ensure that your sessions include a plan for purposeful practice? The answer depends on the mode of instruction and the type of content.

Lecture/Discussion Mode

Consider these questions as you plan for purposeful practice in each session.

- What habits of the mind and what type of thinking are you looking for? (Are you looking for creative brainstorming, novel writing, historical pattern analysis, scientific thinking, etc.?)

  Is the skill a new skill (insurance billing) or a developmental skill (a competency we have been using lifelong such as speaking, writing, problem solving, etc.)? If the skill is new, model it and teach the requisite skills needed to perform it. Have students practice or perform as soon as you think they can perform an authentic part of the task. The goal here is to move from one problem to the next, gradually increasing knowledge in depth and breadth. What resources are available to support the students' learning and progress toward the goal?

  If the skill is developmental, have students perform it early in class and diagnose their strengths and weaknesses. Identify any learner misconceptions and correct them early in the course. Use active discussion and include the voices of many students.
- Are the major parts best practiced separately and then put together at the end or, if the skill is additive, do the students build on the first skill until they are performing the mulitparted task?
- Educational reform expert Grant Wiggins asserts that we need to help students "uncover learning." How will you help them unearth it, connect it, analyze it, question it, prove it, and generalize it?

- What contexts for practice will you provide that will increase in challenge and difficulty?
- Will you integrate group projects and collaborative work?
- What feedback and knowledge of results will you provide and when? How will the students' final work be judged?

Lab and Demonstration Instruction

- What type of skill or application competency is your target goal? (Application competencies include keyboarding, troubleshooting computer hardware/software problems, and performing medical assisting procedures.)
- Do the learners come into your course with experience in this skill but under different conditions of learning? Are learners coming into the course with partial competency? Is it possible that students have already mastered the skill and need to be allowed to test out?
- Will you demonstrate the skills in additive parts or in full? What will best communicate the end goal? Will you have learners attempt to demonstrate the skill following your demonstration?
- What guided practice sessions will you provide? What kind of coaching will you provide during guided practice? Will you allow students to work in pairs and teach each other?
- How soon will you wean the students from guided practice and allow for independent practice? What kind of feedback and knowledge of results will you provide after independent practice? How will the students' final work be judged?

All practice and development is driven by the need to understand what we know and what we do not know. Ask yourself if your practice and development activities will help learners monitor their own learning and judge whether they need more development or if they are performing satisfactorily on the task.

Session Assessment

On-going assessment of the teaching-learning interaction can be among the most useful and informative activities conducted in your course, for instructor and students alike. These assessments are not the hour-long (or more) comprehension or performance assessments. Rather, they are formative assessment techniques that will help you make practical decisions about the progress and direction of your course.

Angelo and Cross, in *Classroom Assessment Techniques*[2], provide strategies for using various formative assessment tools that are quick, engaging, and informative. The following section describes some of their tools and techniques

---

[2] Thomas A. Angelo and K. Patricia Cross. *Classroom Assessment Techniques: A Handbook for College Teachers*, second edition. San Francisco: Jossey-Bass Publishers, 1993.

that are widely referenced in the literature of instructional design and curriculum planning.

One-Minute Papers

Also called Minute Papers or Half-Sheet Responses, One-Minute Papers provide you with fast, written feedback from students. A few minutes before class is

> *"To be able to be caught up into the world of thought—that is being educated."*
>
> —Edith Hamilton

scheduled to end, ask students to answer two questions on a half-sheet of paper or their computer screen. Ask them "What was the most important thing you learned during this class?" and "What important question remains unanswered?" The responses in One-Minute Papers not only tell you if students understood and remember major points, but also indicate whether your course is on track or you need to take some other direction. Note that the questions require students to evaluate their learning—what they think is important and what else they need to know.

One-Minute Papers can also be used for warm-ups, and they work well to assess learning from lecture, lab, group, field, and other learning situations. As for other assessments, take time in the next session to report on what you learned from the One-Minute Papers.

Muddiest Point

The Muddiest Point assessment is similar in administration to the One-Minute Papers, with the main difference being the question asked. The instructor asks students to write down or type a quick answer to the question "What was the muddiest point in [the lab, the reading, the homework, the lecture, etc.]?" Students must, in a few moments, recognize what they do not understand and communicate that in writing.

The technique is an efficient way to identify topics or procedures that need clarification or require additional instruction or activities.

Misconception Check

Do your students have prior knowledge or misinformation that gets in the way of new learning? Assess this by using the Misconception Check. Prepare a list of common misconceptions that students might have and use a few of the most troublesome of these for the activity. Students can help you identify these if you ask them the question "What misconceptions do you think many people have about _____?" Then create a short survey using multiple choice, short answer, or other question formats. You might wish to design the survey as a series of statements and ask students to agree or disagree using a scale of 1 to 5.

When you administer the survey or discuss the results with the students, explain that you need to address misconceptions that might hinder learning. Administer the survey anonymously to avoid possible embarrassment to a student.

Meeting a Challenge
Dealing with Difficult Students

Inevitably, a student of yours will pose a difficulty. This might be one who is unhappy with his or her grade and complains that you have been unfair or unfairly rigorous. It could be students who are argumentative in the classroom, refusing to accept that you do not agree with their point of view. Some students dominate discussions in class or in small groups, making participation by other students more difficult. And some students demand an excessive amount of your time and become angry when you cannot meet their expectations. Here are some tips for dealing with angry, demanding, or dominating students.

1. Prevent many potential difficulties by making the course expectations, requirements, and learning philosophy crystal-clear at the outset. If students know your attendance, class participation, and grading policies, they will be more likely to conform and less likely to object or argue. Put your policies in writing and give the information to the students along with or as part of the syllabus.

2. Post your office hours and honor them! Also, be sure students can reach you by e-mail. Many problems can be averted if students have a way to communicate with you and if you respond promptly.

3. Encourage questions and suggestions during class. This will alert you to any small problems before they swell into big issues.

4. Avoid embarrassing students or making them defensive when you need to correct their answers or redirect their work. Be sure your feedback is positive and constructive.

5. Make sure your evaluation and grading system is clear and then apply it consistently. Sometimes examples of good essays or answers will help confirm your grading standards. Some students may need some guidance in preparing for an exam. If your school offers study skills help, let your students know about it. If a student does complain about a grade, listen to the specific explanation. Respond calmly and demonstrate to the student why the grade is what it is. Be open to the idea that you can make mistakes, and be willing to correct a grade when a student is right.

6. If a student repeatedly argues or disrupts the class, discuss the situation with the student in private. Listen carefully and try to be sympathetic. Sometimes disruptive students need special assistance or are facing difficulties outside the classroom. In these cases, a referral to a college counselor might help.

7. Some students love to participate in class. They like to answer questions and easily contribute to discussions. And though you may appreciate their enthusiasm and willingness to take part in every activity, they may make other students feel left out. When this happens, you will need to find a strategy that allows participation by others without offending the gregarious student. Adopt a system that calls on specific students, such as drawing a name from a basket. When everyone has contributed, return the slips of paper to the basket and start over. Another approach is to say, in a warm, positive way, "Okay. Who else has a comment on this issue?" or "Who besides Susan can answer this one?" If the student is waving an arm, eager to be called on, you might say to the student, "Don't worry. I know you know the answer to this one. I need to see who else knows too."

RSQC2 (Recall, Summarize, Question, Connect, and Comment)

Assess students' recall and understanding of class content and ask them to apply their analytical and relational skills by using the RSQC2. This activity provides students with a structured but nonthreatening opportunity to recall, summarize, and evaluate the course information and process. Use the information to compare their understanding and perspectives on the course with your own.

The following list describes the five components of the technique, which may be used individually or as a group. The activity can refer to the previous class session, a lab, readings, an online unit, and so forth.

1. **Recall.** Ask students to make a list of words or phrases of what they remember as important from the previous class. After students have had a minute or two to write their list, ask them to put the items in order of importance.
2. **Summarize.** Instruct students to summarize the most important points of the previous session (or other learning segment) using only one sentence.
3. **Question.** Ask students to write down one or two questions that they have regarding the last class.
4. **Connect.** Ask students to explain the relationship between a point or two that you provide and the course as a whole.
5. **Comment.** Ask students to write a few comments that evaluate the class. When you do this, give them a criterion for their comments; for example, which aspects of the class were most/least useful, enjoyable, informative, and so forth.

RSQC2, if conducted using all five components, will require a little more in-class time than the One-Minute Papers or the Muddiest Point. If, however, you incorporate the exercise as part of your warm-ups or purpose time, you will find that it may help direct the remainder of the class time and make it more efficient.

Student-Generated Test Items

Discover what students consider key information and fair test questions as well as how well they can answer the questions by asking them to generate test items. The technique helps students evaluate their own learning and identify areas of weakness.

One potential, and important, benefit from this exercise will be the indication of students' expectations for tests, which may be more lax or more demanding than your own. Students should be given feedback on their questions and how closely they parallel or fit the actual course testing.

Pro and Con Grid

The Pro and Con Grid assessment tool has many applications. It is especially useful for courses or topics that involve value judgments because students must think beyond the first impression and examine other possible perspectives. Students will name the pros and cons, costs and benefits, advantages and disadvantages of an issue, approach to solving a problem, a decision, a proposition, or other question. From their lists, instructors can evaluate students' objectivity, imagination, understanding of underlying principles, and their ability to weigh viewpoints.

Categorizing Grid

By sorting terms, phrases, equations, images, concepts, procedural steps, and so forth, students give evidence of how well they understand and remember relationships or groupings. The Categorizing Grid is a paper-and-pencil sorting tool. Given a scrambled list of items and a grid with two to five categories at the top, students place or write each item below the appropriate category.

The Categorizing Grid is probably most useful in introductory courses, regardless of format, where students are learning the terminology of a discipline. If you discover that many students are incorrectly categorizing certain values (for example, terms), provide more examples or clarification for those terms. Also, review the grids to determine categories in which students are weakest.

Empty Outlines

Provide students with an Empty Outline or "study frame" of a chapter or lecture or lab experience and ask them to fill in the main points. You may prefer to use this as a learning or review tool, rather than as an assessment tool. Students will learn to extract key points and organize information from a lecture or presentation.

Using the Empty Outline approach can be time consuming. You might wish to assign it as a homework task rather than as a classroom assignment.

Concept Maps

Concept Maps provide a visual representation of conceptual connections. Your students' maps could be concentric circles, a center concept with spokes, a set of connected ladders, or some other configuration. They are most useful in courses that address theories and concepts, although procedures are also subject to useful mapping.

Students' maps will show you the patterns of their associations, and whether they are organizing information—making the connections—in reasonable ways. Students can compare maps and evaluate the differences.

Be sure to provide some examples of concept maps and review them with students before you ask them to create their own.

One-Sentence Summary

How can instructors assess whether students are understanding and retaining the core or critical information in a large body of information? Asking students for a One-Sentence Summary is one possible way to do this. With this technique, instructors challenge students to answer the who, what, to/from/by whom, when (and for how long), where, how, and why. Students write a long sentence that presents the key information. Instructors of writing may cringe, but others will find that this approach provides them with a useful measure of how well they have communicated the essentials.

Directed Paraphrasing

Asking students to restate certain text material or lecture information—possibly a theory or procedure—in their own words will not only identify areas they do not understand or do not understand correctly, but also give them practice with this very useful study skill.

A particularly instructive variation is to ask them to paraphrase the assigned material in a way they would tell it to their ten-year-old brother. This will determine whether they can paraphrase in straightforward, plain language. If appropriate, you might also ask them to paraphrase the material for a particular person in a related career such as a consumer or a manager.

"Teaching is the highest form of understanding."
—Aristotle

Invented Dialogues

Invented dialogues tap into students' abilities to synthesize information in a creative way, possibly looking even beyond their readings or the lectures. History professors find the technique particularly engaging.

With this technique, students either construct dialogues from actual quotes or write what a particular figure would have been likely to say. Characters might present opposing viewpoints, one might instruct the other, or they might discuss an event, theory, procedure, and so forth.

Invented dialogues challenge students to capture the personality and style of the assigned individuals, as well as their experiences, opinions, prejudices, and so forth.

Wrap-Up and Assignments

Your conclusion of a session should help students remember the major points. It should also provide brief feedback on the session and mention the topic of the next session. Remind students (yes, again) of any assignments or deadlines. Here are some suggestions for session wrap-up.

- Review the major points by summarizing them for the students.
- Ask three or four questions that will elicit the main points from the students.
- Ask a few questions that require the students to answer "in chorus." The questions need to elicit terms or short phrases, not "yes" or "no."
- Ask students to complete a *short* post-session quiz about the main points of the session. Or, ask students to complete a *short* survey to give you feedback about the activities or content of the session . . . was it interesting? Too slow/fast? Fun? Did they learn from it?
- Provide general feedback about the session such as "We've covered a lot of information on this topic today." "You asked some excellent questions today." "Wow! You did a great job today. Congratulations! Let's keep it up!"

- Remind students of assignments or deadlines. In choosing assignments, consider what students should do outside of the classroom to learn new material or reinforce or enhance previous learning. Most students expect reading and regular homework assignments appropriate to the subject matter. These daily or weekly assignments are required in addition to the major course projects and assignments that require higher-order thinking or the integration and/or application of students' learning.

Regular assignments must connect to performance, or enabling, objectives on the session plan level; the assignments must relate to the objectives of that session. Does each of your assignments pass that test? Do they relate to one of the outcomes that you expect of your students?

A routine daily assignment might be one of the following.

- Do problems 15-1A and 15-3A.
- Write out the answers to questions 1–16 on page 235.
- Compose a letter that you would give to a customer to explain your store's return policy.

In each case, the material related to the assignment has been covered in a session or will be covered in the next session. One of your key decisions related to assignments is whether you want your students to do the assignments after you have taught the material or go ahead and do the work prior to it being taught. A major factor in this decision is the ability or motivation level of your students. Some students or even entire classes are able to proceed on their own. This can occur in advanced classes, such as Cost Accounting.

Another factor is the technical nature of the material. In courses in which there is a high level of specialized technical knowledge, such as Statistics, there is a strong chance that you will teach the material in class first. On the other hand, if you have adult working students in a course in Human Relations, they may be able to do the assignments on their own. In either case, the daily assignments could be the same.

Be clear about the details of assignments and your expectations. Provide sufficient detail so students can do them without asking you for clarification. In an on-campus class, present the assignments orally or in writing; in an online class, provide them via the course management system. Assignments of problems or end-of-chapter activities in the text can be simply page and reference numbers, such as "Exercise 6 on page 27."

Wrap-up techniques apply to lab sessions as much as they do to classroom sessions. Since lab sessions are instructor-facilitated, schedule the work so that students finish up with five (or so) minutes left before the end-time of the session. Then use some of the suggestions above or others of your own making.

Some lab sessions are highly individualized; students finish at their own pace and leave the session. If this is your situation, be prepared to wrap up individually with each student, making a few comments about the work. Also, in this situation, ask students to complete the short post-session quiz or short-survey on paper before they leave (or on the computer if it's a computer lab). Put assignment reminders on the marking board or on paper. (Use quarter-sheets or strips of colored paper. Save trees!)

Online sessions should also have a wrap-up. If the session is "live," you can do this via the whiteboard or chat room messaging. If, however, the session is one that students complete independently, program the wrap-up to appear as the last slide or page of the session. End a session with a poll, survey, matching game with the main points, or other review or assessment. Remember to set the confirmation display to show a score and related feedback, preferably something that "sounds like you." If possible, use animation for the feedback. This is one more opportunity to motivate your learners. Post a thank-you for completing a survey, the survey results, and other wrap-up announcements

Using Planning Templates

Where do you get lesson plans for your course? There was a time when every instructor created his or her own plans "from scratch." In today's world rich with resources, however, instructors have many options. Lesson plans ranging in complexity from a bare-bones outline to a comprehensive, highly detailed specification can be found in great abundance on the Internet. Download the files and use them as they are or adjust them to your particular circumstances. Planning templates also are available, offering you the convenience of an electronic form that you complete from scratch, resulting in your own lesson plan creations.

One of the best sources of completed lesson plans can be the publisher of your chosen textbook. EMC/Paradigm, for example, has developed Lesson Blueprints and a wealth of online tools to accompany many of its texts. Individual Lesson Blueprints for the Marquee and Benchmark Microsoft Office 2003 series include the following items.

> Chapter number
> Page numbers in textbook
> Lesson # in week # (class #) as it coincides with the syllabus
> Learning objectives
> End of chapter activity information
> Estimated times
> Student data files (in order of occurrence)
> Equipment check
> PowerPoint slides available
> Lecture/Demonstration notes
> Extra tips for students
> Possible work for advanced students
> Space for writing your own individual notes

Figure 3.5 displays a Lesson Blueprint for a session on "Maintaining Data in Access Tables" in a text on Microsoft Access 2003.

INTERNET RESOURCE Templates

LESSON BLUEPRINT
Application: Access 2003
Section: 1 – Maintaining Data in Access Tables **Topics: 1.7 (Sorting Records) – 1.11 (Backing Up a Database)** **Page number(s) in book:** 16-32 **First lesson in Week 9 (Class 25)**
Learning Objectives:
1) Sort records by a single field and by multiple fields 2) Change margins and page orientation 3) Preview and print datasheets 4) Use Help feature to find Access information 5) Increase row height in a datasheet 6) Compact and repair a database 7) Back up a database
Microsoft® Office Specialist Objective Correlation:

AC03S-2-1	AC03S-3-3	AC03S-3-5	AC03S-4-2
AC03S-4-3	AC03S-4-5	AC03S-4-6	

END OF SECTION ACTIVITIES	
Procedures Check Page 26, 15 short answer questions Skills Review Activities Begins on page 28 Activity 1 – Best fit column widths; find and edit records Activity 2 – Delete and add records in Datasheet view; add records in Form view Activity 3 – Sort records; change page orientation; preview and print Activity 4 – Compact and repair database; turn on Compact on Close feature; back up database	Performance Plus Assessments: Begins on page 29 Assessment 1 – Adjust column widths; edit records; preview and print; turn on Compact on Close feature Assessment 2 – Find and delete records; add records; adjust column widths; change margins; preview and print; turn on Compact on Close feature Assessment 3 – Find and delete records; sort records; increase row height; preview and print; turn on Compact on Close feature Assessment 4 – Back up database; turn on Compact on Close feature Assessment 5 – Use Help feature to find information on designing a database; write memo in Microsoft Word using a memo template that lists steps found in Help and describes the first four steps Assessment 6 – Find company information on the Internet for eight companies; add records; adjust column widths; sort records; change page setup options; preview and print; turn on Compact on Close feature

Estimated Times:
Lecture/Demonstration: 30 minutes - flexible
Section tutorials: 30 – 45 minutes (homework time needed will vary depending on length of lecture/demonstration)
End of Section Activities/Assessments: 1 hour

continued on next page

Student file(s) needed for entire section:	
Topics:	WEDistributors1
Skills Review:	WEEmployees1
Performance Plus:	NPCGrades1
	WBInventory
	PTCostume Inventory1
	JobSearch1

Equipment Check:

No equipment check is required.

PowerPoint Slides Available: Access_Section01, Slides 19–End

Lecture/Demonstration Notes:

In this lesson students learn to sort, change page setup options, use Help resources, compact and repair a database, and back up a database.

LESSON LEAD-IN DISCUSSION

Students learn two important database utilities in this lesson: compacting and repairing a database and backing up a database. Data is the backbone of the business and must be protected. Ask students to consider the impact on a business of a database becoming corrupted, being hacked, or otherwise damaged. Also, what happens if a database becomes largely fragmented and is used to access hundreds of records? The record retrieval time becomes slow and productivity is lost. These scenarios help to reinforce the necessity for database utilities such as compact and repair and back up. Emphasize that the topics are presented in the first section to introduce early the importance of these features. Students will be asked to turn on the Compact on Close feature for every database used in the section. Additionally, students should consider how often backups of the databases for course work should be made. Encourage students to have an extra set of disks for backup purposes.

If you have access to a computer connected to a video display projector, or are teaching students in a computer lab, demonstrate the following tasks. If time is constrained due to previous discussion, focus the demonstration on the tasks preceded by an asterisk.

✓ Have on disk the data file WEDistributors1.

✓ *Open WEDistributors1.

✓ *Open the US Distributors table.

✓ *Click in the *State* column and then click the Sort Descending button.

✓ *Drag the *State* column to the beginning of the table (before *Name*). Select both the *State* and *Name* columns and then click the Sort Ascending button.

✓ *Point out that more than one record exists for the state of New York and that the *Name* column is then used to sort the records alphabetically within the state. Multicolumn sorts usually require that fields be moved in the table in a left to right order defining the sort sequence.

✓ Display the datasheet in Print Preview. Change the magnification to 100% and then display the second page.

✓ Click the Setup button on the Print Preview toolbar and change the page orientation to landscape. Display page 1. Point out that the printout is still two pages long.

✓ Click the Setup button on the Print Preview toolbar and change the left and right margins to 0.2 inch. Notice the printout still requires two pages. Discuss with students that to fit the table on one page you would have to adjust column widths and/or delete a column such as *Street Address2*. Mention that using queries and reports provides more control over the printout and that printing from the datasheet is usually done only for small table printouts.

✓ Close the Print Preview window.

continued on next page

✓ Display the Access Help task pane. Type **keyboard shortcuts** in the *Search for* text box. Click the topic *Keyboard Shortcuts* in the Search Results list. Click the link <u>Navigate in Datasheet view</u> and then <u>Going to a specific record</u>. Read the information about function key F5. Close the Help window and the task pane.

✓ Press F5. Type a record number and press Enter to move to the specific record.

✓ *Ask students to tell you how to increase the height of the rows between the records in the datasheet. Based on Excel experience, students should offer that you point on the boundary line in the record selector bar between the rows and then drag up or down.

✓ *Drag the bottom row boundary for the first record down approximately one-half inch. Ask students to look at the results and describe a difference between changing row heights in Access and Excel. Students should note that the row height changed for *all rows* in the datasheet in Access while in Excel only the row height for the row boundary that was dragged would have increased.

✓ *Close the US Distributors table. Click Yes to save changes to the layout of the table.

✓ *Minimize Access. Open the My Computer or Windows Explorer window (whichever window you normally use to view files) and navigate to the drive and/or folder in which WEDistributors1 is stored.

✓ *Display the details so students can note the file size for WEDistributors1. (File size should be approximately 685 KB.)

✓ *Switch to the Access window and run the compact and repair utility (click Tools, Database Utilities, Compact and Repair Database).

✓ *Switch back to My Computer or Windows Explorer and note the reduced file size for WEDistributors1. (File size should be compacted to approximately 412 KB.)

✓ Discuss how a database should be compacted and repaired periodically to optimize the performance and reduce disk space. Compacting defragments the file.

✓ *Close the My Computer or Windows Explorer window.

✓ *Display the Options dialog box in Access. Click the General tab and show students the *Compact on Close* check box. Tell students it is advisable to turn on the Compact on Close feature for each database so that the file is routinely compacted.

✓ *Click Tools and point to Database Utilities. Point out the Back Up Database option on the Database Utilities menu. Click the File menu and then click Back Up Database. Mention that the two menus access the same feature.

✓ *At the Save Backup As dialog box, show how Access has appended the current date to the current database file name. Click the Save button.

✓ *Students may not have noticed that when you opened the Save Backup As dialog box, the database was closed in the background. When the backup is complete, Access automatically reopens the database. Explain why you have to reopen the database to resume your work.

✓ Discuss the benefits of performing backups on a regular basis not only for the normal security reasons but also to provide a historical record of data. When records are deleted or edited, the backups provide the audit trail that might be needed to look up old information.

✓ *Close WEDistributors1.

WRAP-UP CLASS DISCUSSION TOPICS Depending on time available consider the following topic: Since databases store crucial business information, a backup system is essential for protecting the data. Break students into pairs or small groups and have them design a backup strategy for a typical small business office that uses Access to store information on invoices and customers. The backup strategy should include the frequency with which backups should be done, the media onto which the backup should be copied, the person responsible for the backup, the offsite storage location, and so on.

Figure 3.5. Lesson Blueprint for Marquee Series Microsoft Access 2003.

The Lesson Blueprints provide materials that match quite closely with the elements of a session plan, as described in the preceding section. Learning objectives, for example, become the Session Plan purpose. PowerPoint slides available with the text are identified in the Blueprint and could become the main tool for the warm-up and kickoff. If the instructional approach is lecture or demonstration, the PowerPoint slides coupled with the Lecture/Demonstration notes become the content for the learner interaction part of the session. The Blueprint's Extra Tips for Students and Possible Work for Advanced Students provide additional practice material for learner interaction. Blueprint End of Chapter Activity Information might be used as part of the Session Assessment. Table 3.3 depicts these relationships.

Comparison: Session Plan Elements and Lesson Blueprint Elements	
Session Plan Elements	Lesson Blueprint Elements
Warm-up	PowerPoint Slides Available
Purpose and kickoff	Learning Objectives
Instructional approach and methodology	Lecture with PowerPoint Presentation or Guided Demonstration
Development and practice	PowerPoint Slides Available Lesson Lead-in Discussion End of Section Activites (Procedures Check and Skills Review Activities)
Session assessment	End of Section Activities (Performance Plus Assessments)
Wrap-up and assignment	Wrap-Up Class Discussion Topics

Table 3.3. Session Plan and Lesson Blueprint Element Counterparts.

An overview provided with the Lesson Blueprints offers suggestions for adjusting the session plans to the most common class environments:

In order to accommodate the widest range of teaching environments and preferences, the Lesson Blueprints contain suggestions for more discussion and activity than can be completed in a 1-hour class. This is designed to allow you the flexibility to pick and choose the discussions and/or activities that best suit your teaching style and student population.

Theoretical topics are included if you prefer classroom discussion over guided demonstration. For demonstration style teaching, the lessons include a suggested demonstration sequence that mirrors the order of topics in the chapter. Activities preceded by an asterisk are considered the more important topics from the chapter that should be taught versus topics that students can probably manage to learn on their own.

Times have been estimated based on assigning all exercises and all end-of-chapter activities. These times should be used as a guideline only. Based on student ability and/or if you choose to assign less work, these times may need to be shortened or lengthened. An assumption is included in the time estimates that most of the work in the textbook is assigned as homework. If your classroom is a self-paced working lab, the times shown in the Blueprints will vary greatly from student to student.

Figure 3.6 illustrates another session plan format that is similar, but not identical, to the model presented in this chapter. Designed for a Business Math course, this particular session plan is aimed at teaching the topic of base, rate, and portion. The plan has four major sections.

- Identifying data—course, date, title, textbook, and other resources
- Learning objectives—what you want your students to learn as a result of the lesson
- Six parts of the lesson—

    1. Apperception: the process of setting the stage for that lesson. It is also referred to as "anticipatory set." Students may be thinking of home, work, family, social issues, other courses, and so forth. You must do something immediately to set their minds on your course.
    2. Motivation: the part of the lesson in which you interest and excite students about learning the new material.
    3. Development: the presentation of new material. It can be done with question-and-answer, discussion, lecture, or other methods, depending on course content.
    4. Application: another term for practice. As soon as you have taught a new skill or concept, your students need practice so that you can see if what you have taught has been learned. The need for practice explains why you cannot teach two things at once. There needs to be intervening practice so that you can see if the first "thing" has been learned before you proceed.
    5. Summary: Every lesson should end in some-instructor directed way. One type of summary activity is a series of questions, as shown in Figure 3.6. Another more generic approach is the question "What did you learn today?" Your students need to be able to leave your class saying to themselves "Today, I learned that . . . ."
    6. Assignment: connects this session to the remainder of the course. Today's assignment can be tomorrow's apperception and the cycle starts all over again.

- Comments—space for writing your thoughts about the plan and the lesson itself for future reference.

SESSION PLAN EXAMPLE	
Business 151	November 3, 20XX
Business Math	
Text Chapter 4	
Topic of Lesson: Base, Rate, and Portion	
Learning Objectives: At the conclusion of this lesson, the student will be able to identify the base, rate, and portion in word problems and solve the problems.	
Apperception:	$500 x .20 = ($100) $500/$2,000 = (25%) $75/.05 = ($1,500)

continued on next page

Motivation: What is the meaning of the phrase "part of"? Tell us some things that you are part of. In math, the portion is a number that is part of another number called the base. The fraction of the base that the portion is, is called the rate. BRP problems, as they are called, are the most common type of problems in business math. Today, we will learn the most important aspect of BRP problems, identifying which is B, which is R, and which is P. We will also learn how to solve some basic BRP problems,
Development:
1. You earn $500 a week and save 20% of it. How much do you save? Identify $500 as B, 20% as R, and solve for P as in apperception problem 1. ($100)
2. If you save $500 from a check of $2,000, what percent are you saving? Identify $500 as P, $2,000 as B, and solve for R as in apperception problem 2. (25%)
3. If the $75 a week that you save is 5% of your salary, what is your salary? Identify $75 as P, 5% as R, and solve for B as in apperception problem 3. ($1,500)
Application: In each problem, identify the elements and solve.
1. Three hundred hot dogs are spoiled, which is 6% of the total cooked. How many were cooked? (5,000)
2. We have 500 workers; 50 are out sick. What percent are out sick? (10%)
3. Of 20,000 miles driven a year, 15% are in the city. How many miles are driven in the city? (3,000)
Summary: How do you recognize B? R? P? How do you find B? R? P?
Assignment: Problems 1–8 on page xx.

Figure 3.6. Alternative Session Plan Format.

Notice how the six parts of this lesson plan example correspond with the session plan as we presented it earlier. We've summarized the correlation in Table 3.4. The point to recognize with this comparison and others we make with the session plan elements model is that regardless of the labels we use, the level of detail, or variation by discipline, good lesson planning has certain commonalities.

Session Plan Elements	Example Lesson Plan Elements
Warm-up	Apperception
Purpose and kickoff	Motivation
Instructional approach and methodology	Development
Development and practice	Application
Session assessment	
Wrap-up and assignment	Summary and assignment

Table 3.4. Comparison of Elements in Session/Lesson Plans.

Your collection of session plans for the entire course becomes a valuable record. When your course is over, you can look back on its entirety and review each individual plan to assess what worked and what you can improve. Today's plans are the basis for tomorrow's revisions as you strive to help your students meet the objectives of your course.

Special Considerations in Planning Online Sessions

Planning online sessions or modules or lessons involves many of the same considerations as we've discussed for planning classroom sessions, plus a few others. The richness of online courses varies tremendously, and is often related to the resources and skills of the developer. Publishers who develop online courses to accompany their textbooks may provide colorful, interactive, interesting materials and functions. On the other hand, some published online courses are merely page turners; that is, the content of the textbook displayed on the monitor.

Instructors in some colleges or departments are expected to create their own online courses, usually in Blackboard or WebCT. (See Chapter 2 for criteria to consider in choosing or developing courses.)

If you are developing modules for online courses, plan the module using the parts we discussed for a lesson. Begin with a warm-up, such as a short pretest or survey or a few questions to engage students' thinking. Other beginnings might be a quick video file, animation, or pop-up poll. Be sure that the objectives are clearly displayed. The main part of the module's instruction should have choices for students to master the content—readings, charts, graphs, illustrations, Web tours, scheduled chats, online puzzles or games. Use the interactive tools available to you and the students as much as you can. Whiteboards, threaded discussions, live chats, and e-mail are available with most online courses. Live functions are not appropriate for all courses; students must agree to participate according to a preestablished schedule.

Online work supplements the textbook material rather than replacing it! Follow with a summary and posttest. If the posttest does not provide students with immediate feedback, then try to provide your feedback as soon as possible. If your online course forces students to proceed through a predesignated order of modules, then be sure to point them to their next activity or assignment. Finally, since online courses may never provide opportunity for you to give personal praise, feedback, or motivation to students, remember to add comments at appropriate places in the course, usually when students successfully complete a task, that say "Good Job!" "Congratulations!" "Way to go!" or other positive comment. Figure 3.7 displays an example of a six-element session plan for an online session of a Botany course.

BOTANY ONLINE SESSION PLAN	
Session Name: Healing Herbs	
Warm-up	Review by electronic flashcards
Purpose and kickoff	Herbs and their healing purposes. Image map: diseases and symptoms
Instructional approach and methodology	Reading Unit 6
Development and practice	Exploring (six links)
Session assessment	Matching activity
Wrap-up and assignment	Summary and feedback. Assignment reminder: sketchbook pages, six herbs with detail close-up for each

Table 3.7. Sample Plan for a Session on Healing Herbs in an Online Botany Course.

CHAPTER SUMMARY

- Planning individual sessions begins where course-level planning leaves off, with course and part outcomes established, and the topics, skills, and concepts identified for each part. The first step is to divide the part content into sessions based on the instructional hours available. Then adjust the plan to accommodate an efficient and acceptable balance among on-campus sessions, online assignment hours, reading and project time, and major assessments.

- Prepare a syllabus for distribution in the first class session. An effective learning-centered syllabus defines students' responsibilities, defines the instructor's role, lists student outcomes clearly, establishes evaluation standards and procedures, acquaints students with course logistics, establishes a communication pattern between instructor and students, and includes difficult-to-obtain course materials.

- Prepare to teach course sessions by first considering best instructional practices, which include building background knowledge; teaching essential vocabulary; including reading, communication, and writing; addressing technical literacy skills; providing opportunities for independent learning; and making learning emotional.

- Among the several session planning models that exist, certain essential elements emerge: warm-up, purpose and kickoff, instructional approach and methodology, development and practice, assessment, and wrap-up and assignments.

- Using electronic planning templates can streamline the session planning process and help ensure that all essential elements are included.

- Planning effective online sessions involves many of the same issues instructors need to consider for on-campus sessions. Additional needs include offering choices for the main part of each module's content, using interactive tools as much as possible, including a module summary and posttest, and providing feedback frequently and as soon as possible with assignments and tests.

Think About It: Evaluate Your Skills in Using Various Instructional Modes

Using the scale below, indicate your experience level and confidence in teaching using each of the delivery modes listed. Then rank the delivery systems from most preferred (1) to least preferred (10). Finally, reflect on your experiences and write a few sentences describing your strengths and challenges with each approach.

VE (Very Experienced)
SE (Somewhat Experienced)
NE (Little to No Experience)

Delivery Mode	Experience Level	Rank
lecture		
lecture in combination with discussion		
question-and-answer		
small group/peer-to-peer learning		
independent study		
discussion		
labs and hands-on work		
demonstration		

Discussion Questions

1. Which activities or materials have you found to work best in helping ESL students participate more effectively in your courses?

2. Grant Wiggins, an educational reform consultant and coauthor of *Understanding By Design*, has said, "Our students are good at giving us answers, but they do not know what the questions are." What does he mean? Does his view change the type of questions you would ask your students? Does it change what you would emphasize in your course lectures or demonstrations?

3. Practice and application are essential to learner success. Discuss the techniques you have used to provide quality practice and application sessions. What has really worked? Do the strategies and techniques vary by types of learners? How does guided practice, or coaching, differ from independent practice?

4. So much of instruction is presented through lectures. How are lectures best "replaced" in Web-based learning? What strategies have you tried and which have been successful? How do you plan to address this challenge in future Web-delivered course sessions?

Field Work

1. What field work—for example, research of some type—could you add to a course in your discipline? What would the intended outcomes be? What would students learn? How?
2. Conduct Internet searches to find information on course assessment techniques (CATs) not discussed in the chapter. Write a description of two new techniques you would like to try in your classroom.
3. How are course structures changing on your campus? Research this issue to determine the number of traditional course offerings (lecture or some combination of lecture and another on-campus mode), the number of distance learning courses, and the number of hybrid courses. What are the trends, and how is your administration directing and/or helping you to prepare for the future?
4. LessonBuilder™ by SoftChalk is a product that allows you to build interactive Web pages for a distance learning course. Research this tool and create a simple Web lesson for one of your courses using the free trial download available at www.softchalk.com.

Professional Portfolio: Rebuild Your Session Plans

Review two of your most important session plans. Which parts of those lessons need to be improved? Do the plans reflect best instructional practices? If not, redevelop those sessions using the session parts and best practices presented in this chapter. Be sure to address the often overlooked issues of building background knowledge, teaching vocabulary, incorporating technology, and conveying emotion.

Exceptional Teaching is

Engaging and Action-Oriented

Engaging students' minds, keeping their attention and motivation at the highest possible level, is a huge challenge—and one that is absolutely essential to exceptional teaching. Some students are naturally engaged. They are interested and curious and motivated. Others, however, are not. The job of the exceptional instructor is to engage the minds and energies of as many students in a class as possible and for the greatest period of time. How do you maintain interest and motivate students throughout a course? Here are some important keys to keeping your students engaged.

Incorporate Action Wherever Possible

Almost anything you teach can involve action, such as an application of the idea, a demonstration, a performance. Some courses are naturals for this. Are you teaching art, music, or film? Take advantage of every performance

opportunity you can! Hold an exhibit or recital of student work. Other courses may require a little more imagination. Are you teaching anthropology? Demonstrate excavation techniques. Are you teaching architecture? Have students build models.

Use Students To Teach

This is especially applicable with adult learners. Determine early in your course, whether by discussion or short survey, some of the background and experience of your students. When appropriate, invite student presentations, especially if they include a demonstration. Guide their development of any audiovisual aids that might improve their talk. Assign experienced students to be team leaders on collaborative projects. At the end of the course, find out if any students would like to help with tutorials or presentations for the next offering of the course.

Maintain Your Own Interest

Your own high level of interest and energy is contagious. If you are not interested in the topic, you cannot expect to invigorate anyone else. Demonstrate that you think particular concepts are interesting and important by your gestures, your voice, and your words.

Shake Up the Routine

Teaching can get into a rut, and when it does, learning also stagnates. Every once in awhile, vary the approach of your session. Surprise students with a guest speaker or a quiz. Hold a "Quiz Bowl" or "Jeopardy" session instead of a pencil and paper test. Show a short video. If you are ahead of your plan, use ten minutes for a doodling contest or a creative thinking test or a magic trick. Do something that *you* enjoy, and students will also.

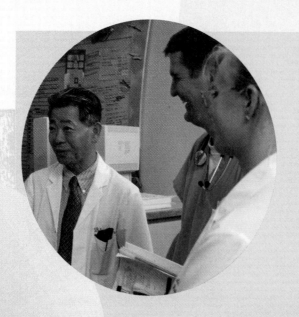

Teach Students to Solve Problems

Problem solving is a high-engagement activity. Learners must actively focus on aspects of a problem and apply their knowledge to the puzzle. (The firing of neurons in the brain actually increases when people solve problems.)[1] This is an important clue for instructors. When the brain is not encoding, retrieving, comparing, evaluating, or otherwise working with information, the result is a bored student.

Although some experts say "Don't teach problem solving; instead give students problems worth solving," exceptional instructors do both. Students need to know the problem-solving steps or tactics or approaches, and they should have meaningful, relevant problems to solve. Depending on your discipline, the steps of problem solving can be simple or complex. Usually the steps include at least the following.

- Define the problem.
- Gather data related to the problem.
- Generate some possible solutions and select one.
- Apply the solution.

- Evaluate the solution. (Is the problem solved?)

Most sciences apply a more complex, detailed approach and use the scientific methods that pertain to that science. Physics, chemistry, and biology instructors seldom have difficulty providing pertinent problems for students to solve. But students in other fields also need to apply these steps to solving real problems. For example, direct your real estate students to determine the value of a property. Ask desktop publishing students to design an annual report to meet certain criteria. International marketing students could design an advertising campaign that sells one product in three different countries.

Teaching might be at its best when students are able to solve new problems using the information and tools the instruction has provided. Not only have students understood and remembered concepts or skills, but they apply them in new situations.

---

[1] According to a 2003 study by Dr. Jeremy Gray of Washington University, brain activity increases in the lateral prefrontal cortex, a brain region associated with memory, planning, and goal-directed activity (*Nature Neurosciences*, March 2003).

Change and Adapt Your Instruction as Needed

If one approach doesn't work, the exceptional instructor develops or implements another. This is part of what keeps teaching dynamic and interesting to instructors.

Make time during your course for reflecting on what is working and what is not. Distinguish between what is working for some students but not for all. Ask yourself how you can motivate the students who have fallen behind. If a student just "isn't getting it," try to think of other ways to help him or her learn. Remember that when a student truly does not understand a concept or what to do, the burden must be on the communicator to help. Get out your notes and idea books and identify some ways to proceed. Do not be afraid to admit to yourself that something didn't work. Denial doesn't help you or the students.

Once you have recognized that something isn't working, do not be reluctant to ask your colleagues for help. Some colleges assign experienced faculty to mentor new faculty or associate faculty. You will soon know—from department meetings and word of mouth—which instructors at your school are most likely to be helpful. If you don't know, ask your chairperson or dean which instructor might be able to give you some tips.

Many concepts or skills need to be taught and retaught. Few of us are one-trial learners. (If we were, schools would go out of business.) The exceptional teacher must be able to teach and reinforce the same concept or skill in various ways to reach students with varying backgrounds, experiences, and abilities. Teacher resources, experience, and experimentation will prove invaluable in developing teaching approaches and skills.

Chapter

4

Delivering Engaging Instruction

I stared. Could it be? My vision went dark except for that one glint of brightness. My seven-year-old feet wouldn't move, and my father reached down and tapped between my shoulders to move me along. Was it a vision? A dream? Right here by the apples and pears and the sweet juicy peaches? She put bananas into her cart. *Bananas! She eats bananas!* I gulped in some air in disbelief. Father tapped me again. Then the worst. He actually *talked* to her. My ears were ringing, so now I was blinded, paralyzed, *and* deaf. "Say hello, Sweetheart." I moved behind Father's right leg, trying to comprehend the momentous discovery. My teacher. My own teacher! My very own teacher was a, a, a *person!*

Learning Outcomes

- Answer the questions "What is engaging instruction for my course?" and "What does an energetic course look like?"
- Determine the strategies that could create a more personal environment for your courses
- Assess the value of learning style theory in the areas of student affirmation, course planning, and course delivery
- Evaluate the primary delivery modes and choose techniques for making them more successful
- Contrast the use of lecture, discussion, question-and-answer, and demonstration instructional modes in traditional classroom and online learning and determine how to maximize each mode for best effect
- Revisit how you communicate expectations of learner performance and determine whether you could communicate your expectations more clearly and at a higher level

What *Is* Engaging Instruction?

Engaging instruction is teaching that captures students' attention, motivates them to concentrate and expend effort to learn, activates the information stored in their brains, triggers their curiosity and inspires them to think and ask yet more questions, and communicates to them that they are capable of learning and expanding their powers of learning. This may seem a little overwhelming at first, but taken in steps, it can be and is done, and is well worth the effort.

This chapter addresses engaging instruction in the context of four principles: creating a personal learning environment; driving an active, energized classroom; establishing authentic contexts for instruction; and communicating high expectations.

Building a Personal Learning Environment

Students' first impressions will set the foundation for all future interactions. They will decide very early, almost immediately, whether they like you, their classmates, and the course. They decide whether they will enjoy the class sessions, the assignments and activities, and, yes, even the assessments. This makes that first class session or first online interaction very important. Instructors who do no more than take roll and hand out a syllabus at the first class session do a disservice to themselves and their students. This session is your greatest opportunity to establish rapport, set student expectations, and ensure that they will be involved actively in their learning!

Ten Tips for First-Day and Ongoing Success

The ten tips that follow are intended to help you succeed in your classroom from the very beginning. Most of these ideas apply to succeeding sessions as well as to your first one.

1. **Use warm-ups to capture students' attention and engage their interest immediately.** If you are positive and eager to start this class, students will know it. (And if you are not, they will know that too.) Here are some possibilities.
   - If you take roll aloud, ask the student what he or she wants to be called. Some students prefer to use nicknames or shortened versions of their names. Also ask students about their interests, their reasons for taking the class, their work, their opinion on a recent event.
   - If the class is large, consider circulating a sign-in sheet rather than taking roll aloud. Randomly ask students questions, getting their names as you do so.
   - Involve the class in a discussion about an issue related to the course, their participation in the course, their goals for the course.
   - If you like theatrics, begin with something dramatic. This could be a startling announcement, an audio clip, a pretest or survey or checklist, a few minutes with an important guest who makes a few comments, or something else related to the conduct of the course or to the course content.
   - Ask learners to write down their answers to four questions that you read aloud to them. Then discuss.

2. **Communicate to the students why the class is important. Lead a discussion on student viewpoints about the importance of the class.** Such a discussion will reinforce student reasons for taking the class or clarify some misconceptions about the goals or content of the course. Student motivation will increase.

3. **Communicate your expectations.**
   Talk with students about what you expect them to do and what you expect them to accomplish. Discuss the amount of time you expect them to put into their learning, and the types, quality, and timing of assignments. Explain what behaviors you expect during class time and the importance of participating in classroom discussions and other activities.

4. **Begin to get to know your students and let them know you.**
   Like the child described in the scenario at the opening of this chapter, many college students are surprised to discover that an instructor has a life outside the classroom, is an interesting person, and has feelings and opinions, especially about students. Revealing yourself as a person will also increase some students' motivation because they will want to please you as an individual, not just as an instructor.

   Telling students something about your background in teaching, research, writing, appointments, awards, and other experience related to the course will help build credibility. Usually, students expect you to be knowledgeable in your disciplines, but giving them information that establishes your expertise and status in the field will result in their feeling pleased about taking the course from *you*. (Of course, you want to limit this to the few most interesting points. Otherwise, you'll risk being viewed as a braggart or egotist.)

Remember that using humor and being able to laugh at yourself or accept a comment or factual correction from a student also tells students something about you!

5. **Let students begin to know each other.**
   Allow five minutes or so for students to introduce themselves to the student next to them, exchange phone numbers and e-mail addresses. Students who feel comfortable in the class—with you and with each other—will more readily ask for assistance or clarification and overcome reluctance to participate in class discussions and other activities.

6. **Provide information about course administration—how the course will function**
   You know what students want to know right away. Probably, most of this information is included on your syllabus. Review the major points, and allow students to ask questions.

7. **Encourage students about their potential learning and performance.**
   Make positive comments about the fact that these students have enrolled in this class. Reassure them that they can succeed in the course. Expect them to succeed and communicate that to them.

8. **Preview the course content.**
   You might begin with an overview of the subject (or career) area and where the learning in this course fits into that area. Provide students with information about the major parts of the course and what they can expect to learn, the major intended outcomes.

9. **Begin the course process!**
   If you are planning small group activities, discussions, active questioning, or other modes of classroom participation during the course, do some of this in your first session. This will make it clear that you expect them to engage in certain behaviors from the very start.

   If you are teaching students who might have difficulty with the material or the skills expected, assure them that you will help them succeed. Tell them that you will be available (office hours, e-mail, telephone) for assistance or that you will arrange study groups or other support. Remind them of any resources the college provides for learning assistance.

10. **Wrap up the session with reinforcement and reminders.**
    Summarize major points. Repeat major expectations. Remind students of assignments they need to begin planning. And once again communicate your energy and enthusiasm about the course and their participation in it.

Use the checklist shown in Figure 4.1 as a reminder when you prepare for the first day of a new course.

FIRST CLASS OR SESSION CHECKLIST
Are you ready to begin? Use this checklist to help make sure.
❑ I am eager to teach this class.
❑ I know how I'm going to begin the session—how I'm going to get students' attention.
❑ I have questions or a survey ready so I can find out about students' backgrounds, expectations, and interests.
❑ My syllabus is ready—and it is clear and informative.
❑ I have notes for students about their responsibilities, activities, and how I will evaluate their progress and achievement.
❑ I am prepared to give an overview of the class and begin the class process.
❑ Students will see me as an objective (fair), committed instructor who cares about them and their learning. They will see me as an interesting person. Students will be eager to return for the next session and so will I!

Figure 4.1. A Suggested First Session Checklist.

Getting to Know Your Students

Exceptional teaching is about helping students learn. To cause this learning means that you need to know who those students are—not just their names, but their backgrounds, strengths, weaknesses, interests, and goals.

Learning the names of your students is an important first step in creating a personal learning environment, for each of us wants to be known as an individual with unique characteristics, not just a number or a face in a group. Here are a few practical tips to help you to master students' names.

In the classroom:

- Use name tags for the first two or three sessions.
- Try various association strategies. For example, you might associate the name and face of Lori Anderson with her initials L.A. for Los Angeles. You can use the association technique with places, comparisons, objects, and so forth.
- While students are involved in group or independent work, repeat their names to yourself as you observe them.
- Assign some type of written work for the second or third session. Collect the papers and return them the next session, calling out the names and handing them to the students directly.

For an online class:

- Insist that your students log in from the very first possible day so that you can begin to learn names.
- Have your students provide a writing sample the first day. You can then attach the student's name to the sample and begin to recognize his or her work.
- Do not forget to use the *Homepage* feature available in the Web class management system being used. Have each student prepare a one- or two-

paragraph composition about himself or herself for the home page. Not only will the instructor(s) have access to this information but so will classmates.

- Depending on what equipment is available, students can fax or scan pictures of themselves and e-mail them to you. Students can also send you their pictures via surface mail.

You can reinforce your recall of students' names by using their names on assignments, examinations, and in class discussions. If Alfred, a student in your class, works as a banker, Marie is another student, and you are teaching about banking, use these or similar words: "Marie walks into the bank to apply for a loan and meets Alfred, a loan officer. What information do you think Marie will need to give Alfred?"

These techniques will help you learn names, but this is just a piece of who your students really are. If you did not ask student background-related questions during roll call, or perhaps did not conduct a roll call, consider using a simple questionnaire during the first session of class (or as an initial online activity). Be careful of treading on student privacy issues; there are many questions you do not have the right to ask. The following questions are typical of what you can ask and can provide data that may help you get to know your students.

- What is your name? (For online students, include address and phone number plus best times to reach the student.)
- What is your major?
- What traditional and online courses are you enrolled in this quarter/ semester?
- What previous courses have you had in this subject area?
- What are your career goals?
- What are your hobbies?
- What interests you about this course?
- What worries you about this course?
- In what ways do you think you may need help?
- What do you hope to learn from the course?
- What are your learning strengths and weaknesses?
- Do you enjoy writing?
- Do you enjoy teaching others?
- What are your technical skills (e-mail, use plug-ins, download from Web sites)? Could you help teach those skills to other students?

Many other questions could be added to this list. Customize it per your college and community, but keep the focus on questions that will tell you most about your students and their learning.

In online courses, students and faculty can learn about each other via chat sessions where questions, responses, comments, and observations can be shared with one another. The user's name appears with whatever is entered by that person. No doubt students will be e-mailing you from time to time with questions. This gives you another opportunity to learn about that student's needs.

Meeting a Challenge
Teaching the Bored Learner

You know them. The students who slouch down in their chairs and watch you with vacant eyes. The ones who do not take notes, ask questions, or raise their hands to participate in a discussion. The ones who might yawn or, pray it doesn't happen, fall asleep. The ones who are last to arrive and first to leave, early if possible. They're bored.

Why do students become bored? Possibly because the material is too advanced for them. They stare at the ceiling or out the window, not understanding the concepts. Or because the course content is too foundational or elementary, and they are not sufficiently challenged. You know what they are thinking: "Yeah, yeah. Blah, blah. I know all this stuff." Or perhaps the material is not relevant to their lives or interests. They enrolled in the class because it was available and they needed the credits. They do the assignments, but seldom do you see them energized in class. Or maybe the instruction is, unfortunately, boring. They've got to be wondering, "Can't we get on with this, please? I can't survive another hour."

Apparent boredom can be contagious. Your job is to figure out why an individual student is bored and then do something about it! But what?

Material Is Too Advanced

It isn't unusual for a student to enroll in a course for which he or she is not adequately prepared. Discuss the situation with the student and explore some options. Here are some possible strategies.

- It may be the case that this individual is in the wrong course and should be redirected to a recommended foundational class.
- The student may need a tutor for help catching up.
- You can pair the student with a willing peer for collaborative learning.
- Assign readings or problems from other textbooks that will help resolve the issue.
- Post some learning units on your Web site or in your course management system that the student can complete.

Course Content Is Too Foundational or Elementary

Again, discuss the situation with the student and explore some options. Here are some possible strategies.

- Redirect the student to a more advanced course.
- If the student already has a firm grasp of the material, substitute (not add) more challenging assignments for the planned ones.
- Plan various choices for assignments and various avenues for reaching stated intended outcomes, making sure that one or two of the choices are more challenging.
- Ask the student to research some aspect of the course and report on it.

- Allow the student to use class time for library research, to work on a writing activity in a neighboring classroom or other location, or complete a related Internet or computer assignment in the computer lab.

Content Is Not Relevant to Their Lives or Interests

Interview the student, probing to determine his or her interests. Ask "What really piques your curiosity? What questions do you want to solve? Why did you think the course topic might be interesting when you chose it?" Then do your best to find resources and create assignments that are related to those interests and questions.

You may need to take a step back and ask if your materials and planned activities are sufficiently "authentic," that is, asking all your students to read and do things that are clearly real world. Review the sections of this chapter related to authentic learning (see pages 144–146) and replan your sessions and assignments.

The Instruction Is Boring

The most common reason that instruction is boring is that the instructor is bored. Students know this. They can see it and they can feel it. If you are bored, it is time for a change.
- Are you feeling healthy? Check your own energy levels. Maybe it's time for a checkup.
- Are you stressed with life and just not feeling excited about this course? Maybe a team instructor or a session trade-out with a colleague will give you a needed break.
- Are you in a rut? Have you taught this class for years and now do it in your sleep, literally and figuratively? Then decide that you are going to turn the course on its head. Ask students what assignment they would do if they could do anything they wished and then help them do it. Throw out the lecture notes and find a guest speaker, video or film, or plan a field trip. Get out of that rut.
- Ask your department for a one-course release time so you can redesign the course. Review new textbooks and resources. Select new intended outcomes and replan the course. Think of activities you'd like to do, but never had time.
- Maybe it's time to offer a new and different course. Find out if you can alternate your current course with a new, experimental one.
- Find course activities that appeal to you, but that you hadn't previously considered. Implement some of those right away.
- Take care of your health, mental and physical, or you'll never get out of the "same old rut."

A side benefit of learning about your students is that it provides information for grouping your students for educational purposes or to help build a personalized environment. You can put students of similar ability together or link students of differing abilities. Grouping allows your students to get to know each other better and can create an atmosphere of mutual encouragement and team camaraderie.

The Learning Style Factor

Discovering each student's preferred learning style offers a major avenue toward personalizing the educational environment. Adult students tend to have developed a greater array of strategies for learning, may be more self-directed, and may be more goal-oriented than younger learners, but the range of adult learning preferences is still sufficiently large to merit consideration in delivering instruction. We discuss three models of learning styles in the sections that follow. As you read the information, remember two important principles:

1. No learner relies completely on one style or another. The styles are general preferences, and most people use a combination of styles depending on the situation and tools available.
2. The importance of learning styles lies not in categorizing individuals, but rather in the *teaching implications* of the styles for your instruction and courses.

The Grasha-Reichmann Student Learning Style Scales

Psychologists and educators have developed many ways to categorize learning styles and tools for identifying learning style preferences. The Grasha-Reichmann Student Learning Styles Scales (GRSLSS),[2] for example, use six categories related to ways that learners prefer to interact with each other and with the instructor in the classroom. The six categories or styles are called independent, dependent, competitive, collaborative, avoidant, and participant. The inventory that assesses these dimensions includes sixty items, such as, "I enjoy discussing my ideas about course content with other students" or "I prefer to work by myself on assignments in my courses."

David Diaz, Ed.D., professor and faculty distance education mentor at Cuesta Community College in San Luis Obispo, California, has conducted research on modes of learning, including the GRSLSS. In an article published in the journal *College Teaching*, Diaz and coauthor Ryan B. Cartnal describe the six styles this way:[3]

---

[2] S. Hruska-Reichmann and A.F. Grasha. The Grasha-Reichmann student learning style scales. In J. Keefe (ed.), *Student Learning Styles and Brain Behavior.* Reston, Va: National Association of Secondary School Principals, 1983: 81–86.

[3] David P. Diaz and Ryan B. Cartnal. "Students' Learning Styles in Two Classes: Online Distance Learning and Equivalent On-Campus," *College Teaching.* Washington, D. C.: Heldref Publications, Vol. 47, No. 4, 1999: 130–135.

1. "Independent students prefer independent study, self-paced instruction, and would prefer to work alone on course projects than with other students." Most courses provide plenty of opportunity for independent study, especially reading assignments and written assignments. Lecture mode works well with independent learners. They may or may not be inclined to participate in discussions. If you assign projects to teams or groups, independent learners will sometimes feel they are wasting their time. Often, they would prefer to complete the project alone. Note, however, that this does not mean you should leave independent learners out of group work. Including these students in group work provides them an opportunity to learn to work more effectively in group situations, a valuable real-world ability.

2. "Dependent learners look to the teacher and to peers as a source of structure and guidance and prefer an authority figure to tell them what to do." Dependent learners perform better when you provide them with a very clear and detailed course syllabus or outline. They are more comfortable and confident completing assignments when your instructions are detailed and your expectations are obvious. When appropriate, provide examples of completed assignments. If you are allowing students to define their own projects, lead a discussion about the characteristics of a "good" project. Encourage all the students to participate in defining the projects.

3. "Competitive students learn in order to perform better than their peers do and to receive recognition for their academic accomplishments." Recognition is a singularly motivating reward in most aspects of our lives, and yet may be too often overlooked in postsecondary education settings. Do not assume that "learning for the sake of learning" is going to be true for all your students. Recognition for accomplishments motivates competitive students more than anything else. Look for novel ways to recognize students' work, and do so on a regular basis. Make comments when you return papers in class; post public notes on the class Web site about positive contributions to classroom discussions or best organized, most succinct, most creative, etc., projects, and so forth.

4. "Collaborative learners acquire information by sharing and by cooperating with teacher and peers. They prefer lectures with small group discussions and group projects."
   Small group assignments work very well with collaborative learners. You'll need to try a few sessions to determine whether all, some, or few of your students work well under these conditions. The mix may vary greatly from term to term. You may have one class in which small groups of students bond, set times to meet outside the classroom, continue to work by e-mail and telephone, and so forth. Another time you might assign tasks to small groups only to have them groan that they aren't learning that way and it is wasting their time. Be prepared to adjust to either situation! If your course plan includes a project, consider providing several options for students to choose from . . . some that could be done collaboratively in teams of two to four students, others that would be independent.

5. "Avoidant learners are not enthused about attending class or acquiring class content. They are typically uninterested and are sometimes overwhelmed by class activities."

The key to deciding how to approach teaching avoidant learners is to recognize the reasons for their avoidance. Some avoidant learners have had negative experiences with education, have low expectations of themselves, and have learned to stay disengaged because they don't understand or don't want to fail to understand. These learners can be overwhelmed by lively discussions they can't follow, lectures that use unfamiliar vocabulary, assignments that would take them days instead of hours, and so forth. Avoidant learners can also be intimidated by instructors who communicate expectations that the learners believe are absolutely unattainable.

Reaching these learners is a huge challenge. Many of the suggestions in this book should help you find ways to engage them. They may respond well to online or CD assignments, where their peers cannot observe them and they can work at their own pace. They might work well with peer mentors, if handled in a sensitive way. Also, you are more likely to succeed if you communicate *realistic, positive expectations* of their performance and provide frequent feedback and recognition.

Finally, some avoidant learners attend class because they are somehow obligated to do so, but believe the material to be irrelevant to their "real" lives. If possible, instructors should find out what interests these students most and then try to build activities that involve those interests.

6. "Participant learners are interested in class activities and discussion, and are eager to do as much class work as possible. They are keenly aware of, and have a desire to meet, teacher expectations."

The challenge of instructing participant learners is to maintain an energy level and sufficient assignments, challenges, and resources to keep them engaged. Provide many options. Participant learners are, generally, successful students because they are motivated to learn and perform. They are not all, however, "A" students, so instructors need to provide activities that allow for participation by students with a varied ability range, not just "honors" activities.

Experiential Learning Theory

David Kolb's inventory,[4] based on experiential learning theory, emphasizes cognitive dimensions, usually described as related to thinking, perceiving,

---

[4] A.C. Baker, P.J. Jensen, and D.A. Kolb. *Conversational Learning: An Experiential Approach to Knowledge Creation*, Westport, Conn.: Quorum Books, 2002.

J.S. Osland, D.A. Kolb, and I.M. Rubin. *Organizational Behavior: An Experiential Approach to Human Behavior in Organizations*, seventh edition. Englewood Cliffs, N.J. Prentice Hall, 2001.

J.S. Osland, D.A. Kolb, and I.M. Rubin. *The Organizational Behavior Reader*, 7th edition. Englewood Cliffs, N.J. Prentice Hall, 2001.

R.E. Boyatzis, S.S. Cowen, and D.A. Kolb. *Innovation in Professional Education: Steps on a Journey from Teaching to Learning.* San Francisco: Jossey Bass, 1995.

D.A. Kolb. *Experiential Learning: Experience as the Source of Learning and Development*, Englewood Cliffs, N.J. Prentice Hall, 1984.

analyzing, remembering, and so forth. The four dimensions of his learning style inventory are

1. Diverging: combines preferences for experiencing and reflecting
2. Assimilating: combines preferences for reflecting and thinking
3. Converging: combines preferences for thinking and doing
4. Accommodating: combines preferences for doing and experiencing

Kolb thought of the four dimensions as a continuum, but the inventory and the styles descriptions support thinking of them as separate dimensions. Let's look at some of the implications of the four dimensions for instruction.

1. Diverging thinkers like to reason from specific information. They prefer detailed, systematic, logical presentations. Lecturing, when it is logical and focuses on specifics, reference materials with organized summaries, and hands-on explorations work well with these students. Be prepared to answer questions about details and specifics.
2. Assimilating thinkers are drawn to accurate, well organized information. They value expertise and "correct" answers. These students do not tend to deal well with ambiguity, but are likely to follow instructions well. As with the diverging thinkers, lectures work well with these students, especially when accompanied by demonstrations or "proof." Instructors in lab or field situations will find the sessions to be more effective if the students have a lab manual or other guide to follow . . . even better if the guide has "answers."
3. Students whose preferred mode in Kolb's framework is "converging" will be most successful when instruction is active and interactive. They also like to know how things connect—the relationships among concepts and processes.
4. The accommodating thinkers are explorers and experimenters. They work well with complex learning and enjoy independent discovery. Instructors will be more effective with these students if they provide many opportunities for independent study, such as student-designed research projects.

Auditory-Visual-Kinesthetic Styles

One early theory of learning styles classified learners as having a predominantly auditory, visual, or kinesthetic (tactile) learning preference. Learners may, and probably do, use all three to some extent. Also, one mode could be used for some types of tasks and another mode used for other types of tasks. The implication for instruction is that we need to use all three modes, for two reasons: (1) so that no learners are left behind because we have not provided appropriate opportunities for them, and (2) because most learners use some degree of all three, with two modes reinforcing the other.

Auditory learners learn by what they hear. You might find them reading aloud to themselves or asking you to explain material from the reading, material that you think is plainly written. They also like to restate what they have read or heard during lecture and discussion to confirm their comprehension. To ensure that you are reaching auditory learners, be sure to tell your class the overview and summary information, rather than only giving a handout; use question-and-answer techniques discussed elsewhere in this chapter; use discussion, brainstorming, and small group techniques; encourage students to ask questions and develop dialog with them.

Some visual learners prefer reading and writing to access and interact with information. Other visual learners process information more effectively when they see visual representations such as charts, graphs, and illustrations. The two modes—text and graphic—are not mutually exclusive. Instructors need to consider both. Ways to do this include using visual aids during lectures; providing outlines and other handouts for reading and notes; posting written information, graphics, PowerPoint presentations, and so forth on the Internet for students to review; explaining graphics and diagrams and having learners draw their own depictions—educational doodles.

Tactile, or kinesthetic, modes emphasize touching and moving. Writing information by hand—taking notes, preparing outlines, etc.—is an important tool for postsecondary instructors to use. Have students take notes, doodle, and use highlighters. Some instructors have students use movement during review sessions; for example, "How many ways have we discussed to hold property title? Hold up fingers!" Other instructors ask students to stand and move around for a short break, and, while doing so, think about something just discussed. Assignments that involve making collections or scrapbooks such as used in botany, biology, journalism, criminal justice, and other courses are often very successful with tactile learners.

"I have never let my schooling interfere with my education."

—Mark Twain

Using Learning Style Inventories to Personalize Instruction

Learning styles inventories abound. Using them can be informative, but time consuming. With the availability of interactive inventories on the Internet, however, the time factor has been reduced. The results of an inventory for a class will indicate some overall characteristics for that group of students—and help an instructor ensure that the activities, teaching approaches, and assessments used during the course are sufficiently varied and with enough options to facilitate all students' participation and learning.

Given the relatively recent surge in distance learning courses, inventories that assess students' preference for classroom as opposed to online learning may not be as plentiful as the classic learning style assessment tools. Thus we offer an instrument, shown in Figure 4.2, that can help students decide if online learning will work for them. The questions will also help them decide if a highly interactive or more self-directed online course will be most effective for them. We recommend that you add an inventory or survey like this at the beginning of your online courses. The inventory offers another benefit: it should help guide your decisions about the choices that you wish to include in your online course to help students accomplish the intended outcomes.

EMC/PARADIGM ONLINE LEARNING STYLES INVENTORY[5]		
Indicate how strongly you agree with each of the following statements. Use this scale: 5 = Strongly Agree 4 = Agree Somewhat 3 = Not Sure 2 = Disagree Somewhat 1 = Strongly Disagree		
1. ____	A very important part of my learning is talking through concepts or questions with other students.	
2. ____	I love to read and I learn very well through reading.	
3. ____	I communicate well through e-mail, discussion lists, and chat rooms.	
4. ____	I need to hear concepts or procedures explained verbally. Reading just isn't enough for me.	
5. ____	When the instructor calls on me to talk in class, I sometimes freeze and don't have much to say. It makes me uncomfortable.	
6. ____	I am comfortable making comments and asking questions in class.	
7. ____	I would rather write a paper than talk in class.	
8. ____	Writing papers and reports is difficult. I would rather talk.	
9. ____	I learn better studying on my own than studying with others.	
10. ____	I prefer projects to complete on my own rather than working on group projects.	
11. ____	My assignments are late more than they should be.	
12. ____	I like to interact with the instructor and other students in class.	
13. ____	I need to interact with other students to really enjoy a class.	
14. ____	I do better with classroom learning than with independent study.	
15. ____	I prefer classes that have small group assignments or lots of discussion.	
16. ____	I like to solve puzzles and mysteries.	
17. ____	If I am going to learn how to do something new, I just dive right in and try it.	
18. ____	If I am going to learn how to do something new, I always read and study the directions first.	
19. ____	If I am going to learn how to do something new, I prefer to begin by having someone show me how to do it.	
20. ____	If I am going to learn how to do something new, I would rather try it on my own. I get impatient when somebody else tries to show me.	
21. ____	I am very organized about my learning.	
22. ____	I like courses that are structured tightly, with clear, detailed directions for assignments.	
23. ____	I like a lot of independence in deciding about projects or papers.	
24. ____	I talk better and more comfortably than I write.	
25. ____	I learn better when I get to know the instructor.	
26. ____	I am uncomfortable with using the Internet for school.	

Figure 4.2. A Sample Inventory to Identify Classroom or Online Learning Preferences.

---

[5]Scoring key and inventory template are available at the Exceptional Teaching Internet Resource Center, www.emcp.com.

Creating an Active Classroom

Exceptional classroom teaching builds and maintains an active, energized classroom. Students and instructors who are alert and paying attention together create an environment that fosters learning and retention. The all-too-familiar lecture-lecture-lecture format may sometimes allow for more imparting of information by the instructor, but this does not mean it is allowing for more internalizing of information by students. Plan and use the allotted time to maximize the potential for active learning. Vary what students are doing throughout the session—listening, thinking, writing, discussing, asking, leading, demonstrating, doing.

In this section we present information and suggestions for lecturing like a pro, using demonstrations and question-and-answer approaches, leading useful discussions and activities in which students collaborate, and providing opportunities for students to learn independently.

Engaging Students in Instructor-Led Approaches

In Chapter 3 we listed various common instructor-led and instructor-facilitated approaches to adopt in the classroom and online. This section discusses some techniques for making the methods and learning more interactive, for getting students involved. As you read these descriptions, think about which learning style preferences are being met by each instructional technique.

Lecture Techniques

The lecture method of teaching—instructor speaks and students listen—has been with us from the beginnings of formal education. Some instructors today do lecture all the time, and there are some who have gone to the opposite extreme, that of pure facilitation and student-generated learning. Neither extreme seems to fit today's effective teaching and learning. A combination of methods, including lecture, is needed for today's students who learn in so many different ways.

The lecture method works best when you present information that is really new to your students. It allows you to present a lot of material in a very brief time. For example, you could deliver a very effective fifteen-minute illustrated talk on the generations of computers. Or you can lecture on the P's of marketing, the steps in the accounting cycle, or the parts of a contract. Topics that contain specific points or lists are usually good candidates for a focused lecture. Here are some guidelines to bear in mind as you prepare to lecture.

- Be organized. If you need to, work from an outline or even a script. Giving the appearance of wandering or being unfocused can cause students to lose interest very easily.
- Keep a user-friendly pace. Too slow a pace can give students a chance to "tune out." Too rapid a pace can create anxiety among your students. You need to select a comfortable pace, one that includes a chance for students to take notes, if that is your intent.

- Use conversational language. Don't use what some call "lecture words," words with multiple syllables that sound impressive. Talk as you would normally talk to your students. Difficult language can put a barrier between you and your students.
- Practice asking questions while you are presenting. Do students indicate that they have understood the presentation? Do you need to clarify? Make mental note of which students seem to be "ahead of you," those who know where you are headed and meet you there.
- Session pretests/posttests. Conduct a brief pretest at the beginning of the classroom session. Alternatively, ask students to write down "What I want to know about (session topic)." At the end of the class, conduct a short posttest, or ask students to write down "What I learned about (session topic)."
- During presentations, stop periodically to ask students if they have questions. Give them time to think about it for a moment before going on.
- Do a check by asking the class if they would like another example of something or of how to do something.
- In a few sessions, ask students if they feel they are learning the material. Ask them what is most difficult for them, what is most interesting, what they'd like to do more often.
- Try to be an interesting speaker. Vary your speed and volume. Work on eye contact. Be enthusiastic. Think of all those qualities that you admire in a speaker and try to emulate them to the best of your ability.

"Professors known as outstanding lecturers do two things; they use a simple plan and many examples."

—W. McKeachie

Lecture formats work well for students who learn best, or very well, by listening and taking notes. Other students' learning, however, suffers in lecture formats. These include learners who learn best by doing or those who need visual reinforcement. These also often include students whose English is not at the same level as native speakers. This reality supports the case for combining instructional approaches in the classroom and for supporting lectures with other modes and activities. Here are some examples of how you can augment your lecturing to make it more effective and reach more students.

- Add visuals to your lecture. Show objects, overhead transparencies, and/or computer-generated slides so that students will see as well as hear.
- Train yourself to use synonyms or short definitions after you have used a term or language that might be unfamiliar to ELL students. Do NOT avoid using the unfamiliar terms or language. Rather, use it and then briefly define or explain it.
- Hand out an outline of the lecture so that students can follow along with you and see where you are headed—and when it will end! This relieves the concern that some students have of the "unending" lecture.

Integrating Technology
Online Polls and Surveys

> Which of the following do you think created the greatest change in American architecture?
>
> - electricity
> - CAD/CAM programs
> - steel
> - assembly lines

Two highly engaging, as well as informative, technology tools are online surveys and online polls. Online surveys may consist of just about any number of questions. Instructors capture the data or run the report after the intended respondents have completed the survey. Polls usually consist of one or two questions. Students or other online users click on their answer to the poll and the results up to that time are displayed immediately.

Custom Surveys

Many learning and teaching surveys are ready and available on the Internet for you to use to assess aspects of your teaching, learning environment, or students. However, you can also create your own custom surveys to use in your course. Learning-related surveys might be constructed to gather information on students' learning styles, their background or experience with the subject matter, their preferences for activities, scheduling preferences for a field trip, their expectations for the course, their evaluation of your teaching or the course overall, and so forth. Content-related surveys might introduce parts of your course or review other parts. For example, a business math course might include a survey asking students to identify how often they have encountered certain real-life business math problems (student loan, credit purchase, payroll, etc.). An international marketing course might gather information on students' notions about interacting with specific cultures or their perceptions about business styles in other countries.

Online Polls

Polls are very brief and quick. They are often used for gathering information about opinions related to current issues or events. You might, however, use them to spark a discussion or debate regarding just about any topic related to your course, whether past, present, or future. "Should" questions, "why" questions, and "which (theory, process, sculpture, product, etc.) is better/worse/faster/cheaper/most accurate . . ." questions make good starters for instant polls. Some can be e-mailed to students directly. Results are reported in simple percentages, bar charts, time reports, response popularity sorts, and in other ways.

Creating Online Polls and Surveys

Instructors need not be technology wizards to create online polls and surveys. Programs are available that allow you to construct the poll or survey online, without downloading any software or uploading the survey or poll to a Web site. Advertising sometimes supports free polls; ascertain the types of advertising that might be displayed for your students before building a poll on a particular site.

One use of surveys and polls that many instructors find particularly appealing is assigning creation, launching, and analysis of surveys and polls to students as projects. These assignments can be simple or challenging; but regardless of difficulty, they may be just the connection you need to grab the interest of a difficult, left-out, or bored learner.

Here is a sampling of sites offering online software, polls, and surveys.

- Web poll software:
  PollMonkey (www.pollmonkey.com/)
  InfoPoll (www.infopoll.com/)
  Quask (www.quask.com/)
  PollPro (www.pollpro.com/)

- Free polling:
  Sparklit (webpoll.sparklit.com/)
  FreePolls (www.freepolls.com/)
  WebSideStory (www.hitbox.com/)

- Online survey software:
  KeySurvey (www.keysurvey.com/)
  QuestionPro (www.questionpro.com)
  WebSurveyor (www.websurveyor.com/)

Hundreds of online survey/polling sites and programs are available. Enter "online polls" or "free online polls" in the search box of your favorite search engine to find more.

- Stop every five to ten minutes and apply what you have just spoken about. Ask questions. Ask for student reactions.
- Put students into groups to discuss the topic. This approach helps you to create a series of "mini-lectures," relatively brief talks on a specific topic.
- Post your lecture notes on a Web class management system such as Blackboard or Web CT, or on your instructor Web page. This relieves the pressure on your students to have to listen and to write at the same time.

What if you find students "tuning out" despite your best efforts to bring the lecture topic to life? Figure 4.3 presents some additional tips for engaging learners and fostering active participation.

Tips for Engaging Learners during Lectures
1. Seek out a different student every day and get to know something about him or her by asking a question related to the lecture topic.
2. Start the class with a puzzle, question, paradox, picture, or cartoon on slide or transparency to focus on the day's topic. Following a video, speech, or presentation, have students write the "muddiest point" they heard. Review key points of the last lecture.
3. Elicit student questions and concerns at the beginning of the class and list these on the chalkboard or whiteboard to be answered during the hour. Start with what the students are thinking. Develop the students' ability to ask questions. The ability to ask questions and to connect dissimilar ideas is a skill of key importance.
4. Have students write (anticipate) what they think the important issues or key points of the day's lecture will be.
5. Ask preplanned rhetorical questions.
6. Stage a figurative "coffee break" about twenty minutes into the hour: tell an anecdote, invite students to put down pens and pencils, refer to a current event, shift media.
7. Show a film in a novel way: stop it for discussion, show a few frames only, anticipate an ending, hand out a viewing or critique sheet, play and replay parts.
8. Have students write something—*anything:* learning memos, summaries, questions, etc.
9. Have students paraphrase the main points of the lesson.
10. Administer a quiz. When a quiz is included in the last part of the lecture, learners retain twice as much of the material presented.
11. Have students prepare test questions and model answers. You will learn what they remember, what they consider important, and how well they understand the material.
12. Have students listen without taking notes. Then put students into pairs or "learning cells" to quiz each other over material for the day. Have them focus on WDWWWHW questions—Who? Did what? To whom? When? How? Why?
13. Have students create a concept map that shows the relationship of the key concepts discussed. Have students explain in their own words what the schematics or diagrams mean.

continued on next page

14. Use the split-in-two lecture (think, pair, share):
   a. Lecture for 20 minutes.
   b. Ask students individually to summarize the main points. Then ask them to work with a partner to see if they can reach a consensus. Finally, have a large group discussion to reach consensus. (10 to 15 minutes)
   c. Lecture for the remaining period of time.

15. PowerPoint and other slide programs provide visual support, both text and graphic, for lectures. The slides or an outline of them can be printed and used as handout material for students to follow, review, or take notes on. Some publishers provide PowerPoint presentations to accompany their textbooks, but creating custom presentations is not difficult.

Figure 4.3. Tips for Engaging Students and Fostering Participation during Lectures.

Teaching by Demonstration or in Combination with Lecture

Demonstrating, or showing, is just as important for some students as lecturing, or telling, is for other students. For example, students who are what Grasha and Reichmann call dependent or avoidant learners, Kolb's diverging and converging thinkers, or visual and tactile learners will respond positively in demonstration situations. Demonstration in connection with lecture can be a powerful teaching tool. For example, you can tell how to fill out a time card, or you can show a filled-out time card, but telling as you are showing how to do it is what will solidify learning.

> "Thought flows in terms of stories—stories about events, stories about people, and stories about intentions and achievements. The best teachers are the best story tellers. We learn in the form of stories."
>
> —Frank Smith

You can demonstrate a wide variety of things. Besides showing how to fill in a form, such as the time card or an accounting worksheet, you can demonstrate a step-by-step process in a software program. For example, you can show your students how to cut and paste in a Word document by demonstrating it yourself.

Ideally, you will have a projection system in your classroom that will allow a computer screen to be shown in a format large enough for the entire class to see it. It may be your own computer or one a student in class operates. You may in fact have a student who will execute the commands and directions as you give them so that the entire class can watch and follow at their stations. You can also demonstrate such activities as how to do a window display in a marketing class or how to burn a CD in your computer class.

Demonstrations can be with physical objects, LCD panels, overhead projectors, chalkboards, or whiteboards. Figure 4.4 lists some tips that will help improve the success of your demonstrations.

TIPS FOR IMPROVING YOUR DEMONSTRATION TECHNIQUE
1. Be prepared and well organized. Practice the demonstration before doing it "live." Follow a list of steps, or keep one handy, to help ensure that you do not skip steps or add in extras.
2. Prepare students by telling them the purpose of the demonstration. Tell them the points or steps or effects/results that you want them to watch for.
3. Use a list of key points that you want to make while conducting the demonstration.
4. Set up the demonstration in a way that is visible to all students.
5. As much as possible, involve the students in the demonstration. Ask them what they think the next step should be or why a certain step is important.
6. Provide students with handouts that will guide them through the demonstration. Ask them to take notes on the handout.
7. Frequently ask students if they understand the procedure. Ask them if they will be able to do it. Ask them if they want you to repeat a step. Ask them what would happen if you did something in a different way or in a different order.
8. Summarize the steps and important points of the demonstration when you wrap up.

Figure 4.4. Tips for Improving Demonstration Technique.

Maximizing the Question-and-Answer Approach

Question-and-answer is a teaching approach that dates back to the Ancient Greeks. In fact, the method is sometimes called the Socratic Method, named after Socrates. The instructor asks a question and the student replies. The instructor then follows with another question based on that response and on it goes. The Socratic Method works well with most types of courses and with most students. Take care, of course, to avoid embarrassing students. How? Use the method on a regular basis so students are prepared. Call on students who volunteer. If a student asks you to not call on him or her, respond that if they volunteer regularly, you will not single them out. Here are some keys to using the question-and-answer approach.

1. Ask a variety of questions. Questions can vary by level (as in Bloom's cognitive domain), type of phrasing (what, why, when, who), and length. By varying your questions, you will increase the likelihood of different students responding. Here is an illustration of how questions about the same topic can be phrased on each level of Bloom's cognitive domain. The topic is classifying Web sites. Notice the connection to the verbs used in the Chapter 2 table on Bloom's taxonomy (Figure 2.2).

   Knowledge: What are the common extensions used in Web addresses? (LIST)
   Comprehension: What makes one site an "org" and another a "com"? (EXPLAIN)
   Application: From the following list, which ones are "gov"? Which are "com"? Which are "edu"? (A list of several sites would be presented.) (CLASSIFY)
   Analysis: Is this college "com" or "edu"? How did you

arrive at this answer? (DISCRIMINATE)
Synthesis: Since our school is an "edu" site, what are some
links that you might expect from here? (DEVELOP)
Evaluation: Here is a Web site. (Show it on the monitor.)
Based on what you might expect to find on a "com" site,
how does it match up? (RATE)

2. Vary the type of response required. You may want just one individual to answer the question or you may want a group response. You may want hands raised or you might encourage a less formal response, such as speaking out.

3. Avoid simple questions whose answers are yes or no. Use sparingly those questions requiring answers of just a name, place, or date. The reasons for these cautions are twofold. First, your goal is to probe, to stimulate in-depth thinking—not parroted one-word responses. Second, by speaking several words to the student's one word each time, you are dominating the class, which is not a shared classroom environment.

4. Listen to responses before you ask the next question, for the responses may cause you to change direction. For example, in a business class you may ask "What type of investment is the most secure and why?" expecting an answer of "bonds, because a fixed return is guaranteed." However, you get the response "It depends on the condition of the economy." This reply should lead you from wherever you initially planned to go to the question "How does the condition of the economy affect the security of investments?" instead.

The question-and-answer method does have its pitfalls. In addition to the risk of embarrassing an unprepared student, question-and-answer sessions can lead to unexpected comments and get the discussion off course. As a final note, if the questions are related to reading or previous lecture material, some of the students might be unprepared, resulting in a failed activity. Avoid the pitfalls and improve the likelihood of enjoyable interactions with your students during question-and-answer sessions by following some of the tips in Figure 4.5.

Enhancing the Question-and-Answer Mode
✓ Call on students randomly—not just those eager to discuss; the rest will stop thinking.
✓ Allow for "wait-time"—after asking a question that requires thought, wait ten seconds *or more* to give students time to formulate a response.
✓ Answer questions with another question; reporter questions (what, why, when, where?); ask follow-up questions (Why? Do you agree? Can you elaborate? Tell me more. Can you give me an example?)
✓ Tell students there is *not* only one correct answer; their job is to think about as many answers as possible.
✓ Withhold judgment—respond to students in a nonevaluative tone. Rephrase what the student just said.
✓ Help students become active listeners—ask students to put down their pencils and listen to the lecture for ten minutes. Request that students not take notes, just listen. After the presentation, ask students to recall or write everything they can from the lecture. Students could also work together in small groups to determine major points.

continued on next page

✓ Ask students to think about their own thinking—"Describe in specific detail how you arrived at your answer." (Think aloud.)
✓ Ask for a summary—"Jane, could you please summarize John's point?"
✓ Encourage students to develop their own questions related to a particular lesson and then assign study groups to answer them.
✓ Use a consistent "thinking skills" vocabulary.
✓ Feign forgetfulness and invite students to bring you up-to-date.
✓ Prelecture, ask for truth statements—ask several small groups to decide on three things they know to be true about some particular issue. This is useful when introducing a new topic that students think they know well, but where their assumptions need to be examined.

Figure 4.5. Tips for Enhancing Your Question-and-Answer Techniques.

Leading Discussions

Many of the benefits derived from question-and-answer sessions apply to discussions. The main difference is that the instructor does not guide as directly or as actively as in the question-and-answer mode. Beginning with a shared experience such as reading an article or a specific problem statement, students comment on each others' comments. The instructor might repeat a student's statement and then ask for comments on that statement, rather than inserting another question.

Another particularly strong vehicle for launching discussion is a case study. The instructor presents students with a situation or challenge a business faces (real-world or hypothetical) and asks them to determine which actions to take. To reach a solution, they need to analyze the situation, pinpoint the problem or issue, and determine ways to solve the problem or resolve the issue.

Cases can be brief or extended. A case can be as simple as "Anthony Jenkins is looking to start a printing business. How should he proceed?" It can be as complex as a multiple-page scenario that includes a firm's organization chart, financial statements, and strategic plan with related questions. You might even teach a course that is entirely case based. For example, business management programs typically include a capstone course in strategic management or business policy, based on the case-study method. Here are some keys to using the discussion approach.

1. Students must be prepared for the discussion. Without some basic knowledge of the topic under discussion, the time spent becomes conversation with little basis for informed viewpoints. Thus, assigned reading or thought prior to the discussion is important.
2. Both sides of an issue need to be aired during a discussion. A discussion is not an attempt to convince a class of a single point of view. Rather, it is a consideration of ideas and their merits.
3. Listening is an important skill in a discussion. You need to listen to your students, who need to listen to you and to each other. Avoid the very natural tendency to repeat a student's answer in order to affirm it. When

you repeat student responses, students will listen to you but do not need to listen to each other.

4. Your position in the class is important during a good discussion. Move around the room, even out of sight at times. Try to move as far as you can from a student who is speaking, for that will encourage the student to speak louder in order to be heard by you, thus increasing the volume for everyone in the class.

5. Integrate yourself into the discussion only if it bogs down or if you want to do so. Move the discussion to higher levels as it proceeds. Periodically, ask a question or summarize what has been said, or introduce a new idea. You are both a participant and a facilitator in the discussion approach to learning.

6. During the discussion, briefly note key points and issues on a chalkboard or a whiteboard. At the end of the entire discussion, use the notes to summarize conclusions, including consensus points as well as points of disagreement.

Gauge the effectiveness of the session by student participation. If students do not ask questions or make comments, the discussion has left them out. If students get off track and need redirection too often, they may not be prepared to discuss the main topic or question yet. If students seem bored or irritated, they probably are. They may be feeling that they are not benefiting from the discussion. (Avoid this by telling them at the outset the benefits that you expect them to derive—and challenge them to do so.)

To enliven your class discussions and to encourage more student interaction, consider the suggestions shown in Figure 4.6.

TIPS FOR FACILITATING LIVELY DISCUSSION
✓ Stage a change-your-mind debate, with students moving to different parts of the classroom to signal change in opinion during the discussion. Boredom has more to do with alienation and passivity than actual dislike of the subject.
✓ Conduct a "living" demographic survey by having students move to different parts of the classroom: for example, size of high school, rural vs. urban, consumer preferences.
✓ Require your students to assume the role of professional in the discipline: ask them to think like a philosopher, literary critic, biologist, agronomist, political scientist, engineer. By giving students something worth thinking about, problem solving will occur naturally.
✓ Use an opinion questionnaire as a basis for discussion (see Figure 4.7 for an example).
✓ Distribute a list of the unsolved problems, dilemmas, or great questions in your discipline and invite students to claim one as their own to investigate.
✓ Utilize "think-pair-share" groups—Allow two or three minutes of time to think, followed by two or three minutes of discussion with a partner. Then open up the entire class to discussion.
✓ Consider giving each group member a role, and rotate the responsibilities: • recorder • facilitator (ensures that all members are participating) • checker/auditor (ensures that all work is quality and done on time)

Figure 4.6. Ways to Enliven Class Discussions.

WHAT IS YOUR OPINION?	YOUR OPINION?		HOW CERTAIN?		
	Agree	Disagree	On Shaky Grounds	Moderately Confident	100% Confident
"Dumbing down" curriculum is a factor in the decline of national test scores.					
Deep breathing helps students think.					
Some students are born to be instigators (disruption for a purpose).					
The way students think and process information is innate.					
Neural growth in the brain happens when we finally solve a problem.					
Neurons do not process steady states. They only see change.					
Boring environments physically thin the cortex.					
Individuals filter out new information if it doesn't fit their current view.					
Authentic work is original; revising others' work does not fall into the area of authentic work.					
There is not a direct correlation between intelligence and genius.					
If you give students choices, they will be more committed to the work.					

Figure 4.7. A Sample Opinion Questionnaire to Use in Launching a Discussion.

Implications for Online Classes

The main "lecture" technique online is, of course, presentation of written material. Reading, whether online or hard copy, works well for many learners. Other learners, however, will be more successful using other modes to acquire knowledge and skills. Do not limit online instruction to reading!

For students who need to hear information explained, use audio CDs or downloadable files. Some instructors tape their live classes and then edit them for distribution to students in parallel online classes. Online courses do have the capacity to store large files for download as well as to program short audio clips that might explain, for example, vocabulary terms. Video streaming also brings information to students via sound. You will need good technology assistance to create videos to stream or even to stream commercial ones.

Provide images, animations, charts and graphs, and other ways to visually display information or procedures. This is especially important for students who rely on visual input for learning. In many cases, you will be able to get permission to scan and display images from books for educational purposes. Depending on your discipline, you will also find a wealth of useful visual presentations that you can link to on the Internet and either assign or recommend that students use.

For one-way instruction, slide presentations made from PowerPoint or other programs can incorporate both text and graphics. These presentations can incorporate animations, and have the added advantage of allowing you to determine the sequence in which the information is presented. Partner these presentations with online quizzes or interactive functions to reinforce learning and increase involvement of learners.

Interacting with students in an online course can happen "live," as in a chat room. Many students can be included in a chat room discussion, or it could be just two students or just you and one student. You and your students type questions and responses in real time.

Most online courses provide virtual classrooms with whiteboard technology. In addition to allowing instructors to enter text, whiteboards give instructors tools for drawing lines and boxes, displaying Web site pages and writing on them, and creating slides, all while students are viewing the whiteboard "live." In contrast, E-mail and threaded messages are "delayed response" functions.

> *"The secret of teaching is to appear to have known all your life what you learned this afternoon."*
>
> —Anonymous

Scheduling effective chats can present a challenge. However, some instructors with small classes use live chat to meet with individual students once a week or for special explanations or to conduct individualized assessments in modified essay test format.

Consider using chat rooms for virtual office hours, either "open door," so that any students can view and join the discussion, or by appointment to answer a student's questions privately.

Engaging Students in Instructor-Facilitated Approaches

Instructor-facilitated approaches, that is, approaches in which the instructor guides student work without directly leading the work, are critical tools in your repertoire. These approaches range from guiding collaborative learning through group interactions or projects, managing and guiding student mentoring and presentations, offering appropriate choices for independent learning, and using online assignments.

Enhancing Group Work—Collaborative Learning

You may well be a brilliant speaker. You engage students' interest, deliver information clearly and directly, and use a lively, entertaining style. Even so, students need to do more than listen to you. Group work is another way to involve students in the learning process. Groups can be fixed-member groups, established at the start of the course and continuing through the course, or one-time groups, formed for a specific purpose. Groups can be randomly assigned, preassigned by you, or just allowed to form. Groups should be neither too big nor too small—three- to five-member groups work well.

Regardless of how groups are formed, there are some strong advantages to collaboration: (1) all students get the chance to participate; (2) group work encourages brainstorming without fear of teacher criticism or public reaction; (3) groups simulate teamwork on the job, a critical skill in the twenty-first century; and (4) you have another opportunity to assess student learning as you move from group to group observing, listening, and asking and answering questions.

Some keys to effective group work are the following.

- Set a time limit on group activities. For example, if you are charging groups to develop a partnership agreement for a business of their choice, add to the charge "You have twenty minutes." Without a time limit, groups can feel no pressure to get the job done.
- Establish the purpose of the group before you move your students into the group. If you first form the groups without direction, you are leaving your students unfocused until you get their attention a second time to explain the purpose of the activity.
- For reporting on the group work, have the group select a spokesperson. However, ask the group to rotate the spokesperson after he or she first reports. Rotation allows others to have the chance to practice leadership and communications skills.

Group work activities will vary significantly from discipline to discipline, course to course. In all cases, the groups should report something—their results, interactions, differences of opinion, success, and so forth. Figure 4.8 offers a few ideas for group activities.

Group Activities That Work
✓ Grade quizzes and homework assignments in class and require corrective learning. Compare answers, discussing similarities and differences.
✓ Solve a problem related to the course. This could be related to generating ideas about how to approach a problem (steps to follow? survey? scientific method? where to start?) or to develop possible solutions and evaluate them. You might assign all groups the same problem and then compare the results, or give each group a different problem.
✓ Create something (in class) related to the course material. Depending on the topic, it could be a list of questions or observations or ideas, a diagram or chart of relationships or of a process, a step-by-step procedure, a time line, a literary review or critique, a set of survey or interview questions, or any of hundreds of other activities limited only by your imagination.
✓ Introduce pressing problems to solve and brainstorm the next day. Example: How would you design an entrepreneurial program in the Inuit language, which has no word for *money* nor a concept of profit?
✓ Introduce ethical issues.
✓ Encourage students to take a different view from yours.
✓ Use invented dialogue and have students write conversations with famous or historic people. Example: Interview Napoleon and Caesar on their leadership styles.

Figure 4.8. Suggestions for Successful Group Activities.

Invite Students to Teach

If the class is small enough and time is sufficient, each student or a few selected students can make individual presentations to the class. Adult learners, in particular, have life or work experiences that could be instructive for students. Individual presentations should have a definite time limit, and could be anywhere from two to ten minutes. Sometimes a longer presentation is acceptable. In most cases, you will want to preview the student's presentation materials and make suggestions before the student actually presents. Another way to deal with this is to invite students to submit a presentation description, outline, and list of slides or materials, and then select a few for class presentation.

Individual presentations can be done in a panel format, with three to five students presenting some aspect of the topic and the whole panel taking questions from the remainder of the class.

Occasionally it is also a good idea to let students work individually. For example, you could have ready a list of prelecture questions for students to work on when they arrive. Similarly, follow your presentation of a concept or completion of a talk or lecture by distributing a page with questions about the main points or with questions about how to apply a technique or concept they've just heard about. This allows *all* students to review what they've heard, think about the questions, and attempt to answer them. And it helps you vary the ways that you provide for students to engage their thinking.

Best Practices for Independent Study

Provide varied opportunities for students to work on their own. When you are planning such activities, include some for students who have less experience with independent learning or who are not as comfortable in this mode. Also provide more challenging options for students who enjoy working independently and are successful doing so. Here are some suggestions that will increase the probability that your independent learning activities will be positive learning experiences for your students.

1. **Expectations.** Independent learning activities are most likely to be successful when instructor and students have a shared understanding of the intended outcomes. From the outset, communicate your expectations for the learning that should happen as a result of the independent activity.
2. **Directions.** Describe the activities in detail and, when possible, give examples of completed work to serve as models. Directions for submitting the work should be clear, including deadlines.
3. **Discussion/review.** Schedule times on a regular basis to review the independent learning. Use positive discussion techniques to create an energized atmosphere for discussion of the projects. Show your excitement about students' learning and their projects. These sessions will enable you to monitor students' work and to foster their motivation.

4. **Feedback.** Check on students' progress regularly and provide meaningful feedback, that is, feedback that recognizes what students have accomplished in a positive way and provides guidance for the next steps or continuation of the work.

5. **Organization.** Students working independently should have good self-starting skills and good self-monitoring skills. They need to know if they are learning and if they are focused on the right skills. When appropriate, provide them with criteria so that they can learn to judge their own learning effectiveness.

Implications for Online Classes

An effective way to infuse an online course with action is to design engaging and rigorous assignments. Students will need to submit their work to you online or by e-mail or by sending or delivering some hard copy or physical product. Remember that most students can e-mail photos, either taken with digital cameras or scanned, and this could significantly increase the range of potential assignments. Some instructors have students videotape or audiotape projects such as interviews, field trips, or performances.

Blackboard and WebCT allow instructors to establish groups of students who can then work together on projects, share information, send e-mail within their group, and perform other functions. This technology is especially useful for collaborative learning.

Framing Instruction and Learning within Authentic Contexts

"Tell me and I forget. Show me and I remember. Involve me and I understand."

—Chinese proverb

Authentic contexts reflect what happens in the "real world." We ask students in a literature course to think like reviewers or authors, students in a pharmacy course to think like pharmacy technicians, students in sociology courses to think like sociologists, etc. The learning activities conducted in authentic contexts are somewhat different from those conducted in "traditional" environments: they mirror those activities as they are carried out in nonclassroom settings. Outside the educational environment, for example, writing is done not for a teacher but for customers, employees, coworkers, colleagues, patients, constituencies, and many other reading audiences. In the real world, the purpose of writing is not usually to provide evidence of comprehension or learning or writing skills, but to inform, persuade, direct, manage, sell, communicate ideas and decisions, and so forth. Figure 4.9 summarizes some of the characteristics of traditional learning, real-world activity, and authentic learning for selected subjects or topics.

INTERNET
RESOURCE
Templates

AUTHENTIC LEARNING CONTEXTS			
Subject	**Traditional Learning**	**Real-World Activity**	**Authentic Learning**
Math	Math is taught as calculations and abstractions.	Math is used to make purchasing decisions, compare sales results, create mixtures.	Math is presented in specific contexts: business math, math for chemistry, math for social sciences, math for transportation, and so forth.
Writing	Almost all writing happens as homework; it is primarily done by individuals, not pairs or groups; it often emphasizes explanations; it is usually written for the instructor.	Writing happens on the job; it is more often collaborative; it often emphasizes summarizing or distilling information and representing it; it is almost never written for an instructor; it is written for very specific audiences.	Writing happens in the classroom as well as for assignments; some writing is collaborative; assignments emphasize writing for a real purpose with specific audiences.
Speaking	Discussions focus on comprehension of academic material.	Discussions focus on negotiating, selling, directing, etc.	Discussions demonstrate comprehension of concepts and skills as they are used to negotiate, sell, give directions, summarize, persuade, and so forth.
Reading	Reading is often foundational or focused on academic material. Seldom do students perform "applied" reading.	Reading is applied, and often nonacademic. For example, reading is done to get instructions or directions, determine policies and procedures, or obtain information needed to make decisions.	Foundational reading is assigned as necessary. Students also practice "applied" reading.
Thinking, Problem Solving	Thinking and problem solving are focused on understanding and remembering, often related to learning academic material.	Thinking and problem solving are focused on planning, assessing success or effectiveness, and making decisions.	Students are asked to solve problems representative of real- world situations. Instruction and problems use simulations and other approaches to provide decision-making contexts.

Figure 4.9. Comparisons of Traditional Learning and Authentic Learning for Selected Academic Areas. (Developed by Barbara G. Cox, PhD, consulting editor, *Exceptional Teaching*.)

In authentic contexts, the emphasis is on the value of related disciplines, along with communicating and problem solving. The real-world interconnectedness is appreciated and reflected in the curriculum. For example, elements of an authentic context for learning Pharmacy Practice would include the following.

Communications (reading, writing, speaking):
- Writes summaries of information, data, or decisions for different appropriate audiences, e.g., patients (consumers), med techs, physicians, researchers, or advertising copy
- Uses language of pharmacy effectively

Problem Solving, Decision Making:
- Interprets medical documents and systems reports
- Implements processes appropriate to each business function

Interdisciplinary Connections:
- Troubleshoots and corrects math errors
- Uses foundational chemistry knowledge
- Reads and locates structured medical forms
- Relates to various persons/roles (consumers, pharmacists, drug retailers, etc.)
- Uses math related to pharmacy practice

Holding High Expectations of Students

High performance happens in a positive environment of high expectations.

> *"The main hope of a nation lies in the proper education of its youth."*
> —Erasmus

The significant effects of instructor expectations on the performance of students have been well documented in studies of the Pygmalion Effect, or Self-Fulfilling Prophecy. In education, this phenomenon begins with an instructor's formation of an opinion and expectations about a student's abilities that are communicated by various cues, some subtle, some not. The student adjusts performance or behaviors to conform to the instructor's expectations, essentially, verifying the instructor's view. The implication, one compellingly validated by a multitude of studies, is that when instructors have high expectations of students, the students rise to meet them. When instructors have low expectations of students, the students, unfortunately, match those.

Establish Expectations Early in the Course

Always begin with the highest of expectations for all of your students. Anything less is a disservice to them and their education. Communicate the expectations from the outset by including them explicitly in your syllabus and your comments to the class during the first session.

When you describe or discuss assignments, indicate that you expect everyone's work to meet certain standards. Describe the standards and provide examples of completed assignments that meet those standards. Give a real-world rationale for the standards. Indicate that you want students to do this because in the real world they will be doing this.

Here are a few reminders to help you check to see if you are communicating high expectations.

- Do you know what you expect from students?
- Do you provide clear directions, examples, standards, and priorities for your students?
- Have your students acknowledged and agreed to your expectations?
- Do your students understand how their performance affects the course of the class process?
- Do your students understand how their performance relates to real-world standards?

Foster and Maintain Student Motivation

The time you spend with students in the classroom is critical to their success. This is your greatest opportunity to foster their motivation. Students respond to recognition of their ideas or work—whether spoken or written, or even a smile or nod of the head. Here are a few ideas.

- Provide frequent positive feedback, for groups and for individuals. Respond to student statements and questions with a positive comment or question: "Excellent!" "How did you know that?" "How did you think of that?" "You all surpassed my expectations!" "This is one of the best presentations I've ever observed." "You've made a lot of progress!"
- Provide feedback when you hand back student work. If the class is a size that allows you to walk around the room and hand material to individuals, try to make a positive, constructive comment about the work to each student. Avoid sarcasm or negative statements. Save criticism for written feedback or one-on-one situations.
- Activities, whether individual or group, that have a tangible outcome give students something they can see when they're done. "Products" such as charts, lists, diagrams, written material, drawings, results of experiments, and journal entries give students a sense of accomplishment.
- Tell students that you hold very high expectations of their performance. Repeated comments such as "I know you'll do well with this project," or "You can do this! I know you can!" will reinforce their self-confidence and enhance motivation.

- The nature of the activities in class will make a difference in student motivation. Activities, whether group or individual, need to challenge students' thinking. Activities need to be authentic. Asking students to solve new problems, apply new ways of looking at old information, or use new tools and skills will communicate that you have confidence in their learning and increase their confidence in themselves. If activities do not engage students' imagination and higher-level thinking, they will soon become bored and lose interest. This does not mean that activities must be difficult. It does mean that they should be fun and captivate student interest.

"Good teaching is one-fourth preparation and three-fourths theater."

—Gail Godwin

CHAPTER SUMMARY

- "Telling isn't teaching." "Real" teaching engages students' curiosity and attention, inspires them to think, motivates them to concentrate, and communicates to them that they are capable learners. Doing this requires building a personal, nonthreatening environment, creating an active, energized classroom, using authentic contexts for learning, and holding high expectations.

- Understanding students' learning styles and the implications of those learning preferences for instruction offers an important tool for personalizing the learning environment.

- Creating an active classroom means infusing every teaching approach with ways for students to interact with and work the skills and/or content being taught. For online courses, design engaging and rigorous assignments that are executed through a variety of media.

- To frame instruction and learning within authentic contexts, develop activities that mirror the real-world work of the discipline. Emphasize the connections to foundation competencies, such as communicating and problem solving, and to interdisciplinary skills.

- Begin every course with the highest of expectations for all of your students, for research demonstrates that learner performance correlates strongly with instructor expectations, a factor known as the Pygmalion Effect or Self-Fulfilling Prophecy.

THINK ABOUT IT: Evaluate Your Instructional Delivery Skills

Mark each item on a scale of 1-5. Use 1 to represent "very able" and 5 for "need extensive training or help."

INTERNET RESOURCE
Checklists

	Face-to-Face	Distance
1. Presenting lectures		
2. Guiding interactive discussions		
3. Handling difficult questions		
4. Encouraging wide participation		
5. Team teaching		
6. Managing small group/peer-to-peer learning		
7. Managing labs and hands-on work		
8. Coaching individual students		
9. Teaching by demonstration		

continued on next page

	Face-to-Face	Distance
10. Planning engaged and action-oriented learning		
11. Keeping students' attention		
12. Planning effective quizzes and assessments		
13. Motivating bored or underachieving learners		
14. Including learning strategies for remedial students		
15. Including learning strategies for accelerated students		
16. Creating a personal environment		
17. Modeling authentic skills in the context of the discipline		
18. Accommodating different learning styles		
19. Monitoring and adjusting learning based on learner feedback		
20. Using appropriate technology to teach		

The skills listed below directly impact the success of distance learning instruction. Review and rate each skill area for distance delivery only.

	Distance
1. Projecting your personality online	
2. Posting course materials in advance	
3. Creating instructional modules using visuals, audio, and multimedia	
4. Providing unambiguous directions throughout the instruction	
5. Ensuring that materials are easy to use	
6. Providing engaging opportunities for online discussion	
7. Organizing discussion threads by topic	
8. Guiding online discussion groups	
9. Providing varied opportunities for students to apply learning	
10. Writing discursively and clearly in all communications	
11. Writing e-mails to answer individual student questions	
12. Writing e-mails or using a broadcast tool to communicate to the full class	
13. Using the Web to plan class extension activities	
14. Using online grade books	
15. Returning student phone calls and coaching by phone	
16. Creating a sense of community by incorporating social aspects of learning	
17. Encouraging students to track their own progress and assignment completion	

Discussion Questions

1. One of the warm-ups presented in the chapter stressed the importance of letting students get to know you "as a person." Do you agree? If yes, what does that really mean? How important is it and how personal should the relationship become? If no, why not?

2. Problem solving is a worthy goal for most subject areas. Do you teach an approach for problem solving and if so, for what skills? Are students becoming better problem solvers? Do the skills transfer to other courses?

3. Review the learning styles defined by Grasha and Reichmann. Reflect on your learning experience and determine your own learning type. Then, reflect on the students in one of your courses. Does one style dominate? Or do most of your students fit into three or four categories? Which style or learner is the most difficult for you to relate to and to teach? Which is the easiest? How does your own learning style influence the way you teach?

4. What are two techniques, other than those mentioned in the chapter, that you have used to encourage learner participation and make your teaching more active? What were the results? What changes did you observe in student attitude and performance?

Field Work

1. Observe a willing colleague's classroom session. Answer the following questions:
   a. How did the instructor begin the session?
   b. What presentation types were used?
   c. What types of student participation did you see?
   d. How did the instructor wrap up the session?
2. Consider the chapter suggestions for warm-ups and wrap-ups. Which ones suit your style? Which ones would best engage your students?
3. Some courses are naturals for including action-oriented learning while others require more imagination. What are the performance opportunities for your course? What could your students demonstrate or create as evidence of learning?
4. Review the content of one of your courses and determine the specific reading and writing skills needed for this course. To help ensure student success, which ones should receive direct instruction in the course?

Professional Portfolio: Matching Activities and Learner Styles

Reflect again on the categories of the Grasha-Reichmann Student Learning Style Scales. Select two instructional sessions that are critical to student understanding of the course goals for one of your current classes. For each type of learner, what instructional activities could you include to foster success? Consider this same question for both instructor-led and instructor-facilitated sections of the course.

Exceptional Teaching is

Assessment-Driven

Or we could have said: Exceptional teaching is circular. We plan educational outcomes, deliver instruction, and assess the outcomes. Then based on continuous assessment results, we plan again, deliver, and assess again. The process continues until as many students as possible are successful in meeting the course outcomes. The key to this cycle is continuous feedback and, even more important, adopting the belief that the course or unit is not over when students turn in their tests.

Teach to the Test?

Decisions about what and how to test end up driving what and how you teach. In other words, what is on the test does indeed affect what you teach. We have all heard the phrase "Don't teach to the test" and have argued the merits and the meaning of the phrase. But it is your expert judgment and decision making that we need here. What if the test is worth the focus? The answer depends on the test itself. If

the test is a quality, valid assessment, teaching to the test can be a strong instructional approach. If the test is poorly planned or misses the main focus of your instruction, teaching to the test is wasteful, possibly damaging, and certainly inefficient. Class time, a very scarce resource, has been spent on the wrong skills and the wrong learning. On the other hand, tests or assessments that capture the habits of the mind, that focus on the essential questions of the subject, and that require authentic performance or production are tests worth teaching to.

As you decide what and how to test, ask yourself: Will this test contribute to student learning? Will the test enable me to provide feedback on learning and ways to reach the learning outcomes? Will I be able to identify areas in which instruction has failed to help students achieve the outcomes and then know how to adjust the course plan and activities accordingly? Remember, you can use both concept and performance tests in the same course. In fact, multiple test venues give students a better chance to evidence what they know. In the past, testing programs focused on the question "*Is* the learner smart?" Now that we know more about how the brain works and understand the implications of different learning styles, the question is "*How* is the learner smart?"

Continuous Assessment and Feedback

Why is feedback so vital? Continuous feedback during the course is the only way for students to know what they know and what they do not know (but may think they know). We have all had students who think they know but do not. We have also had students who do know but doubt that they do or do not realize they know. The goal of continuous assessment and feedback is to get students to recognize what they know and to be able to monitor their own learning. How do we achieve this outcome? By capturing an immediate picture of the student's learning and identifying any misconceptions that will impede learning. Quick, continuous assessments familiar to most instructors might be weekly tests, pop quizzes, or unit tests. Other possibilities include class assessment techniques such as lecture reconstruction using concept maps, outlining and note taking on key points, test item writing, creating a frequently asked set of questions covering the main issues, and pro/con grids.

Variety in the form and format of assessment is important. It keeps your course interesting. But it is the feedback that students

are waiting for. Feedback does not give a grade or judgment category. It is designed to be qualitative, motivating, and personal. It is not intended to answer in a summative way whether students have arrived or have "it." Feedback answers the questions: What of "it" do I have? In which areas am I strong? Where am I weak? What, in the world, do I do next?

To move students toward the goal of self-monitoring and to nurture a positive learning environment, check your feedback for these characteristics.

- Feedback should be timely. Give feedback as soon after the behavior or performance as you possibly can.
- Feedback should be clear and specific. Tell students the basis for the feedback. Discuss the characteristics of the student's work that led to the feedback. As with all instruction, use clear language that the student can relate to.
- Feedback should be personal. If this is written feedback, write the student's name before the comments ("Henry, you've captured the essence of Johnson's argument. Good job!")

- Feedback should encourage response and interaction. Students need the opportunity to discuss feedback, to consider and explain their performance further. The added interaction should build positive communications as well as give the instructor some insights into the assignments or other teaching.

The End Game

Final letter grades are powerful. They can inspire or deflate. Today's effective educators often delay formal grading as long as possible. The reason for this is that grades, if given too early in the course, serve to demotivate students. Believing they cannot succeed, students will drop the course long before they have really given the course a chance. We have known for some time that the rate of learning among individual students varies significantly. Some get it immediately, some take the expected time, and some take longer. If given the opportunity, this latter group will most definitely learn but will take longer to do so. This is as true in college as it was in first grade. Delaying formal grades avoids the risk of communicating failure too early in the course and chancing that students will drop out not to return to this class again.

In addition to the issue of timing, we know that no single assessment is a perfect measure of what a student knows or can do. This is why conducting multiple assessments, even multiple types of assessments, provides instructors with a better picture of their students' mastery. An instructor will have a much better picture of a student's grasp of Howard Ball's influence on graphic design and airbrushing techniques if the student writes an essay, answers questions, and demonstrates early airbrushing than if the student just answers ten questions.

Though time for developing, administering, and evaluating assessments is precious, using multiple assessments is the most effective and most certain way to assess all the important outcomes of your course. Ongoing assessment in multiple forms moves us closer to every student answering "Yes" to the big questions: Am I here? Do I have it? Is my work complete?

Chapter

5 Assessing Learning

George had been sitting at the small table by the window for nearly two hours, and his legs were getting a little stiff. The sunlight fell across the page, where he was reading about how to sail the *June Bug.* Grandfather had given George and his two younger sisters the small boat as a special Fourth of July surprise. George squinted at one diagram and then another, struggling to visualize how the illustrated maneuvers would actually look if he were in the boat out on the lake. He pictured himself, steady and sure, pulling this and tying that, sail catching the breeze. For a fleeting moment, he was Pirate Pete, in tricornered hat and black eye patch, headed round the point to his cove.

George read and reread the instructions until he was fairly certain he knew exactly what to do. He tested his memory, asking himself questions about each of the major steps. Just a little more reading to make sure, and then he would announce to Grandfather that he had it all figured out and was ready for the adventure. Time for a break. George stretched his legs to shake out the stiffness. Inhaling deeply, George looked out the window. His gaze focused on the far shore against the horizon, where—what's this?— his two younger sisters had sailed the *June Bug* and were laughing gleefully at their success.

Learning Outcomes

- Analyze the major types of assessment venues and explain their purpose along with the advantages and disadvantages for various course types
- Plan, administer, and score course-appropriate assessments
- Create and use different types of authentic assessments, including the use of rubrics for essay, product, and performance tests
- Create student opinion polls and use the information constructively to improve course plans
- Participate in peer coaching evaluations and offer suggestions based on Exceptional Teaching principles

Why Assess?

Assessments contribute to the teaching/learning experience in several ways. In addition to helping you and your students determine what they have learned, assessments can help you motivate them. Assessments also help guide your instruction—its pace, approaches, and content—and the results will indicate the effectiveness of your teaching.

Before you determine and implement a final assessment plan for your course, you should be familiar with various types of tests and their strengths and weaknesses. You should also have a philosophy of assessment, one that guides your decisions about what types of tests to use for what purposes. Decide also how you are going to use the test results to evaluate students' overall performance.

The Functions of Assessments

Assessments play the following key roles in the teaching/learning experience:

- **Helping you decide where to begin**
  Pretests administered at the beginning of a course will tell you if your plan for the course is starting at the right place. Results will indicate whether you need to review some foundational concepts or skills before diving into the heart of the course or if, on the other hand, students have already mastered certain content and you can move over some learning more quickly than you had thought.
- **Comparing or classifying students, usually for purposes of placement or grouping**
  Depending on your course, the degree of individualization you visualize or need, and the degree of grouping you must do for some learning, pretests and other early diagnostic assessments will be useful.

- **Determining what course components (concepts, skills) you might need to reteach or teach using a different approach**
  Each assessment throughout the course, whether quiz or poll or performance test, will provide information about the effectiveness of the learning activities so far. Based on that information, you will make decisions about the next steps.
- **Motivating students**
  Use assessments to motivate students, either to convince them they do not know what they think they know, to reinforce their effective learning strategies, or to improve learning strategies that are not working for them. Provide feedback, not just scores, when you give assessment data to students. Scores may "speak for themselves," but sometimes they give the wrong message.
- **Helping students see what they have learned and what they still need to learn, i.e., helping students learn to monitor their own progress**
  Many students are able to monitor their own learning and attainment of intended outcomes without feedback from assessments and instructors. These tend to be the exceptions, however. Assessments help students learn to monitor what they know or don't know, can or cannot do.
- **Determining a course grade for each student**
  Assessments might not be the exclusive means of determining a course grade for each student, but their role is usually critical. Because grades will or might be used in the future to evaluate students' college performance either for career considerations or for other college admissions, the accuracy and validity of the assessments are also critical.
- **Determining the overall effectiveness of your teaching**
  The cumulative information generated by the assessments throughout the course together with final examination or performance scores, student evaluations of the course, and other feedback will help instructors see whether and to what degree their teaching and their course plan implementation were effective.
- **Meeting accreditation requirements**
  Assessment data can contribute to evaluation of instructors and courses and the programs or divisions that offer those courses. This data can feed college decisions about program and course offerings, including how to expand or improve them.

An Assessment Philosophy

Assessments can serve various purposes, but how do you decide their function in *your* instruction? Before planning an assessment strategy for a course, establish certain principles about assessment and evaluation—a philosophy that will guide you. The ten items that follow might form the core of your philosophy, or you or your school might have others.

1. Assessment should contribute to students' learning by asking them to apply their skills in out-of-school or workplace situations.
2. Timing, content, and form of assessments should be planned as an integral part of the course design. From the beginning, assessments should be consistent with the course content, approach, and intended outcomes.
3. The purpose of every assessment should be clear.
4. The type of assessment—its content and format—should be appropriate for the purpose. It should measure what it is intended to measure, meaning it has *validity*. Three types of validity that relate to your work as an instructor are face, content, and criterion/concurrent validity. *Face validity* refers to whether a test appears to measure what it is supposed to measure. *Content validity* asks whether a test is properly "balanced" with regard to the important material to include—are the questions representative of the entire scope of what is meant to be tested? *Criterion/concurrent* validity tells us whether a test result is consistent with what is expected or with other performances of an individual.
5. Assessments should be scored as consistently and objectively as possible. When an instructor's (or other evaluator's) judgment is required for scoring or grading, a set of criteria should be developed and applied consistently. This characteristic is called *reliability*. For purposes of your classroom assessments, you will want to examine your own scoring of essays, projects, portfolios, products, and other assessments to ensure that your judgments are consistent. One way to help ensure this reliability is to develop criteria or rubrics to guide your judgments. We will discuss rubrics in more detail later in this chapter.

6. Assessments should provide students with feedback on their learning. And feedback should, as much as possible, provide direction for review or ways to reach intended outcomes.
7. Assessments should emphasize intellectual traits of value: analytical reading, thinking, decision making, and research skills along with individual creativity and individual intelligence.
8. Assessments should be conducted at specific, planned checkpoints. They should not become a burden to instructors or students.
9. Assessments should be conducted in a positive learning environment, with every effort made to lower students' test anxieties.
10. Assessments should allow students to demonstrate their accomplishment of outcomes in various ways, including ways that fit their individual learning styles.

Developing an Assessment Strategy

With an assessment philosophy as a foundation, you are ready to develop a strategy that encompasses the number, level, and type of assessments and incorporates them into a grading scheme.

Begin thinking about major assessments when you are planning your course, as was discussed in Chapter 2. Answering the following questions will help you get started.

- Do I want a course pre-assessment?
- Do I want a course comprehensive assessment—one that will determine students' mastery of the major intended outcomes for the entire course?
- Do I want pre-assessments for each unit or part?
- Do I want comprehensive assessments for each unit or part—ones that assess students' mastery of the major intended outcomes for that part?
- Do I want interim or checkpoint assessments that assess students' mastery of intended outcomes of learning chunks within units? How many? How often?
- Once my system is in place, will my students know that I value *how* and *how well* they think?

Once you've answered the course-level questions, you will know approximately how many assessments you wish to include and their general place in the course. Then you will need to decide which type of assessment you want to administer or assign for each of these.

Types of Tests

Student assessment approaches fall into two broad categories: traditional cognitive tests, which historically have been known as "objective tests," and performance-based assessments, which require students to demonstrate what they have learned. Within the two broad categories are subcategories that include several formats, as shown in Figure 5.1.

TRADITIONAL COGNITIVE TESTS		PERFORMANCE-BASED ASSESSMENTS		
Selected Response	Constructed Responses	Products	Performances	Process-Focused

multiple-choice
true-false
matching
	fill in the blank
	short answer
	label a diagram
	visual
	  representation
	✓ concept map
	✓ flowchart
	✓ graph/table/
	  matrix
	✓ illustration
		essay
		research paper
		log/journal
		lab report
		story/play/poem
		photograph
		  exhibit
		physical model
		video/audio
		  product
		spreadsheet/
		  database
		art work
		portfolio
			oral
			  presentation
			demonstration
			dramatic
			  reading or
			  performance
			enactment
			debate
			recital
			role play
				oral questioning
				observation
				interview
				process
				  description
				"think aloud"
				blogs

Figure 5.1. Types of Tests.

Best Uses of Traditional Cognitive Testing

Traditional cognitive tests are usually best suited for testing information recall, comprehension, analysis, and application. Courses that ask students to master facts or courses that cover foundational learning in an early part often use this type of testing to its best advantage. The strengths of traditional tests lie mostly in their reliability and efficiency, as well as accuracy of scoring. Instructors of very large classes rely heavily on these tests for those reasons; that is, the feasibility of administering performance assessments for a large number of students is severely limited by the time required for scoring or evaluating them.

"we have the most tested but least examined students in the world."

—D. P. Resnick

Because these tests can be administered quickly, especially short quizzes and polls, they can provide timely feedback to students, which should help them understand what they have mastered and what they need to address. It helps them take responsibility for their learning, including setting objectives and goals for themselves in the learning process. Results from quizzes and polls can serve to stimulate discussions in class or to group students for collaborative learning.

Best Uses of Performance-Based Testing

Traditional cognitive tests are criticized for being contrived and not representative of how students will use their new skills or thinking in the real world. For that, we need authentic, or performance-based, testing.

What do we mean by authentic tests? Authentic assessment values and emphasizes real-life contexts. Multiple-choice or other tests seldom measure one's ability to perform tasks on the job. People conduct interviews, write advertising, design landscapes, build schools, write stories, analyze budgets, and perform other tasks without ever stopping to complete a test along the way. Authentic tests try to measure students' abilities to do these things (as they pertain to the course) in ways as close to reality as possible. Authentic assessments have the added advantage of increasing student engagement with a course and student motivation. Creating a clay sculpture for an art class is much more interesting than taking a pencil-and-paper test about sculpting techniques. This is not to say that the pencil-and-paper test does not have value. Often, both types of testing are used and contribute to the overall evaluation of student performance.

Authentic assessments use a variety of approaches, depending on the discipline, instructor and student inventiveness, available resources, and other factors. Authentic assessments ask students to integrate what they have learned and apply it to resolve an issue, solve a problem, create something new, work collaboratively, or use their written and oral communication skills. Authentic assessments stress the process of learning as well as the outcomes of learning.

Meeting a Challenge
Teaching the Advanced Learner

Students who are very quick learners or who have background or external experience with the subject matter and skills of a course may advance more quickly than others. As we mentioned in Chapter 4, these students may be at risk of boredom or irritation at the pace of the course.

Ask yourself if you need to adjust your thinking about "coverage-based" instruction—that is, do you feel compelled to ask all students to do all the same work? If so, you will need to give up this notion fairly quickly.

How do you make assignments or activities more challenging for advanced learners? Here are some suggestions.

- Graduate the rubrics. This means that the assignment or activity is essentially the same for all students, but the advanced students' task has other facets to it, making it more complex.
- Assign more challenging extended readings, using library, Internet, and other resources.
- Use more real-world applications or simulations.
- Allow advanced learners more flexibility in defining their assignments, topics, resources, and so forth. Give them more independence in planning and designing and monitoring their learning.
- Include tasks that require more research or problem solving.
- Design assignments that require them to apply the learning in more creative ways.
- Create assignments that ask them to reorganize information and present it from a new perspective, apply it in a novel context, or prepare some visual representation of relationships.
- Advanced students might be able to take "giant steps" in their learning, rather than work through all the in-between steps. They might be more challenged by being shown a result and trying to figure out how to get there.
- For students who have moved through materials and activities very quickly, assign work that requires them to explore a concept, topic, or procedure in more depth.
- Make a learning contract with advanced students, listing what they can do and what they must do to succeed in the course.

Selecting Types of Assessments for a Course

Choosing the type of assessment for all phases of your course, from pre-assessment to the final exam or performance, revolves around several factors. Consider the following questions.

- What is the main purpose of the assessment? What do I want to know about students' understanding, skills, or progress?
- What type of learning is being assessed? Factual knowledge? Application of knowledge? Skills? In-depth understandings?
- What type of assessment will be most appropriate for this purpose? How can students best demonstrate their mastery?
- What other types of assessments have I already included (or will include) in the course?
- How feasible is the assessment? How much time is available for the assessment?
- How will I score or grade the assessment? How much time will I need?
- How will I use the assessment results? What feedback will be possible for me to provide following the assessment?
- Will I allow students to demonstrate what they have learned using their preferred learning style?

Figure 5.2 illustrates part of an assessment strategy for a Pharmacology and Pharmacy Practice course, developed around the questions above. The instructor has planned seven assessments for Unit 1: a unit pretest plus three checkpoint tests and three outcome tests. She uses traditional cognitive testing for the pretest and checkpoint tests since she intends to test information recall and wants the tests to be efficient, quick administrations, and yet inform her of whether the students are keeping pace and the course is on track. She will give students feedback so they know what they might need to do to catch up, if necessary. The instructor plans more authentic assessments for the major unit outcomes. These require students to use actual materials, such as prescriptions, labels, and pharmacy materials, to dispense drugs appropriately. She also provides a scenario or case-study essay exam that requires higher-level problem solving.

COURSE: PHARMACOLOGY AND PHARMACY PRACTICE UNIT I: PHARMACOLOGY OUTCOMES		
OUTCOMES	**ASSESSMENT TYPE**	**COMMENTS: PURPOSE AND RATIONALE**
Demonstrate a working knowledge of the principles of drug action in the body and individual cells, drug dosages, routes of administration, and interactions.	Pretest: Multiple choice.	Determine foundational skills and knowledge. Verify starting point for course. Most feasible type.
	Checkpoint Test: Multiple choice, Fill-In, etc.	Test recall. Terminology check. Confirm that course is on track.
	Checkpoint Test: Multiple choice, Fill-In, etc.	Test recall. Test and reinforce learning of drug-action principles. Check knowledge (recall) of dosages, administration, and interactions.

continued on next page

| Interpret drug labels and dosage information and dispense as prescribed.

Use drug references to accurately identify generic and brand equivalents.	Checkpoint Test: Error Identification.	Test ability to identify potential problems with dosages, administrations, or interactions.
	Outcome Test: Short answer on generic/brand equivalents.	Test ability to use drug references to check generics for brands and vice versa. Authentic testing using actual drug references.
	Outcome Test: Lab-type practice-based assessment in the pharmacy.	Test ability to dispense according to label/dosage information. Authentic assessment.
	Outcome Test: Scenario-based essay/short answer.	Test ability to identify potential problems with dosages, administrations, or interactions and indicate solution. Test relational information and problem solving.

Figure 5.2. Unit Assessment Strategy for a Pharmacology and Pharmacy Practice Course.

Blending the Approaches

Notice that by using various approaches to assessments instructors can better match the assessment to the intended outcome, using traditional cognitive assessments to test recall of facts and performance-based assessments for testing skills, creativity, and relational learning. Using a mix of assessment types allows students to demonstrate their learning in various ways. Students who are poor at completing forced-choice tests, or who are very lucky at them, can demonstrate their learning in ways that better represent their accomplishments. Furthermore, the variety of approaches to assessment can complement the learning styles represented in your classroom. This is one of the points addressed in Figure 5.3, which summarizes key considerations in developing an assessment strategy.

GUIDELINES FOR TESTING AND ASSESSMENT
The goal of assessment is to reduce the gap between teaching and testing. What will quality work and thinking look like?
✓ Find out what your learner already knows. Survey learner skills and knowledge in the first week of the course.
✓ Use a variety of classroom assessment techniques. Gather feedback in the first three weeks of the class and use it to modify your course plan.
✓ Delay grading as long as possible. Students need to give and get feedback on their learning before they are evaluated for grades.
✓ If one of your goals is self-directed learning, give students instruction and practice in self-assessment. Students need to internalize the criteria by which they will be judged.

continued on next page

> ✓ Provide numerous models and examples of what quality work looks like. Many students know what constitutes poor-quality work but do not understand what constitutes high-quality work. Include in the syllabus examples of the types of items that students will see on the final test.
>
> ✓ Have students prepare test questions and model answers. You will learn what they remember, what they consider important, and how well they understand the material.
>
> ✓ Incorporate test items that go beyond recall and basic comprehension. Teach students what kind of response the test item is calling for at each level (application, analysis, inquiry, evaluation).
>
> ✓ Give tests, assignments, and problems that are worth solving and thinking about.
>
> ✓ Administer more quizzes and tests that count and allow students to drop one from the grading formula. Use a variety of test types.
>
> ✓ Grade and give feedback on the test as soon as possible. Require corrective learning.
>
> ✓ Use student feedback to inform your teaching. Assessment is not over when they turn in the test.

Figure 5.3. Key Considerations in Developing an Assessment Strategy.

Creating a Grading System

By thinking through the types of assessments that will measure students' achievement of course and unit outcomes, you will have already established a hierarchy of the major grading components. This provides a basis for weighting the scores and entering them into a grade calculation system. First, though, decide if you will include nonachievement factors, for example, effort and attendance, in your grading scheme.

Including Nonachievement Factors in the Grade

The issue of measuring student performance in behaviors unrelated to the subject matter of a course is not easily resolved. Studies and surveys indicate that a majority of teachers and students recognize academic achievement as the most important grading component. Academic achievement includes competency in three areas: (1) subject matter skills and concepts; (2) thinking and problem-solving skills; and (3) foundation communication and technology skills. Yet research by Cross and Frary[1] indicates that a significant portion of teachers routinely grade students on their effort (participation and completion of work), behavior (following classroom and school policies), and attendance. Employers have also weighed in on the subject, citing the importance of employees' attitude and their willingness to show up for work on time.

> *"what one has to do usually can be done."*
>
> —Eleanor Roosevelt

The solution seems to lie in a compromise. Experts recommend that teachers consistently provide students with feedback on nonachievement factors, thus emphasizing their importance, but that grades be confined to achievement, that is, the attainment of course outcomes.

---

[1] L.H. Cross and R.B. Frary. "Hodgepodge Grading: Endorsed by Students and Teachers Alike." *Applied Measurement in Education.* Vol. 12, No. 1: 53–72.

Weighting Scores

When you have decided on all the assessments for your course, you will want to assign a weight to each of them. The weight refers to the relative importance of each assessment in the total evaluation of a student's performance. Then create a spreadsheet or other record-keeping system to record student scores and calculate totals. Let's say you have decided to administer four quizzes, a midterm examination, and a final examination. You also assign students a project that counts as part of their grade. You also plan to administer some one-minute papers and other short assessments, but these are anonymous and do not count toward a grade, so you do not include these in your spreadsheet.

A spreadsheet for the Unit I assessments described in Figure 5.2 might look something like Figure 5.4 below, after all scores have been entered.

Figure 5.4. Sample Grading Spreadsheet.

To weight the scores to get the Overall Unit Weighted Score, the instructor entered this formula: =D5*0.1+E5*0.1+F5*0.1+G5*0.2+H5*0.25+I5*0.25 for Row 5 (total = 100%), and then copied it down the column to get scores for the entire class. This shows in column J.

The instructor creates a similar sheet for each unit in the course, making the job of determining each student's final grade relatively simple and quick.

Planning the Content and Delivery Mode of Assessments

Should you write your own tests and performance assessments or can you trust that the tests that accompany textbooks are reliable, valid, and authentic? Many instructors would probably choose to write their own assessment instruments if they had the time, the energy, and the expertise. In reality, most college instructors use existing assessment products—particularly the objective type—for practical reasons, but also because textbook publishers offer effective testing tools in a wide variety of media, many of which the instructor can modify or customize.

Sources and Delivery of Objective Tests

Traditional cognitive tests can be classified by source of questions and by type of media. Source refers to the origin of the test questions such as the instructor, printed tests that accompany the textbook, or computer-generated test banks. Media refers to the delivery format such as hard copy, computer hard drive or CD/DVD, or Web/Internet.

Many consider instructor-prepared tests to be the best source. You prepare the test questions based upon what you have discussed in class or online, as well as what you have covered and hold your students responsible for from the textbook. This type of test most closely approximates what you have taught and what you perceive to be the performance objectives of the course. The major downside is that you may be "reinventing the wheel" if there are valid tests already available from other sources. Instructor-prepared tests can be offered as hard-copy tests or online through a course management system. Typically, instructors can also add their own questions to an online test.

Textbook-publisher prepared tests accompany nearly every modern textbook. Sometimes these are hard-copy tests, ready for the instructor to photocopy and administer; in other cases, the publisher provides the test on disk or makes it available for download from the company's Web site. The major advantage of these tests is that they are ready to use. Their major disadvantage is that the items are not in the instructor's words and, worse, they may not emphasize the aspects of the course the instructor considers most important. These tests are, naturally, based on the textbook and do not include in-class or online assignments, presentations, and discussions.

Computerized test banks also accompany nearly all textbooks today. Instead of complete, ready-to-administer tests, the test bank provides many questions from which you can choose and then generate a test. One advantage of using test banks is that you have control over the emphasis or weight of testing specific concepts or skills. You can also control the type of item, that is, true/false, fill-in, and so forth. Like the prepared tests, however, the items reflect only the textbook material and not the emphasis or language students have heard in class or online. However, as was noted above, many test generator systems allow individual instructors to add their own questions.

With Internet and online technologies, we can now deliver instruction to students in ways not available to us a decade ago. Likewise, we can conduct assessments in new and exciting ways. In some cases, as in distance education, all assessments might be online. In other situations, instructors use online assessments as an additional evaluation method. This accomplishes two important goals: (1) It gives instructors more tools with which to meet different student learning styles. (2) It provides opportunities for maximizing the validity of student evaluations through rechecks (test/retest) and comparisons of student learning in more than one mode.

Online tests may be part of a publisher's supplementary products, provided with a textbook adoption. These have the same content drawbacks as other publisher tests; that is, they may not have the intended content emphasis. The instructor cannot edit most of such tests, so they lack flexibility. They do, however, allow students to complete the assessments at times the instructor decides. Scoring is usually automatic, and students receive immediate feedback.

Some publishers provide "cartridges" for online course management systems such as Blackboard and WebCT. Instructors using these products can edit tests to add, delete, or revise items, as well as to adjust the relative weight given to items and to assessments. This gives the instructor much more control over the content and other aspects of the assessments.

Instructors creating their own online courses using a course management system have the greatest degree of control over the testing content, format, and weighting. The time required to develop the assessments, however, might be a major drawback. Scoring in course management systems is usually automatic and gives students their results along with feedback, depending on instructor choices.

Evaluating and Using Existing Objective Tests

In many cases, you will be using tests that you did not create. How do you evaluate those tests and decide how to use them in your course? What weight do you give them? When do you throw them out and start over?

Begin at the same place you would if you were creating them yourself: course planning. Determine which interim, unit, or overall intended outcomes you are going to test and when. Then examine the tests that you have available to you and decide where they will best fit. You might decide that some of the tests are not appropriate. Here are some common reasons.

- The items on the test do not match the information being presented in class.
- The items are skewed too heavily toward one concept, skill, or group of these.
- The items are poorly written. Students won't know what is being asked. (This is not common with major publishers.)
- The level of questioning is not appropriate. The items are too easy or too difficult.
- The test is the wrong length. It takes too much or too little time.
- The items emphasize only recall from the text. They do not ask students to do anything with their learning such as analyze, synthesize, or problem solve.

Solutions

If you cannot discard the tests and create ones that are more suitable, you do have some options. Some possible solutions include the following.

- Weight the class assignments more heavily than you weight the tests.
- Use portfolios and as many performance assignments as you can. Inform students that their essays, projects, reports, etc., will be an important part of their grade.
- Modify the test by deleting or lining through items that are confusing, too easy, or too difficult. Also, delete some items testing a given concept or skill if the test places too much emphasis on that area.
- Omit some of the tests and rely on the ones that are more appropriate.
- Supplement the tests with a few items that require more authentic performances from the students—items that require higher-level cognitive responses such as analyzing, synthesizing, and applying what has been learned. In addition to writing brief essays or paragraph responses, ask students to draw, chart, or diagram, as appropriate for the content.

Sources and Delivery of Authentic Assessments

Many instructors prefer to create their own authentic, or performance-based, assessments because they can quite easily zero in on the skills and knowledge they want students to demonstrate. Test-writing time is also much shorter than with objective tests, although evaluating students' work may take longer, especially if one includes the time required to develop sound, comprehensive rubrics.

Most authentic assessments belong to one of three types: performance tests, portfolios, and self-assessments. Performance tests ask students to use their learning in various authentic contexts. Examples of performances include

- completing a tax return for a small business
- debating a political issue in class
- making a sales presentation
- collecting botanical samples and assembling them in a project or reporting on them
- performing data entry for a keyboarding class
- creating a PowerPoint presentation that would be used to train therapy dog trainers
- designing a report format for an annual report
- writing a screenplay
- painting a portrait

Portfolios represent a long-term view of student learning. This approach provides a view of student improvement and progress, as well as material for overall performance assessment. What goes into the portfolio varies greatly by course, instructor, and student. Some possibilities are essays and reports (rough drafts and subsequent drafts); self-assessments and peer evaluations; notes, diagrams, artwork, or photographs of artwork; journaling, observation, or interview notes and summaries; completed forms; and disks or CDs with spreadsheets, databases, and other computer work.

> "The ultimate goal of the educational system is to shift to the individual the burden of pursuing his education."
> —John W. Gardner

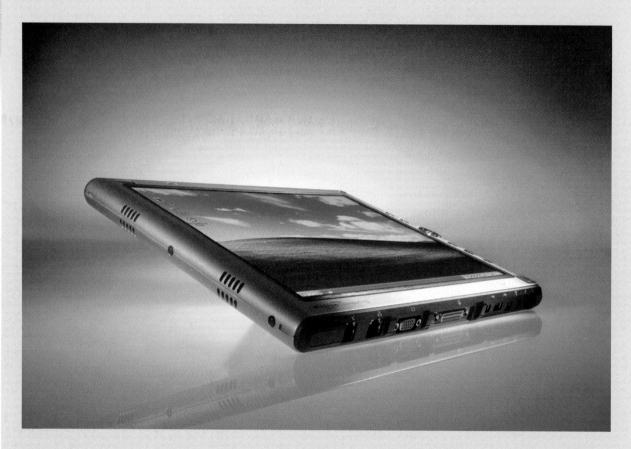

The hardware that is producing the greatest revolution in instruction and learning technologies has to be the Tablet PC. These small, lightweight, go-anywhere computers use a touch screen for input. Some models are convertible, with attached keyboards. Others are "slates," which do not have keyboards, although most can be connected to one.

Users write on the touch screen with a stylus (penlike device), although one model also allows finger-touch entry. A program called Microsoft Windows® Journal and some others will convert the user's handwriting to text. The system allows students to take notes in class, sketch ideas or diagrams, and move images and text around on a page with the stylus. Describing its features, Microsoft says: "Record, organize, and search notes—even sync them with audio/video recordings—creating the ultimate three-ring binder." Its size and functions, as well as support for wireless networks, mean it can be used in many more situations than a regular notebook PC and can share views and documents. Now students can write field notes directly onto/into their computers instead of using a clipboard with pen and paper!

This description of the Tablet PC may sound a little ho-hum, but the applications that we are seeing in education are anything but. The following examples should give you a much better idea of how these applications are changing instruction and learning. The question we think you'll ask shortly will be "When can I have one?"

Student-Side Uses

One fairly well known project comes from MIT. For its iCampus Project, students used Tablet PCs as part of a mechanical engineering competition. Rather than gathering in one place with pens, papers, and whiteboard to brainstorm, and then manually transfer designs into a CAD program, students sketched designs and entered math equations directly into Tablet PCs. Revisions were much faster, and the connectivity kept them communicating.

Another example comes from Texas. At the University of Texas at Austin, Geographic Information Systems (GIS) students used Tablet PCs to complete some of their fieldwork. ArcGIS software allowed them to make notes directly onto maps.

Tablet PCs will improve student efficiencies in any note-taking situations, but, as these examples demonstrate, they are especially useful in courses that ask students to create drawings, charts, or other visual representations.

Instructor-Side Uses

On the instructor side of this picture, Tablet PCs add efficiency and improve communications. They can take you beyond your current computer use in the classroom, even if you are using projected images from your laptop. For example, imagine yourself in the lecture hall with the display of your Tablet PC projected onto the wall or screen. The image is an anatomy image that you animate to demonstrate blood flow or cell changes or some organ functions. You change the display to an illustration and mark it up with your stylus to emphasize major points. Then you switch to a blank screen and write out a formula or calculation or notes in response to a question from a student. Your next display is a diagram, and you drag images into various portions of the diagram to demonstrate relationships. Then you seamlessly incorporate Excel, Java, Web animations, and some simulations into the presentation. After this, maybe you display four review questions and ask students to respond to the questions, and if they have PCs networked with you, they will enter their answers right then and there. All done? E-mail the entire lecture to all the students for them to review, annotate, or expand.

Of course, the Tablet PC provides you with all the course management, communication, word processing, Internet, and other tools that you already rely on. And like the students, you can use your Tablet PC in the field, making observations and notes for your next lecture, evaluating student participation, or commenting on, well, anything.

Tablet PCs are now available from at least seven different manufacturers, and specialty software increases continually.

Portfolios offer other advantages. They involve students in the assessment process to a greater degree. Students are more aware of their progress and performance, and more able to monitor their improvement. In addition, the variation that portfolios allow contributes to increased connections with students' learning styles.

Self-assessments ask students directly about their learning, participation, skills, or accomplishments. Students might respond orally or in writing. Questions to address might include the following.

- What can you do now that you couldn't do before this activity (lesson, course, etc.)?
- How well will you be able to apply this learning (skill, approach, technique, process, etc.) to specific situations in the real world?
- Describe your ability to work collaboratively with others.
- How confident are you that you can _____ (do something)?

Developing Reliable and Valid Tests

As with many other aspects of effective teaching, the major work in creating authentic assessments is the thinking part, the planning. This process consists of three steps.

- **Step one: Define instructional targets and accomplishments.**
  Begin by describing in writing the type of product you expect from the learner. What content areas will you emphasize? What can or should the learner be able to do?
- **Step two: Design an illustrative task.**
  The main outcome of step two is to generate an assessment "task" that satisfies two principal criteria: (1) the task is challenging and motivating for learners to pursue; and (2) the task is representative of the performances or skills you intend to assess. Tasks that meet these criteria reflect the tasks students will encounter in the world outside academia. The tasks have more than one acceptable answer or solution, they are relevant, and they accommodate multiple intelligences. Another important characteristic is that the tasks require students to exhibit metacognitive skills: they reveal how students go about solving a problem.
- **Step three: Design a scoring rubric.**
  A rubric is a predetermined set of criteria that is used as a guideline for evaluating a student's performance. We use rubrics as tools to help evaluate performances fairly and consistently. Rubrics also have the advantage of giving students a clear, direct communication about your expectations. Any assessment that is not a "right or wrong answer" test can benefit from using a rubric.

Rubrics generally consist of several criteria and several performance levels. Instructors evaluate the student's performance for each of the criteria, assigning a level for them. Figure 5.5 shows an example for an essay in a political science class.

CRITERIA	POOR (1)	GOOD (2)	EXCELLENT (3)
Relevance to current events			
Organization of points			
Quality of analysis			
Quality of resources			
Originality of topic and/or approach			
Clarity of writing style			

Table 5.5. Sample Essay Rubric.

In this example, the performance levels are "poor," "good," and "excellent." In many cases, instructors write a description for each criterion for each level. In other words, they define "poor," "good," and "excellent" for each criterion.

Since the criteria are not all equally important, a rubric usually includes a weighting for each one. In the sample rubric above, for example, the originality of topic and/or approach might be worth only half of the value of quality of analysis or only three-fourths of the value of clarity of writing style. To accommodate these differences, assign values to each criterion. One easy way to do this is to assign a "1" to the least important criterion and then assign higher values or weights to the remaining criteria. Figure 5.6 displays a completed rubric for a student paper using weighted values in our sample rubric.

CRITERIA	POOR (1)	GOOD (2)	EXCELLENT (3)	WEIGHT	TOTAL
Relevance to current events		x		1	2
Organization of points			x	2	6
Quality of analysis			x	3	9
Quality of resources	x			2	2
Originality of topic and/or approach			x	1	3
Clarity of writing style		x		1	2
Total (possible 33)					24

Figure 5.6. Sample Essay Rubric with Weighted Values.

In this example, the essay has scored 24 out of a possible 33, or 73 percent.

As a final step in developing your rubric, test it with a few trial essays and adjust the rubric as needed. Maybe you need five levels rather than three. Maybe you discover a criterion that you tend to use, but forgot to put in the rubric's list. Once you are satisfied with the way the rubric works, rescore the trial essays and the remaining ones.

The rubric illustrated above works well for a concepts course in which the performance being assessed centers on building a body of knowledge and being able to apply it in problem-solving and analytical thinking situations. Designing a rubric for a skills course such as medical assisting or word processing or stainless steel welding, in which the performance being assessed is a set of hands-on skills, requires an additional step. You need to confirm your standards with the criteria applied in the workplace, which sometimes involves a certification exam. Here are some approaches to consider.

- Collect examples of student and expert work that span a wide range of quality.
- Interview experts in the discipline on how they define quality.
- Examine characteristics or descriptors of the work that distinguish good from poor samples.
- Differentiate between the essential and nonessential aspects of successful performance.
- If a specific certification is desirable, locate as much information about it as possible and incorporate the certification skills in your assessment and rubric.

Determining the scoring standards for evaluating quality work is really the essence of alternative assessment. Without rubrics, the assessment task remains an instructional activity.

Evaluating Existing Tests

Acknowledging market demand, publishers increasingly are offering performance-based tests with their textbooks. If prebuilt tests are available to you, either from a publisher or perhaps from your department, consider the suggestions in Figure 5.7 to help you decide how to use them.

CRITERIA FOR ENSURING QUALITY OF EXISTING PERFORMANCE TESTS
✓ Do the assessments require students to use and exhibit their knowledge base, technical skills, and problem-solving abilities?
✓ Do the assessments match well with your course outcomes?
✓ Do students' ways of producing the products approximate that of the experts as closely as is feasible?
✓ Are examples of good and "almost good" quality products available to learners?
✓ Are complete rubrics provided for grading the assessments? If so, do the rubrics include criterion checklists prepared in consultation with excellent performers, those who receive the performers' products, and experts in the field?

Figure 5.7. Criteria for Evaluating Performance Tests.

Solutions

Other than the obvious solution of preparing your own authentic assessment should existing tests prove unsatisfactory, consider one of these options.

- In certain courses, for example, a marketing course, an ideal authentic assessment might be having students develop a marketing campaign. However, this option may not be practical because you lack the necessary software or other classroom resources. Instead, offer a simulation that has students think through the process and document their thinking.

- If the rubric is incomplete, add the missing material. Doing so would likely take less time than creating a new rubric on your own.
- Some performance assessments may be excellent examples of authentic, on-the-job work, but they lack a foundation skills component such as a written description of the student's product, a written evaluation of the finished product, or an oral presentation describing the work. In such instances, add the requirement, making sure the expectations are clear and complete.

Administering Tests

Students do not follow directions!

The statement above is a common refrain among instructors. As such, it directs us to the importance of addressing test administration issues, including the clarity of written and verbal directions. Unclear or misleading directions can affect students' scores unjustifiably, thus invalidating the test.

Administration Issues for Objective Tests

Objective tests are among the easiest for instructors to administer and score, especially with a little preparation. Yet they also require proctoring and extra attention to the clarity of the instructions, both written and verbal.

Some form of proctoring should be operating throughout the assessment session, whether by the instructor or another reliable, trustworthy, mature person. The proctor's job is to maintain order, ensure a quiet test environment, and handle any problems or disruptions. The proctor watches for any instances of cheating and should know the college's policy for handling them. All assessments, even those given to classes of very mature, honest students, need proctoring so that the data is considered credible for any future use such as in program evaluation.

Instructions for the test made verbally by the instructor or proctor must be absolutely clear. Students need to hear the procedures, even if they are the same as for previous assessments. They should know how to mark the test, how much time they will have, and what tools they may use such as calculators, dictionaries, their notes, or other class materials. In a course session prior to the assessment, tell the students about the test, including material to be covered; the structure of the test (if applicable), such as "Part I is calculations and Part II is word problems"; how you will score the test, for example, how many points will be assigned to each item; how the percentage or other score will be calculated; and (if applicable) how the letter grades will correspond to scores. Give them any test-taking tips that you can. Should they guess? Should they go through the test two or three times? Should they read each question and any response choices at least twice? Tell them what will not be tolerated: cell phones, iPod®s or Walkman®s, talking, food, coffee, and cheating of any sort. If the test will use bubble forms for electronic scoring, tell students exactly which form and where to get them and what they cost (or if you are going to provide them) and tell them what type of pen or pencil they need to bring for marking them. Also, give them clear directions about marking on these forms and what to do if they want to change an answer.

At the time of the test, repeat the administration information before distributing the tests, as well as additional instructions, for example, to place all books and materials under their seats, or to distribute themselves so that only two (or some other number) students are at each table, and so forth.

Tell students what to do when they finish the test. If they finish the test before the allotted time is up, can they give you their work and leave? Or should they wait until the entire class is finished? When you announce that it is time to stop, be clear and firm. Then tell students what you want them to do with their papers, for example, pass them to the aisle, bring them to you, or exchange them for grading.

If you are administering an online assessment, provide students with clear information regarding the time(s) that the test will be available to them, any necessary password to access the test, whether the test is timed, and what will happen if they use more than the allotted time.

Administration Issues for Performance-Based Assessments

"A good education should leave much to be desired."

—Alan Gregg

The points made previously about test administration also apply to performance-based assessments that are conducted in testing situations, usually essay tests or lab or field tests, with a few additions.

Administration of essay tests should include information about blue books and other materials that students should bring with them. Also, many students will benefit from practice questions and model answers being made available before the test so that they have a better understanding of what will be expected of them.

When giving a hands-on test in a software lab, the instructor or lab assistant should make sure that all needed equipment is working properly; the programs required for the assessment are installed and operating as expected; necessary passwords or access codes are programmed; and any disks, CDs, or other test materials are ready for the students. Use proctors to prevent cheating, or if proctors are not available, provide different versions of the data file students use in completing the assessment. For example, for a desktop publishing test requiring students to create and format a newsletter, distribute three different data files containing the text for the document. Enforce a time limit, since it is important for students to understand that the workplace is deadline-driven and each person is evaluated not only on the actual work done but also on the amount of time taken to complete a task. Be sure that students know what to do with their finished assessment, such as save the file to a disk and submit it, save the report and e-mail it to the instructor, or print a hard copy.

Preparation for science lab or field tests can be very complex. Be sure all needed samples, specimens, tools, materials, and whatever else might be relevant to that assessment are ready and well organized before the assessment begins. Some of these assessments will lend themselves well to reporting forms or answer sheets. Others will result in a product, a labeled collection, drawings or diagrams, and so forth. Procedures are important aspects of many such tests, and sometimes the assessment asks students to solve a problem a certain way. For example, an automotive repair class might be asked to fix a carburetor, with the intended outcome being a working carburetor. Students should know what to expect and be prepared to participate in the assessment. Some performance-based assessments will need specific plans and procedures that the instructor establishes. Examples include debates, role-playing, recitals, demonstrations, and oral interviews.

Scoring Tests and Dealing with Complaints

You can minimize the number and severity of complaints from students about their grades if you communicate your grading criteria as clearly as you possibly can at the beginning of the course. Your grading process or criteria should be easy for students to understand. Repeat them immediately prior to the test administration.

With traditional cognitive tests, student responses are either correct or not. You will not need to worry about in-depth discussions of why a particular student's response is not acceptable. However, students may wish to argue that none of the choices on an item is correct, or that more than one answer is correct. By the time you have administered a test two or three times, you will probably have corrected or deleted such items. Until then, keep an open mind about these items—neither you nor the publisher of your textbook is infallible— and adjust student scores accordingly. The key might have an error, or the item and its response choices may be subject to more than one interpretation. And be patient. Remember that students who question an item's response are thinking about the possibilities.

You might, on occasion, administer a test whose level of difficulty is not appropriate. Students do not usually complain about tests that are easy. They will, however, object to tests that are too difficult, that is, tests with questions that are ambiguous or that include material not covered. Judge whether a test is too difficult by the overall performance of the class. If all students have performed poorly, you might need to adjust your grading criteria for this assessment . . . and adjust the assessment or the course pace for the next term.

One of the perceived drawbacks of performance assessments is that their administration or completion and scoring can be much more time consuming than traditional tests. Another potential problem is that inconsistencies in grading can creep in. Using rubrics helps solve both of these issues.

Rubrics are designed to make quality work "definable" and more objective. Over the weeks of the course, you will have shown students several examples of quality work. Further, if students have had input into the standard-setting process, they are much more likely to understand clearly what is expected of them in a performance and what distinguishes "A" work from "B" work, making grading complaints much less likely. Indeed, one of the main goals of alternative assessment is to help students internalize the standards and recognize if their work satisfies the criteria for quality work. This is exactly what is expected and needed in real-life job situations.

Using Course Management Systems to Evaluate Student Performance in Online Classes

Course management systems such as Blackboard and WebCT include tools for creating assessments. Prepackaged courses include tests for the course, but instructors can write their own items if they wish. The systems will score the forced-choice items, that is, the multiple choice, true/false, matching, fill-in, and ordering items. Students get immediate feedback on their performance on these tests, and the scores are automatically placed in the grade book where the instructor can view them. Assessments can be password protected and they can be timed. Most instructors administer these tests as open-book assessments. Using the time-limit feature, however, is one way to preclude students from looking up every answer in the text.

Online courses also allow instructors to administer additional tests that the instructor must score. Items that require short answers or short essay answers, for example, are easy to create.

Students in courses requiring other physical work can submit it online. Longer papers, including graphics, can be submitted online. Blackboard's digital dropbox makes such submission relatively friendly.

Instructors who assign collaborative projects can require students to use group communication and presentation systems on the CMS. Students can also submit digital photographs of their projects, making evaluation of physical projects feasible, although not perfect. The systems will accept short digital videos and sound files as well. Of course, if you are certain your system is adequately virus proofed, you can allow students to submit work as attachments to e-mail messages.

Instructors can use the grade book in the course management system or some other grade book. Online grade books have the advantage of automatically entering student scores for any assessment they can score. They also will allow the instructor to specify weight values for each assessment. Students can monitor their own progress and see how they are doing compared to the class averages.

Online grade books are downloadable. Instructors can save the grade book data and open it in an Excel or other spreadsheet program. Once in the spreadsheet, scores can be adjusted and instructor-scored assessments can be included. Instructors who teach distance education or hybrid courses that require in-class final examinations, for example, can enter the final exam scores into the same spreadsheet that they've saved with students' online scores.

The lesser demand on instructors' time for small classes allows for additional types of assessment. CMS programs allow live chats with a group of students or with individual students. The program will record the entire chat, and the instructor can later review the session and credit students for various levels of participation. If class size is sufficiently small, an instructor can conduct one-on-one chat-session assessments. Doing this requires significant organizational skills and planning. Sessions need to be scheduled by appointment, and questions need to be at least partially prepared in advance. The advantage is, of course, that this approach provides distance students an opportunity to demonstrate their learning in an individual situation. Students and instructor have the ability to direct or redirect the topic of discussion. Students can demonstrate what they have, indeed, learned, rather than having to document via an "objective" test what they have not learned.

> *"I forget what I was taught. I only remember what I have learned."*
>
> —Patrick White

The potential for cheating is a problem that bothers distance education instructors to varying degrees. How can you know that a student is doing his or her own work? How can you be sure that a student has not shared the answers of an online test with his or her peers? Maybe you can't. You can, however, ask students to verify or certify to you that they have done their own work, completed their own exercises themselves, and taken the exams on their own. Sharing answers can be minimized by setting up tests so that items are drawn at random from large pools of items. Each student will be presented with a different set of items. As previously mentioned, setting a time limit on the assessments will also help reduce potential for cheating.

Using Assessment Results and Feedback to Improve the Course and Your Teaching

A critical function of assessment and evaluation is improvement of a course and the instructor's teaching. Use student performance, student evaluations of your teaching and the course, and evaluations by your colleagues to identify opportunities for improvement.

Student Performance

Every student assessment is also a course and instructor assessment. Following each student assessment, examine the overall performance. Did students do very well on one part of the assessment and poorly on another? Maybe the instruction dwells too long on one part of the content and less time could be dedicated to that course aspect next time. A finding like this could also indicate that certain content or skills may need to be retaught, perhaps using a different approach. Did students do poorly on the exam as a whole? Try to diagnose the problem and identify whether the difficulty lay in student time and application, a difficult or complex reading assignment, a high number of new concepts to master, or a vague or confusing instructor presentation that needs to be reworked.

Student Evaluations of the Course and Your Teaching

The value of student evaluations of courses and instructor performance will depend on the questions and the manner in which they are presented. An instructor could easily write an evaluation form of two to three hundred questions. We recommend, however, that you limit the questions to a maximum of twenty, and then give students an opportunity to make open comments. Questions will vary from course to course because course components vary. Did the course use teaching assistants? Team teaching? Guest speakers? Field trips? Studio or laboratory work? Computer lab? Online assignments? You will want to get student feedback on each major component.

Figure 5.8 presents a list of twenty questions that could be used to evaluate the instructor and the components common to most courses: textbook and other readings, lectures and discussions, assignments, and assessments. You would ask students to indicate their level of agreement with each question, using a scale of one to five, with one being strongly disagree and five being strongly agree.

STUDENT EVALUATION OF COURSE
_____ 1. Instructor treats students fairly and with respect.
_____ 2. Instructor makes expectations and course objectives clear to students.
_____ 3. Instructor's lectures and explanations are well organized, clear, and direct.
_____ 4. Instructor engages the interest of the students.
_____ 5. The instructor uses clear, interesting examples that aid understanding and remembering.
_____ 6. Instructor sees when students need additional explanations and provides them.
_____ 7. Instructor cares about students' learning.
_____ 8. Instructor guides students to focus on the most important aspects of the course.
_____ 9. Instructor gives clear directions or instructions.
_____ 10. The course environment is appropriate for learning.
_____ 11. The textbook for this course is clear and understandable.
_____ 12. Additional readings, Web resources, and other materials were appropriate for the course and promoted understanding of course concepts and/or development of skills.
_____ 13. The course includes enough activities to promote learning.
_____ 14. Activities and exercises are interesting.
_____ 15. Activities are clearly related to course content and objectives.
_____ 16. Assignments are valuable and students learn from them.
_____ 17. Workload for this course was reasonable.
_____ 18. Exams and quizzes were fair.
_____ 19. Exams and quizzes assessed my learning accurately.
_____ 20. I am pleased with my participation and learning in this course.

Figure 5.8. Questions for Evaluating a Course and the Instructor.

Some assessments simply list an aspect of the course and ask the student to rate each aspect on a scale from one to five, with one being poor and five being excellent. Here is a sample list.

1. Instructor knowledge of topic
2. Lecture organization
3. Speaking skills of instructor
4. Clarity of lecture

5. Instructor enthusiasm
6. Instructor interest in students
7. Discussion leading skills of instructor
8. Instructor respect for students
9. Instructor patience
10. Instructor responses to questions
11. Textbook clarity
12. Textbook reading level
13. End of chapter quizzes
14. Other readings
15. Interest level of assignments
16. Variety of assignments
17. Time allowed for assignments
18. Learning gained from assignments
19. Fairness of grading
20. Test difficulty level

Peer Evaluation and Coaching

An underutilized but important way of evaluating one's teaching effectiveness is by having other instructors observe your classes and give you feedback. This process is called peer evaluation and coaching. Peer evaluation is an integral part of some school cultures, but not as welcome in others. Even in the latter type of institution, you can invite a peer to observe your class and give you constructive criticism.

Some keys to an effective system of peer evaluation and coaching include the following.

1. Establish clear criteria. Simply having someone watch your on-campus class or sit in on a live chat in your online class has value, but is more valuable if the person has some focus during the visit. For example, you may wonder if you appear well organized or if you call on all your students. If your fellow instructor is aware of these points in advance, the feedback will be more useful.

2. The goal of the peer review is mutual benefit. You and your peer(s) should visit each other's class; this is not a one-way street. Serving in the role of an evaluator of another's class and watching someone else's strengths and areas needing improvement helps you become a better instructor.

3. Peers should give you a report for your professional improvement. These are not to be used for administrative evaluation, unless that is part of your contractual agreement. An important goal of peer evaluation is improvement without threat of penalty.

4. Peer evaluation will benefit from expanding beyond a single classroom visit. Arrange regular visits, including outside-class activities such as post-visit conferencing, chatting about teaching methods, and reviewing your syllabus and tests. Your peer can move into the role of mentor to you, helping you to develop as an effective instructor through the years.

CHAPTER SUMMARY

- Assessments serve multiple roles in the teaching/learning process: indicating what students have learned, comparing students, motivating students, guiding and evaluating instruction, determining grades, and meeting accreditation requirements.

- A comprehensive assessment strategy addresses the choices of pre-assessment, final course outcomes assessment, unit or part tests, and interim checkpoints.

- Two major categories of assessments are traditional cognitive tests and performance-based tests.

  ◆ Traditional cognitive tests are usually forced-choice tests, require little time for administration or scoring, and are best for testing students' recall.

  ◆ Performance-based testing is more authentic and may include the testing of student accomplishments through essays, hands-on demonstrations, labs, interviews, and a huge number of other possibilities. These may take more time to plan, prepare, administer, and evaluate, but educators generally deem these tests to be more valid indicators of students' learning than traditional cognitive tests.

- Creating a grading system requires assigning a value or weight to each assessment and entering the data and grade calculation formulas into a spreadsheet or database program. In addition to measuring learners' achievement of the course content outcomes, instructors may choose to evaluate nonachievement factors such as effort. Most educational experts recommend that instructors grade students based only on the attainment of content-related outcomes.

- Some instructors create their own objective tests, but a majority use the tests their textbook publisher provides, either in hard copy, CD, or online format. Some publishers also include tests in the course cartridges they provide for online course management systems such as Blackboard and WebCT. Instructors can modify the tests if they choose.

- Instructors tend to create their own authentic tests because they can tailor them specifically to their instruction. Although writing time is shorter, grading time is longer. Developing an authentic assessment involves the steps of defining the instructional target, designing an illustrative task, and designing a scoring rubric.

- Key issues in administering and grading tests are providing clear directions, implementing proctoring and other techniques to prevent cheating, ensuring that the necessary software and other materials are available, listening with an open mind to students' complaints about scoring, and using strong rubrics for evaluation.

- Course management systems can accommodate both objective and authentic types of assessments. Objective tests are scored immediately and scores are entered automatically into the system grade book. Authentic assessments in a CMS could include papers, collaborative projects using the group communication feature, and short digital videos and sound files.

- Do not overlook the importance of using assessment results and specific student evaluations to improve your course and your teaching.

- Consider asking a peer to observe you and critique your teaching effectiveness. Be sure to make that person aware of your goals and any specific methods or behaviors you want evaluated.

Think About It: Evaluate Your Assessment Program

How do you know when you have an effective assessment plan? The three big questions are

1. Does it assess what I want to assess? In other words, does it assess how well students have reached intended outcomes?
2. Is the assessment an accurate reflection of students' learning?
3. Does it provide the information I need for proceeding with instruction and/or evaluating students?

After these come questions about the length of the assessment, time allowed, physical environment of administration, clarity of instructions, and so forth. That said, use the checklist on the next page to evaluate your assessment program. Then devise solutions for problematic areas.

Course Name: _____			
Assessment Component: Ongoing, Formative Assessments	Yes	No	Solution
1. Are a sufficient number of assessments included to keep you on track?			
2. Are the assessments sufficiently short and spaced out so they are not burdensome?			
3. Are the assessments conducted at the appropriate, useful times in the flow of the course?			
4. Is there an assessment for each major intended outcome?			
5. Are the assessments varied in type, format, and length? In other words, have you varied them sufficiently enough that you will have data on student performance even if a student does not work well with one type of assessment or another?			
6. Do assessments address any interdisciplinary learning such as writing or technology skills?			
7. Is the level of difficulty appropriate? Not so difficult as to intimidate students or dampen their motivation? And not so easy as to mislead them about their accomplishments?			
8. Do students have the opportunity to provide feedback on the assessments?			
9. Do the assessments ask for more than recall?			
10. Do the assessments ask students to apply what they have learned in authentic contexts?			
11. Do the assessments include tasks or items related to knowledge, skills, critical thinking or problem solving, and student attitudes or motivation?			
12. Do the assessments provide the information to plan the next steps |such as reviews or changes in activities or assignments? (Did/Will you use it? Do you have a plan for using it?)			
13. Do the assessments meet your school's requirements?			
Assessment Component: Overall End-of-Course Assessment			
14. Is the assessment comprehensive? Does it address all the major intended outcomes of the course?			
15. Is the assessment culminating? Does it bring together the knowledge and skills developed throughout the course?			
16. Does it meet your school's requirements?			
17. Does the assessment require students to apply what they have learned in an authentic context?			
18. Will this assessment together with the smaller assessments provide you with sufficient information to evaluate students' overall performance?			
Online Assessments			
In addition to the questions above, consider the following: 19. Are the assessments easily accessible?			
20. Is the online assessment platform (program) easy for students to use?			
21. Are explanations for completing the online assessment clear and direct?			
22. Is the online assessment nonthreatening?			
23. Does the assessment provide students with immediate feedback?			

Discussion Questions

1. Should instructors use prepared tests from publishers? Why? Why not?
2. Do you agree with the philosophy of assessment points presented on pages 158–159? Why? Why not?
3. Is the development, administration, and evaluation of authentic tests worth the time and effort involved? Why? Why not?
4. Should grading systems include the nonachievement factors discussed in the chapter? How do you justify including them or omitting them? In which situations does including nonachievement factors make the most sense? Which factors are more important? If you include effort, behavior, and attendance in your grading system, how much weight should each component have?

Field Work

1. Obtain all the testing materials available for your textbook from the publisher. Compare the assessments with the textbook content. Compare them with your course action plan and intended outcomes. How well aligned are the assessments with the course you have planned?
2. Which kinds of assessments do your department colleagues use? Check with instructors teaching the same type of course, for example, a computer applications course or an allied health course, to find out how they assess similar skills.
3. Do employers in your area expect colleges to teach good work habits along with specific job skills? Research what employers in fields related to your courses say about which skills are most important to assess.

Professional Portfolio: Design a Rubric

Develop an authentic assessment as part of a final exam for a course you currently teach or have previously taught. Be sure to include accommodations for students with disabilities. Then, following the three-step plan presented in the chapter, write a scoring rubric that includes several criteria and performance levels, along with a weighting for each one.

Appendix

E-Learning (Distance Learning): Frequently Asked Questions

"You go online to get information. You stay online because of the relationships you form."

What is e-Learning?

E-learning refers to instructional activities delivered or mediated by electronic technology. The term is often used interchangeably with distance learning, online learning, Web-based learning, and computer- or multimedia-based learning. When used in the context of online learning, e-learning refers to a full, Web-based distance learning course or to the online elements of a hybrid course (a hybrid course uses the best features of face-to-face instruction with online modules and learning management). These instructional elements are accessed via the Internet and can contain reading material, interactive readings, video segments, Flash tutorials, assignments, projects, and tests.

Online, hybrid, traditional course? What is the difference?

Traditional courses are on-campus courses typically presented in lecture or lab settings using face-to-face instruction. Online courses are partially or completely off-campus courses delivered by Web course management systems (CMS) that contain self-directed learning modules, sometimes referred to as application blocks. Hybrid courses use a combination of both approaches.

In traditional courses, students physically have to come to the course. In online or hybrid learning, the course goes to them. Online or hybrid course elements are delivered using a Web-based learning platform. Online distance learning can be delivered anywhere, at anytime, to anyone. Such flexibility is not possible in traditional learning.

What are the benefits of online learning?

- Online learning shifts the time and place of learning and allows students to learn when it is convenient for them. As a result of this flexibility, online courses can reach more students.
- By necessity, online courses provide more personalized coaching from both other students and from the instructor.
- Online courses typically provide more alternative resources and learning aids.

- Online courses require more communication with the instructor and with groups of students (though not face to face).

Which is better – online, hybrid, or traditional?

Most research comparing the three instructional models has shown no significant difference in student learning. All three types of courses fill a need from the student's and the school's perspectives. Online courses extend their geographical boundaries and go where the students reside, allowing students to learn at their own pace. They give students creative control over the course. More importantly, online learning supports a profound increase in communications and interactions. Web or online learning facilitates more student-to-teacher, student-to-student, and student-to-content interactions. Traditional face-to-face instruction offers more "social" learning and learning that benefits from inspiring lectures, live group interaction, modeling, and discussion. It tends to incorporate strategies for teaching higher-order thinking goals but that may change with improved instructional media on the Web.

The trend for individualization in all venues is the key; individualization is blending the approaches and blurring traditional course lines. Instructors should concentrate on the strengths of each format and use the learning characteristics of each medium to its best potential. All three formats are here to stay.

What platforms are available for online and hybrid teaching?

Successful Web courses typically rely on the usability and effectiveness of a course management system for course delivery. A CMS provides a standard course structure that is easy to navigate and understand. WebCT and Blackboard are the most frequently adopted CMS platforms, but there are many from which to choose. Here are a few: Asymetrix Toolbook, Ecollege, Learning Space, The Learning Manager, Top Class, Web Course in a Box, and All Students Must Learn. All platforms offer relatively standard and comparable tools for instructors and students.

What standard tools do Course Management Systems offer?

Tools designed to encourage participation, interaction, communication are:

Journals
Announcement boards
Help documents
Real-time chat
Whiteboards that support mathematical symbols
PowerPoint presentations with audio
Bulletin boards
Discussion forums
Drop box for submitting documents
Content applications blocks or modules
Linked Web resources

Tools designed to help deliver and structure the course are:

Syllabus
Class rosters
Grade book
Calendar
Resource lists
Import and export capabilities
Quiz and testing platforms

What are learning cartridges and e-packs?

Publishers use different names to refer to their prepackaged course materials. These course materials come preloaded in a CMS and support a particular text or media product. They typically include a syllabus, assignment sheets, course objectives, Web links, PowerPoint slides, additional readings, activities, projects, and quizzes.

How do the course management systems handle interactive and multimedia elements?

Interactive and multimedia elements are essential and often replace the instructional activities (lectures and demonstrations) typically provided by a face-to-face instructor. These can include video/audio clips, PowerPoint presentations with discussion questions and audio, Flash animations, links to CD/DVD materials, links to online work, and Web-programmed multimedia. Often, instead of delivering packaged content such as a lecture, these content modules encourage students to uncover the material through research and inquiry methods. Currently, CMS products are somewhat limited in their capability to present and manage dynamic interactive learning activities. The developers of major platforms are working on systems to integrate e-workbooks and multimedia in their systems.

What are some tips for creating effective courses?
* Set up virtual office hours and keep them.
* Modularize the content and identify clear start and stop points.
* Don't just put a lot of paper documents online. Be selective about which papers and what information will be useful and accessed by the learners. Post documents in HTML format.
* Consider creating a separate e-mail account for class e-mails. (Note that both Blackboard and WebCT include e-mail accounts.)
* Create or provide a variety of interactive experiences.
* Make sure students know exactly what they are to do and when they are to do it.
* Given that your content is likely to be geared toward the average learner, add remediation and enrichment activities for those who need them.
* Make Web assignments and group chat activities mandatory but offer students some choice on how to complete the assignments.

- Provide frequent, regular feedback via e-mail or other venues throughout the course and especially at the end of sessions and modules. Make sure that students always know what to do next.
- Require students to check their e-mail every day.
- Place copyright disclaimers on pages where intellectual property rights are involved.
- Use links as a way of adding content to your course.

What are some guidelines for making your first online course a success?

Recognizing that the teaching environment is different, you may find it challenging to teach an online course for the first time. In particular, you will need to manage your time in a new way. Here are suggestions to consider that will help make your first online class a success.

- Limit the number of students enrolled in your online class. While there is not a universal class size limit for an online course, twenty students per instructor is the limit many schools have adopted. As class size increases, the number of communications between the instructor and each student decreases, thus reducing the instructor's effectiveness. The inability to maintain regular student/instructor communications contributes to an increased student dropout rate and/or the inability of the student to master the performance objectives.
- Set up regular checkpoints to indicate where students need to be with regard to required assignments. Frequent monitoring helps minimize student procrastination. It also serves as a signal that you need to communicate with a student who misses a deadline.
- Provide guidelines for student user names and passwords. To function in the world of the Internet, individuals must struggle with a variety of user names, passwords, and PIN numbers. Anyone who has forgotten any of them knows how frustrating and time-consuming it can be to correct the situation. Suggest that for a user name in your online class, students use the first letter of their first name and their last name. Depending on the CMS used, there may or may not be a period after the first letter of their first name. For passwords, have students use the last four or five numbers of their social security number.
- Provide alternatives for assessing how students will function in an online environment. If possible, meet with your students for an in-person orientation session at the opening of the online class to reinforce what they must do to successfully complete the course and the role that you will play to make sure they are not falling behind.
- Do not customize the course too much. Many instructors using a CMS want to change the graphics, the screen background color, the introduction/announcement page, etc. Leave these things for your second or third online course.
- Keep your assessment plan simple! Stick to the basics; have the students transmit only critical items to be graded. Do not bury yourself in

attempting to evaluate every single thing the students do. Use peer-to-peer evaluation where appropriate.

- Where possible, use the support materials the publishing company provides. The next time around, make changes based on your first experience.
- Get feedback from your students. What did they like? What could be changed? How? Did they accomplish their goals? Document any changes you will make the next time the course is offered.

Are course management systems difficult to learn?

Learning to use a course management system is similar to learning how to use application software such as a word processor, spreadsheet, database, and/or graphic presentation package. The basic features will likely meet your needs, but the more you learn about the enhancements and special functions of the course management system, the more powerful an application it becomes.

Whether you are using Blackboard, WebCT, or some other course management system, it is imperative that you know how the system functions, which features are available to you and to your students, and where to go for help. Generally, schools that offer online courses have a staff person who coordinates online courses and provides workshops or seminars on the course management system being used by the school. Another way to gain the necessary knowledge and expertise to be an effective online instructor is to team teach a course with an experienced instructor.

Still another alternative is to enroll in an online course either as a guest or student the quarter or semester before your class is offered. You will experience how the system functions from a student's point of view and get countless ideas about how to set up your course for success.

Does the publisher of the course materials provide any support?

Most publishers provide a Help Desk or Hotline support to assist you. Here are examples of questions about the online class that can be answered by the publisher's representative(s).

- Of the interactive work and quizzes posted, what should be graded and what are the alternatives for keeping an online grade book?
- How do I change the course objectives, the syllabus, and the assignments provided by the publisher?
- How can I add quizzes and change existing quiz questions?
- How do I use the Dropbox feature to have students transmit work done offline?
- How can I change the Welcome page?
- How do I add/delete students from the class?
- How do I hide/unhide icons?

In addition to onsite support and support from the publisher, the company that owns the course management system you are using provides opportunities for teachers to learn how to use the features. For example, Blackboard offers a Web site that includes a dedicated Help Desk. To access this Web site, go to: http://cartridges.blackboard.com. WebCT also provides a Web site with product information and training for instructors. Access this Web site at www.webct.com/products/viewpage?name=products_training.

What I can expect about communicating online?

Compared to traditional courses, you will be doing much more writing and will need to hone your e-mail writing skills. Students in computer chat or discussion groups are less inhibited than in face-to-face classrooms and participation is evenly distributed across group members. Quiet students and ELL students, particularly, will participate more than in face-to-face classes because speaking is not required.

Because e-mails and online writing often lack context compared to face-to-face instruction, you may need to send more than one round of follow-up e-mails to ask for amplification and clarification.

How do I use the tools to communicate in an online class?

While the telephone offers a familiar method for communicating with students enrolled in your online class, the preferred methods are e-mail, chat rooms, and discussion forums. A telephone call provides an opportunity for instant response to questions, but telephone communication also presents obstacles. Will the student/instructor be available to answer the telephone call? Will you get into a scenario of playing telephone tag? Are you being called or calling a student at a time when the person is concentrating on some important activity? Telephone contacts are best reserved for consultations and more serious interventions. Communication between instructor and students via e-mail can be done anytime of the day or night, anywhere you are located, and any day of the week. Course management systems such as Blackboard and WebCT have their own e-mail component that stores the names and e-mail addresses of the instructor and all students enrolled in the class, provides the ability to send and receive attachments, and keeps a record of what has been sent and received. The e-mail system in your course management system has the features and functions commonly found in commercial e-mail systems. You must stress that students need to access and check their e-mail at least once a day.

Another common communication feature found in course management systems is a chat room This tool is designed for small group collaborative work. Depending on which course management system you are using, the tool may go by other names. To make the most of the chat feature, have your students log in to the chat room on a selected day of the week during a set time period, for example, Tuesday evenings from 7 to 8. During the chat session, the students and instructor can direct questions and responses to one another. No doubt the question from one student and the response from the instructor will be helpful to other students in the class as well.

Course management systems typically have some type of bulletin board. Again, depending on the system, the name could differ. Use the bulletin board to convey a reminder or message for the day or to post thoughtful questions for student response and debate.

Gary S. Moore in *You CAN Teach Online!*[1] provides a good summary of the benefits and purposes of e-mail, threaded discussion, and chat room tools. See Table A-1.

Another feature found in course management systems is the calendar, which, unlike the bulletin board, can display upcoming events, activities, reminders, and due dates not only for all the days in the current month, but for future months. The calendar also can provide a review of past events.

What do I need to do if I buy a publisher's e-course?

If you have selected a publisher's program that provides all of the course content, study guides, syllabus, assignments, and tests, you most likely will not change the existing materials. Your primary activities will include:

- Setting up an information page that includes the course number and name, your name, telephone number, e-mail address, office hours, etc.
- Entering information in the calendar feature that the students need to know during the duration of the online class. This includes reminders about when work is due, test days, school events, and school vacations.
- Personalizing or expanding the course in the section of the course management system generally called Content or Lecture, where you can enter information about the course, tips to the students, and/or additional content.
- Deleting, adding, or changing assignments and tests to be completed. Also add or change due dates.

Tool	Description	Uses
E-mail	An asynchronous tool that allows you to send or receive messages at any time to one person, a subgroup, or an entire class. Documents and other file types may also be attached and sent.	1. Respond to individual student questions or concerns. 2. Make class announcements. 3. Encourage class to collaborate on projects using e-mail.
Threaded Discussion	An asynchronous tool that allows you to post assignments to an entire class. Documents and other files types may also be attached and sent. These remain in a central site where the class may view the questions/assignments and respond at flexible times. The responses are recorded and may be viewed by the instructor and class members.	1. Post periodic discussion questions to which students are required to respond. 2. Post assignments for peer review. 3. Post graphics, tables, and pictures at the site and ask students to describe, explain, or comment on the posted materials. 4. Use the site for collaborative student projects.

continued on next page

---

[1] Gary S. Moore, Kathryn Winograd, Dan Lange. *You CAN Teach Online! The McGraw Hill Guide to Building Creative Learning Environments, First Edition* (New York: McGraw-Hill, 2001).

Chat Room	A synchronous tool that requires all participants be present online at the same time. The chat room may be typed text, live voice, or a combination of the two. Many chat rooms also support document sharing, whiteboarding, and posting URLs so that participants may view the same Web site simultaneously. Some chat rooms support video conferencing as well.	1. Allows small group collaboration. 2. Experts may be invited to present to the group. 3. May be used by instructor for advising and holding office hours. 4. Provides high level of interaction but often not as useful as threaded discussion in inviting thoughtful reactions.

Table A-1. Key Interactive Tools in Web-based Courses. (Source: *You CAN Teach Online!* by Gary S. Moore, Kathryn Winograd, and Dan Lange.)

What if I want to change the information provided in the template or e-course?

If you plan to change or add to the program provided by the publisher, you can download to your word processor whatever is to be changed, make the changes, save the document as a *doc* file, and save it again as an *htm* file. Remember that when you are saving a document as an htm file, there can be no spaces in the file name. The htm file can then be uploaded to your online course. If you are adding something that is not provided by the publisher, you can create the information in your word processor and follow the same steps for saving and uploading the document.

Are there guidelines for developing or selecting effective presentations for online classes?

If you are teaching an online course where the students do their work offline but transmit their work, check the syllabus, take quizzes/tests, check assignments, and send e-mails online, you will be more inclined to develop or select presentations for your class. You can develop printed lectures that include text, graphics, pictures, and other forms of animation using Flash to expand on the chapters being covered in the course textbook. The only difference is that the student generally reads or views the lecture on the screen rather than listens to it. These lectures are entered into the Lecture feature of the CMS. (In some systems, this feature is called Content or Course Content.) You can enter lectures for multiple chapters so that the students access only the lecture from the chapter they are currently completing.

Many publishing companies provide additional presentations that include graphic illustrations, animated images, voice, video clips, and text to coincide with particular sections of their texts. These presentations are generally recorded on CDs and/or DVDs and either come with the text or are sold separately. Students can access these presentations offline.

Other excellent resources for ready-made presentations that can be uploaded to your online class may be available from the publisher in an "Internet resource center" (the name varies depending on the publishing company), which can be accessed by students or instructors. Students can access this resource without a password; instructors, however, receive a password from the publisher, which gives them access to instructor-sensitive information such as tests and teaching hints.

What are some good ways to get to know my students?

Orientation meetings and on-campus tests provide opportunities for face-to-face contact. Another way to get to know your students is through a questionnaire that each student completes and returns to you via e-mail or surface mail. Possible questions are:

1. What is your name, address, and phone number? (The course management system typically provides them with an e-mail address.)
2. Which days of the week and times are you generally available?
3. What is your major or areas of interest?
4. What are your goals for the course?
5. Have you taken online courses in the past? If so, what course(s)?
6. What are your hobbies and interests?
7. What type of work or career are you pursuing?
8. What kinds of jobs and/or volunteer experience have you had in the past two years?

The answers to these questions will help you formulate a picture about each student enrolled in the online course. Other strategies for getting to know your students include:

- Having students send you a recent picture either by scanning it into their computers and electronically transmitting it or sending it to you via surface mail.
- Using the Web CMS Homepage feature as the site where students compose a one- or two-paragraph autobiography. Information should include where they are from, their major, their future plans, what they plan to do with the knowledge gained from this class, personal characteristics, etc. You also can post data about yourself.
- Setting up a weekly chat session where you and the students can pose questions, exchange information, and discuss issues.
- Requiring students to send you a weekly e-mail with a report on what they accomplished during the week, what they learned that is or will be most helpful to them, and content areas that were easy to digest or areas where they need help.

Getting to know your students is the key to success in any online course. The more you know about your students, the easier it becomes to provide for their individual needs.

How do I ensure that my students know how to function in an online program?

Another important task to address when teaching an online class is to provide appropriate information to the students so they know how to function in the course management system. Publish the information in a booklet and give it to students during an orientation meeting. Or, if the students do not come to campus for a meeting, e-mail or surface-mail the booklet to students. Information in the booklet should address the following points:

- Who does a student contact if she/he has questions, needs help, or has problems? Include a name, phone number with days of the week and times of the day for calls, and an e-mail address that can be used 24/7.
- What hardware, software, and text are required? Where or how do students get their texts?
- Instructions for logging on to the online class, including a unique code for initial access to the class, plus guidelines for establishing passwords and entering the appropriate class.
- Instructions on how to use the features of the course management system, including e-mail, chat, drop box, calendar, self tests, quizzes, and help.
- Guidelines for submitting work to the instructor, requirements for checking e-mail, and class requirements and assignment due dates.
- Tips for students on setting personal goals and motivating themselves.

How do I provide authentic and meaningful opportunities for interactivity between and among students and faculty?

Developing interactivity applications requires some imagination. Blackboard, WebCT, and other course management systems have a built in e-mail feature. As the instructor, you can create a distribution list that contains all the students in your class, or you can divide the class into teams and create a distribution list for each team. Then use the feature as a vehicle for interactivity.

As an example, assume that you are teaching a course in Microsoft Word, and all the students in your online class have completed the chapter on customizing documents. You want to be sure that the students have mastered the Merge and Compare feature so you e-mail them a business letter with numerous errors. In the e-mail you instruct them to use the Merge and Compare feature to correct the errors. Within 24 hours, each student is to return the letter to you as an attachment that shows the changes the student made. You then send a corrected copy of the letter to the students so they can compare results.

Another possibility for interactivity in online classes is to use the Chat feature for a group project. Assume that your class in Clinical Medical Assisting logs on to your class on Tuesday evenings from 7 to 8 p.m. After everyone logs on, you enter a series of symptoms and the students are to type their responses identifying the ailment. When the first response comes in, enter the question "Is this correct? If not, what is the correct diagnosis?"

Still another means of providing interactivity is to use the Student Presentations feature (may also be called Group Presentations) for collaborative work. This feature provides space for student teams to upload and exchange files for presentation to the instructor or the rest of the students. For example, a student team in a Telecommunications class could be assigned a project to develop a strategic plan for voice, data, and video telecommunications for a healthcare facility that has three branches within a city.

Other features that can be used to provide interactivity applications include the Calendar, Bulletin Board (sometimes called Blackboard or Whiteboard), and Student Homepages. The purpose of implementing interactivity applications is to get students involved, get them to think and react, and encourage them to make decisions.

Index